MCSE Exam Notes™:
NT® Server 4

Gary Govanus and
Robert King

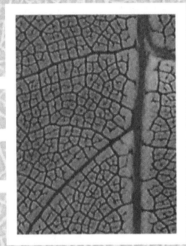

San Francisco • Paris • Düsseldorf • Soest

Associate Publisher: Guy Hart-Davis
Contracts and Licensing Manager: Kristine Plachy
Acquisitions & Developmental Editor: Neil Edde
Editor: Ronn Jost
Project Editor: Emily Wolman
Technical Editor: Ron Reimann
Book Designer: Bill Gibson
Graphic Illustrator: Michael Parker
Electronic Publishing Specialist: Bill Gibson
Production Coordinator: Eryn L. Osterhaus
Indexer: Rebecca Plunkett
Cover Design: Archer Design
Cover Illustrator/Photographer: FPG International
Screen reproductions produced with Collage Complete.
Collage Complete is a trademark of Inner Media Inc.
SYBEX is a registered trademark of SYBEX Inc.
Exam Notes is a trademark of SYBEX Inc.

Library of Congress Card Number: 98-85463
ISBN: 0-7821-2289-2

Manufactured in the United States of America

10 9 8 7 6 5 4 3 2 1

To my best friend, and my wife, Bobbi.

—Gary

To my wife Susan.

—Bob

Acknowledgments

People keep trying to teach me patience. Someday it may take! There are many people who have been tried severely during the writing of this book, and I'd like to thank them all: my loving wife Bobbi; my two daughters, Dawn and Denise; Brandice and CJ for giving up time with their grandfather; Mom and Dad for understanding why we couldn't visit; Neil Edde, for giving Bob and me the chance; Ronn Jost, our Editor, for nursing us through; Ron Reimann, our Tech Editor, for making sure we didn't lie to you; and Project Editor Emily Wolman, Production Coordinator Eryn Osterhaus, and Designer and Desktop Specialist Bill Gibson, for all the hard work they put in over the course of this project. To all, thank you.

—Gary Govanus

I always thought that writing a book would be easy—it's just teaching on paper, right? Little did I know just how much sacrifice would be involved. Unfortunately, most of the sacrifices were made by my family. For that (and more) thanks first go to my wife, Susan, and my daughter, Katie.

I'd also be remiss if I didn't thank the guys at The Endeavor Group in Reno (`www.endeavor-net.com`) who donated a couple of their great computers to my home lab so I could test before I typed.

Lastly, thanks to the fine folks at Sybex for giving me the opportunity to write this book.

—Bob King

Table of Contents

Introduction   *viii*

Chapter 1   Planning   1

- Plan the disk drive configuration for various requirements.   3

- Choose a protocol for various situations.   20

Chapter 2   Installation and Configuration   35

- Install Windows NT Server on Intel-based platforms.   39

- Install Windows NT Server to perform various server roles.   48

- Install Windows NT Server by using various methods.   58

- Configure protocols and protocol bindings.   76

- Configure network adapters.   87

- Configure Windows NT Server core services.   96

- Configure peripherals and devices.   112

- Configure hard disks to meet various requirements.   127

- Configure printers.   139

- Configure a Windows NT Server computer for various types of client computers.   155

Chapter 3   **Managing Resources**   **161**

- Manage user and group accounts. **164**

- Create and manage policies and profiles for various situations. **182**

- Administer remote servers from various types of client computers. **193**

- Manage disk resources. **198**

Chapter 4   **Connectivity**   **227**

- Configure Windows NT Server for interoperability with NetWare servers by using various tools. **229**

- Install and configure remote access service (RAS). **239**

Chapter 5   **Monitoring and Optimization**   **261**

- Monitor performance of various functions by using Performance Monitor. **263**

- Identify performance bottlenecks. **279**

Chapter 6   **Troubleshooting**   **285**

- Choose the appropriate course of action to take to resolve installation failures. **287**

- Choose the appropriate course of action to take to resolve boot failures. **290**

- Choose the appropriate course of action to take to resolve configuration errors. **301**

- Choose the appropriate course of action to take to resolve printer problems. **309**

- Choose the appropriate course of action to take to resolve RAS problems.   **317**

- Choose the appropriate course of action to take to resolve connectivity problems.   **320**

- Choose the appropriate course of action to take to resolve resource access and permission problems.   **328**

- Choose the appropriate course of action to take to resolve fault-tolerance failures.   **332**

Index   *341*

Introduction

If you've purchased this book, you are probably chasing one of the Microsoft professional certifications: MCP, MCSE, or MCT. They are all great career builders. When you glance through any newspaper's want ads, you'll see employment opportunities for people with these certifications; finding qualified employees is a challenge in today's market. If you are certified, it means that you know something about the product, but more importantly, it means that you have the ability, determination, and focus to learn—the greatest skills any employee can have.

You've probably also heard all the rumors about how hard the Microsoft exams are—believe us, the rumors are true! Microsoft has designed a series of exams that truly test your knowledge of their products. Each exam not only covers the materials presented in a particular course, but also covers the prerequisite knowledge for that course. This means two things for you—that the first exam can be a real hurdle and that each exam *should* get easier since you've studied the basics over and over.

This book has been developed in alliance with the Microsoft Corporation to give you the knowledge and skills you need to prepare for one of the key exams of the MCSE certification program: *Implementing and Supporting Microsoft Windows NT Server 4.0* (Exam 70-067). Reviewed and approved by Microsoft, this book provides a solid introduction to Microsoft networking technologies and will help you on your way to MCSE certification.

Is This Book for You?

The *MCSE Exam Notes* books were designed to be succinct, portable exam review guides that can be used either in conjunction with a more complete study program (book, CBT courseware, classroom/lab environment) or as an exam review for those people who don't feel the need for more extensive preparation. It isn't our goal to "give the answers away," but rather to identify those topics on which you can expect to be tested and provide sufficient coverage of these topics.

Perhaps you've been working with Microsoft networking technologies for years now. The thought of paying a lot of money for a specialized MCSE exam preparation course probably doesn't sound too appealing. What can they teach you that you don't already know, right? Be careful, though. Many experienced network administrators have walked confidently into test centers only to walk sheepishly out of them after failing an MCSE exam. As they discovered, there's the Microsoft of the real world and the Microsoft of the MCSE exams. It's our goal with these *Exam Notes* books to show you where the two converge and where they diverge. After you've finished reading through this book, you should have a clear idea of how your understanding of the technologies involved matches up with the expectations of the MCSE exam makers in Redmond.

Or perhaps you're relatively new to the world of Microsoft networking, drawn to it by the promise of challenging work and higher salaries. You've just waded through an 800-page MCSE study guide or taken a class at a local training center. It's a lot of information to keep track of, isn't it? Well, by organizing the *Exam Notes* books according to the Microsoft exam objectives, and by breaking up the information into concise, manageable pieces, we've created what we think is the handiest exam review guide available. Throw it in your briefcase and carry it to work with you. As you read through the book, you'll be able to identify quickly those areas you know best and those that require more in-depth review.

NOTE The goal of the *Exam Notes* series is to help MCSE candidates familiarize themselves with the subjects on which they can expect to be tested in the MCSE exams. For complete, in-depth coverage of the technologies and topics involved, we recommend the *MCSE Study Guide* series from Sybex.

How Is This Book Organized?

As mentioned above, this book is organized according to the official exam objectives list prepared by Microsoft for the *Implementing and Supporting Microsoft Windows NT Server 4.0* exam. The chapters coincide with the broad objectives groupings, such as Planning, Installation and Configuration, Monitoring and Optimization, and Troubleshooting. These groupings are also reflected in the organization of the MCSE exams themselves.

Within each chapter, the individual exam objectives are addressed in turn. And in turn, the objectives sections are further divided according to the type of information presented.

Critical Information

This section presents the greatest level of detail on information that is relevant to the objective. This is the place to start if you're unfamiliar with or uncertain about the technical issues related to the objective.

Necessary Procedures

Here, you'll find instructions for procedures that require a lab computer to be completed. From installing operating systems to modifying configuration defaults, the information in these sections addresses the hands-on requirements for the MCSE exams.

NOTE   Not every objective has procedures associated with it. For such objectives, the "Necessary Procedures" section has been left out.

Exam Essentials

In this section, we've put together a concise list of the most crucial topics of subject areas that you'll need to comprehend fully prior to taking the MCSE exam. This section can help you identify those topics that might require more study on your part.

Key Terms and Concepts

Here, we've compiled a mini-glossary of the most important terms and concepts related to the specific objective. You'll understand what all those technical words mean within the context of the related subject matter.

Sample Questions

For each objective, we've included a selection of questions similar to those you'll encounter on the actual MCSE exam. Answers and explanations are provided so that you can gain some insight into the exam-taking process.

SEE ALSO For a more comprehensive collection of exam review questions, check out the *MCSE Test Success* series, also published by Sybex.

How Do You Become an MCSE?

Attaining Microsoft Certified Systems Engineer (MCSE) status is a challenge. The exams cover a wide range of topics, and require dedicated study and expertise. This is, however, why the MCSE certificate is so valuable. If achieving the MCSE status were too easy, the market would be quickly flooded by MCSEs and the certification would become meaningless. Microsoft, keenly aware of this fact, has taken steps to ensure that the certification means that its holder is truly knowledgeable and skilled.

To become an MCSE, you must pass four core requirements and two electives.

Client Requirement

70-073: Implementing and Supporting Windows NT Workstation 4.0

or

70-064: Implementing and Supporting Microsoft Windows 95

Networking Requirement

70-058: Networking Essentials

Windows NT Server 4.0 Requirement

70-067: Implementing and Supporting Windows NT Server 4.0

Windows NT Server 4.0 in the Enterprise Requirement

70-068: Implementing and Supporting Windows NT Server 4.0 in the Enterprise

Electives

Some of the more popular electives include:

70-059: Internetworking Microsoft TCP/IP on Microsoft Windows NT 4.0

70-087: Implementing and Supporting Microsoft Internet Information Server 4.0

70-081: Implementing and Supporting Microsoft Exchange Server 5.5

70-026: System Administration for Microsoft SQL Server 6.5

70-027: Implementing a Database Design on Microsoft SQL Server 6.5

70-088: Implementing and Supporting Microsoft Proxy Server 2.0

70-079: Implementing and Supporting Microsoft Internet Explorer 4.0 by Using the Internet Explorer Administration Kit

---

TIP This book is part of a series of *MCSE Exam Notes* books, published by Network Press (Sybex), that covers four core requirements and your choice of several electives—the entire MCSE track!

Where Do You Take the Exams?

You may take the exams at any of more than 800 Sylvan Prometric Authorized Testing Centers around the world. For the location of a testing center near you, call (800)755-EXAM (755-3926). Outside the United States and Canada, contact your local Sylvan Prometric Registration Center. You can also register for an exam with Sylvan Prometric via the Internet. The Sylvan Web site can be reached through the Microsoft Training and Certification site, or at http:// www.slspro.com/msreg/microsoft.asp.

To register for a Microsoft Certified Professional exam:

1. Determine the number of the exam that you want to take.

2. Register with Sylvan Prometric. At this point, you will be asked for advance payment for the exam. At the time of this writing, the exams are $100 each. Exams must be taken within one year of payment. You can schedule exams up to six weeks in advance or as late as one working day prior to the date of the exam. You can cancel or reschedule your exam if you contact Sylvan Prometric at least two working days prior to the exam. Same-day registration is available in some locations, although this is subject to space availability. Where same-day registration is available, you must register a minimum of two hours before exam time.

3. After you receive a registration and payment confirmation letter from Sylvan Prometric, call a nearby Sylvan Prometric Testing Center to schedule your exam.

When you schedule the exam, you'll be provided with instructions regarding appointment and cancellation procedures and ID requirements, and information about the testing center location.

What Does the NT Server 4.0 Exam Measure?

The people who write the exams for Microsoft want to make sure that you are a well-rounded network administrator. The MCSE designation is kind of a Liberal Arts degree in Networking—you need to know something about multiple topics.

That philosophy shows in the Server exam and in the way the questions are worded. As you study, try to think like an exam writer. What would you write questions about?

- Is there special terminology that Microsoft uses?

- Are there tips presented on things such as troubleshooting?

- Is there a specific way of doing something, stressed over and over?

- Is there something about the subject that is very specific, such as minimum requirements or command-line switches?

The NT Server exam measures how well you understand the concept and how well you know the procedures. You should know the reasoning behind procedures as well as the procedures themselves. If you know the subject matter and understand the product, you should do great on the exam.

How Does Microsoft Develop the Exam Questions?

Microsoft's exam development process consists of eight mandatory phases. The process takes an average of seven months and contains more than 150 specific steps. The phases of Microsoft Certified Professional exam development are listed here.

Phase 1: Job Analysis

Phase 1 is an analysis of all the tasks that make up the specific job function based on tasks performed by people who are currently performing the job function. This phase also identifies the knowledge, skills, and abilities that relate specifically to the certification for that performance area.

Phase 2: Objective Domain Definition

The results of the job analysis provide the framework used to develop exam objectives. The development of objectives involves translating the job function tasks into a comprehensive set of more specific and measurable knowledge, skills, and abilities. The resulting list of objectives, or the objective domain, is the basis for the development of both the certification exams and the training materials.

NOTE The outline of all *Exam Notes* books is based upon the official exam objectives lists published by Microsoft. Objectives are subject to change without notification. We advise that you check the Microsoft Training and Certification Web site (**www.microsoft.com\train_cert**) for the most current objectives list.

Phase 3: Blueprint Survey

The final objective domain is transformed into a blueprint survey in which contributors—technology professionals who are performing the applicable job function—are asked to rate each objective. Based on the contributors' input, the objectives are prioritized and weighted. The actual exam items are written according to the prioritized objectives. The blueprint survey phase helps determine which objectives to measure, as well as the appropriate number and types of items to include on the exam.

Phase 4: Item Development

A pool of items is developed to measure the blueprinted objective domain. The number and types of items to be written are based on the results of the blueprint survey. During this phase, items are reviewed and revised to ensure that they are as follows:

- Technically accurate

- Clear, unambiguous, and plausible

- Not biased toward any population, subgroup, or culture

- Not misleading or tricky

- Testing at the correct level of Bloom's Taxonomy

- Testing for useful knowledge, not obscure or trivial facts

Items that meet these criteria are included in the initial item pool.

Phase 5: Alpha Review and Item Revision

During this phase, a panel of technical and job function experts reviews each item for technical accuracy, then answers each item, reaching consensus on all technical issues. Once the items have been verified as technically accurate, they are edited to ensure that they are expressed in the clearest language possible.

Phase 6: Beta Exam

The reviewed and edited items are collected into a beta exam pool. During the beta exam, each participant has the opportunity to respond to all the items in this beta exam pool. Based on the responses of all beta participants, Microsoft performs a statistical analysis to verify the validity of the exam items and to determine which items will be used in the certification exam. Once the analysis has been completed, the items are distributed into multiple parallel forms, or versions, of the final certification exam.

Phase 7: Item Selection and Cut-Score Setting

The results of the beta exam are analyzed to determine which items should be included in the certification exam based on many factors, including item difficulty and relevance. Generally, the desired items are answered correctly by 25 to 90 percent of the beta exam candidates. This helps ensure that the exam consists of a variety of difficulty levels, from somewhat easy to extremely difficult.

Also during this phase, a panel of job function experts determines the cut score (minimum passing score) for the exam. The cut score differs from exam to exam because it is based on an item-by-item determination of the percentage of candidates who would be expected to answer the item correctly. The experts determine the cut score in a group session to increase the reliability.

Phase 8: Live Exam

Once all the other phases are complete, the exam is ready. Microsoft Certified Professional exams are administered by Sylvan Prometric.

Tips for Taking Your NT Server Exam

Here are some general tips for taking your exam successfully:

- Arrive early at the exam center so that you can relax and review your study materials, particularly tables and lists of exam-related information.

- Read the questions carefully. Don't be tempted to jump to an early conclusion. Make sure you know *exactly* what the question is asking.

- Don't leave any unanswered questions—they count against you.

- When answering multiple-choice questions that you're not sure about, use a process of elimination to get rid of the obviously incorrect questions first. This will improve your odds if you need to make an educated guess.

- Because the hard questions will eat up the most time, save them for last. You can move forward and backward through the exam.

- This exam has many exhibits (pictures). It can be difficult, if not impossible, to view both the questions and the exhibit simulation on the 14- and 15-inch screens usually found at the testing centers.

Call around to each center to find out whether they have 17-inch monitors available. If they don't, perhaps you can arrange to bring in your own. Failing this, some people have found it useful to quickly draw the diagram on the scratch paper provided by the testing center and use the monitor to view just the question.

- Many participants run out of time before they are able to complete the test. If you are unsure of the answer to a question, you may want to choose one of the answers, mark the question, and go on—an unanswered question does not help you. Once your time is up, you cannot go on to another question. However, you can remain on the current question indefinitely when the time runs out. Therefore, when you are almost out of time, go to a question you feel you can figure out—given enough time—and work until you feel you have it (or the night security guard boots you out!).

- You are allowed to use the Windows calculator during your exam. However, it may be better to memorize a table of the subnet addresses and write it down on the scratch paper supplied by the testing center before you start the exam.

Once you have completed an exam, you will be given immediate, online notification of your pass or fail status. You will also receive a printed Examination Score Report indicating your pass or fail status and your exam results by section. (The exam administrator will give you the printed score report.) Exam scores are automatically forwarded to Microsoft within five working days after you take the exam, so you do not need to send your score to Microsoft. If you pass the exam, you will receive confirmation from Microsoft, typically within two to four weeks.

Contact Information

To find out more about Microsoft Education and Certification materials and programs, register with Sylvan Prometric, or receive other useful information, check the following resources. Outside the United States or Canada, contact your local Microsoft office or Sylvan Prometric Testing Center.

Microsoft Certified Professional Program—(800)636-7544

Call the MCPP number for information about the Microsoft Certified Professional program and exams, and to order the latest Microsoft Roadmap to Education and Certification.

Sylvan Prometric Testing Centers—(800)755-EXAM

To register for a Microsoft Certified Professional exam at any of more than 800 Sylvan Prometric Testing Centers around the world, or to order this *Exam Notes* book, call the Sylvan Prometric Testing Center number.

Microsoft Certification Development Team— http://www.microsoft.com/Train_Cert/mcp/examinfo/certsd.htm

Contact the Microsoft Certification Development Team through their Web site to volunteer for participation in one or more exam development phases or to report a problem with an exam. Address written correspondence to:

> Certification Development Team
> Microsoft Education and Certification
> One Microsoft Way
> Redmond, WA 98052

Microsoft TechNet Technical Information Network— (800)344-2121

This is an excellent resource for support professionals and system administrators. Outside the United States and Canada, call your local Microsoft subsidiary for information.

How to Contact the Authors

Gary Govanus can be reached at ggovanus@psconsulting.com.

Bob King can be reached at bking@royal-tech.com.

How to Contact the Publisher

Sybex welcomes reader feedback on all of their titles. Visit the Sybex Web site at www.sybex.com for book updates and additional certification information. You'll also find online forms to submit comments or suggestions regarding this or any other Sybex book.

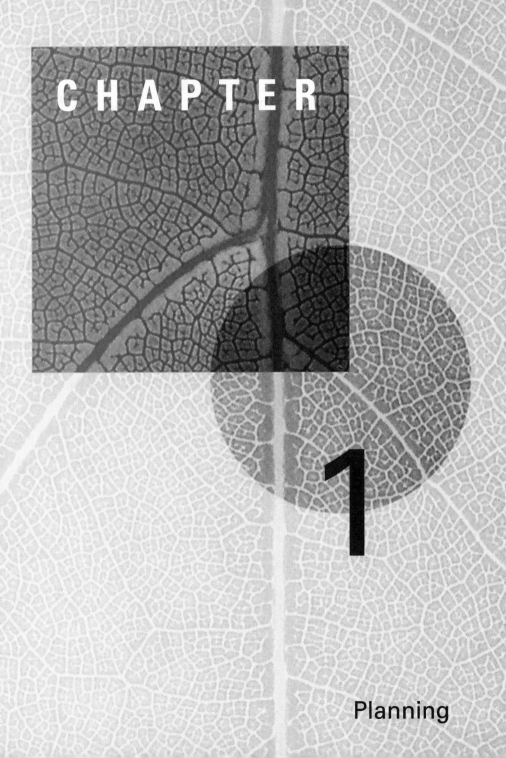

CHAPTER

1

Planning

Microsoft Exam Objectives Covered in This Chapter:

Plan the disk drive configuration for various requirements. Requirements include: *(pages 3 – 19)*
- Choosing a file system
- Choosing a fault-tolerance method

Choose a protocol for various situations. Protocols include: *(pages 20 – 34)*
- TCP/IP
- NWLink IPX/SPX Compatible Transport
- NetBEUI

Someone very wise once said that proper planning prevents poor performance. However, many people don't have the luxury of planning a network. When they took their job, the network was handed to them, blemishes and all. If you are one of the fortunate people who get to plan and design your network before instituting it, the learning curve will be much shorter and much less painful. If you inherit a network, and see something that is confusing, ask yourself why the previous administrator did it that way. A common thread may run through all of the decisions that were made. Once you understand the philosophy of the network, things will be less confusing.

Planning can be time consuming. It starts with questioning and goal setting. First, determine the goal of the network. This goal will drive many of the questions that follow. If your network is to provide file, print, application, and messaging services to an office of 20 people, the questions take one form. If your network is to provide communication services for a network of 20,000 people spread over several continents, the questions take an entirely different form. The NT Server exam assumes that the network you will work with is relatively small.

Planning starts with the basics. First, you need a server (a server is just a computer on steroids). What do you have to put into that computer to make it most effective for the needs of an organization now and in the future? The basic components of any computer are the processor, memory, and disk subsystem. This is pretty straightforward, but which processor, how much memory, and which disk subsystem should you use? For the purpose of this book, an Intel processor—at least a 486/66—and lots of memory—256MB (although this is well past the minimum 12MB RAM requirement to run Server 4)—were settled on. The disk subsystem is a little more complicated.

Plan the disk drive configuration for various requirements. Requirements include:

- Choosing a file system
- Choosing a fault-tolerance method

Planning your hard drive configuration starts with the purchase of your server. As you begin to contemplate the data and applications that you will store on the server, you will get an idea of the overhead involved. If you purchase hardware that can support the expected workload, it will have a positive impact on your users.

NOTE   Even though this is a "short" objective, there is a lot of information. Disk technology is an ever-growing arena. The information presented here (or in any written materials) represents the technology that was current at the time of writing. As a systems engineer, you will be responsible for keeping up to date on new advances in disk subsystems.

Critical Information

Many different types of disk systems are available in today's market—IDE, EIDE, SCSI, SCSI-2, Ultra-SCSI, Wide-SCSI, etc.—and the list grows every day. There are advantages and disadvantages in every choice. Your choice will usually be a compromise between budget, capacity, and speed. Examine your budget and buy the biggest, fastest system you can afford.

Since the disk subsystem is usually the slowest subsystem on a server, you shouldn't "buy for price." Upgrading later to a faster disk system can be expensive and time consuming. Since storage technology constantly changes, no book can explain all of the available options. However, here is a short list of the technologies that are commonly used on today's servers.

Controllers

There are numerous disk technologies on the market today, with more on the horizon. Table 1.1 lists some of the more common technologies used in servers, with their data transfer rates, advantages, and disadvantages.

T A B L E 1.1: Comparison of Disk Technologies

Type	Approximate Data Transfer Rate	Advantages	Disadvantages
IDE/EIDE	Up to 8.3MB per second (IDE) and 16.6MB per second (EIDE)	Included on most modern motherboards	Limit of two drives per controller

T A B L E 1.1: Comparison of Disk Technologies *(cont.)*

Type	Approximate Data Transfer Rate	Advantages	Disadvantages
IDE/EIDE (continued)		Easy to configure (just add drive to CMOS) Least expensive hardware	Traditional IDE drives were limited to 540MB; enhanced IDE has a work-around for larger drives, but not all BIOS will recognize large drives
SCSI	5MB per second	Standard, mature technology Moderately expensive hardware	Must understand SCSI installation, termination, and IDs
FAST SCSI	10MB per second	Speed	Little more expensive
FAST-20 or ULTRA SCSI	20MB per second	More speed	More expensive
ULTRA SCSI-2	40MB per second	Most speed	Most expensive next to RAID drives

Busmaster Controllers

Some controllers have an on-board processor designed to off-load processing from the CPU. The CPU passes a data or write request to the controller and can then continue with another task. The controller's processor handles the details of the request and interrupts the CPU only when the requested function has been completed. Busmastering is very common on high-end (SCSI) controllers, and is often used on servers.

Caching Controllers

Some controllers have their own memory. When the CPU needs to write data to disk, the data can be written into this memory. This process is extremely fast. The controller then writes the data to disk on its own. As in busmastering, the goal is to free up the CPU as quickly as possible.

WARNING   It is imperative to have a good UPS (uninterruptable power supply) on a server using a caching controller. Once the CPU has finished passing the data to the controller, it considers the data to have been written to disk. If power is lost before the data are flushed from the cache, no fault-tolerance system would be aware of the problem. This is usually not a big issue since most controllers have limits on how long data can sit in cache—but it's better to be safe than sorry.

Hardware-Controlled RAID (Redundant Array of Inexpensive Disks)

RAID technology is designed to add fault tolerance to a disk subsystem. In a RAID system, a duplicate of all data is stored on another disk (this is a simplification—RAID will be discussed in more detail later in the "Choosing a Fault-Tolerance Method" section). If one disk dies, the data can be rebuilt on the fly. Some controllers have RAID technologies built into the hardware.

Once you have chosen a type of disk subsystem and installed the hardware, you must configure those disks for NT. So, the discussion will now focus on partitioning your disks and choosing a file system.

Partitioning

Before a hard disk can be used by an operating system, the hard disk must be partitioned. When you partition a hard disk, you define the boundaries of a physical area on the disk. This area can then be formatted for use by an operating system such as Microsoft Windows NT.

You can use partitioning to organize your data by creating a "boot" partition that contains only NT system files, and another partition to hold your data. On a dual-boot computer, you can create separate partitions for each operating system so that each system file has its own physical space. An organized hard disk makes it easier to find your data.

Proper choices can make managing your disk space easy. Poor choices won't kill you, but could make upgrading difficult—you might end up with two operating systems that just won't get along on one partition.

On the physical level, a disk must be partitioned before an operating system can use its storage space. A partition is made up of unused space on the drive. The unused space will be used to form either a primary or an extended partition. You can create a maximum of four partitions on each disk.

A *primary partition* has the necessary configuration to be used by an operating system for the boot process. You can create up to four primary partitions on a single disk. This allows you to isolate the system files from multiple operating systems on a single drive. One of the primary partitions will be marked as active—this is the partition that will be booted from.

Once a partition is created, it must then be formatted. Formatting sets up the basic housekeeping or accounting system on the partition to allow files to be stored and retrieved successfully by the operating system. While several formats exist, the most popular is file allocation table (FAT). Almost every operating system can read FAT, including DOS, Windows 95, Windows NT, UNIX, and Macintosh.

In addition to FAT, advances in the file systems have developed more mature formats such as HPFS, FAT32, and NTFS. High performance file systems (HPFS) was developed for use with OS/2, and NT file system (NTFS) was developed for use with Windows NT. However, these file systems are not designed to be read by other operating systems such as DOS.

You can set up a computer to dual-boot NT and Windows 95. To accomplish this, the partition must be formatted with the FAT file system (which will be discussed later in the "Choosing a File System" section). Note that NT cannot read a partition formatted with FAT32 (a file system available on Windows 95 SR2), so do not use this file system on machines on which you intend to dual-boot NT and Windows 95.

Primary partitions cannot be subdivided further. One way to get around the four-partition limit is to use an extended partition. There can be one extended partition on each disk (it *does* count against the four-partition limit). The *extended partition* can be subdivided into multiple logical disks, each of which will be given a drive letter by the system.

Like a primary partition, an extended partition is created from unused space on the drive. Since there can be only one extended partition, you usually create it last and use all of the remaining space on the drive. You can then divide it into logical drives for management purposes.

NT dynamically assigns drive letters to each partition using the procedure shown in Figure 1.1 and listed below.

1. Beginning with disk zero, the first primary partition on each drive is assigned a consecutive letter (starting with the letter C).

2. Beginning with disk zero, each logical drive is assigned a consecutive letter.

3. Beginning with disk zero, all other primary partitions are assigned a letter.

You can override these default assignments in the Disk Administration tool by choosing Tools ➤ Assign Drive Letter. This process will be illustrated in the "Necessary Procedures" section.

Understanding Partition Numbering and ARC Paths

Windows NT assigns each partition an identification number, as shown in Figure 1.2. NT uses the partition number in an ARC path (defined later in this section) to locate the needed area on a disk for read and write operations. For troubleshooting, you need to know how NT assigns partition numbers.

FIGURE 1.1: Assigning drive letters

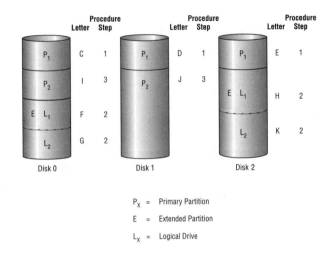

P_X = Primary Partition

E   = Extended Partition

L_X = Logical Drive

FIGURE 1.2: Assigning partition numbers

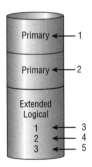

NT assigns a number to all primary partitions first, starting with the number *one,* and then assigns an ID to each logical drive in the extended partition (if one exists).

NT uses the partition numbers in an ARC (advanced RISC computing) path to find the partition. You must understand ARC paths, both for the exam and for real-world troubleshooting. An ARC path will look as follows:

multi/scsi(a)disk(b)rdisk(c)partition(d)

Each *a*, *b*, *c*, and *d* will have a value, as listed in Table 1.2.

T A B L E 1.2: ARC Path Components

Component	Definition
multi/scsi	Identifies the type of controller. If the controller is a SCSI device with the BIOS *not* enabled, this value will be *scsi*; for all others, it will be *multi*.
(a)	The ordinal value of the controller. As each controller initializes, it is given a value—the first will be given a value of *zero,* the next *one,* etc.
disk(b)	SCSI bus number; for *multi*, this value is always *zero*.
rdisk(c)	For non-SCSI disks, this will be the ordinal value of the disk. It is assigned in the same way as *(a)* above.
partition(d)	The ordinal value of the partition (as described above).

ARC paths will be discussed again in Chapter 6, "Troubleshooting."

Choosing a File System

NT supports three different file systems:

- FAT (file allocation table)
- NTFS (NT file system)
- CDFS (CD-ROM file system)

NOTE Since CDFS is a specialized file system used for CD-ROMs, it will not be discussed here.

FAT File System

The FAT file system has been used since the earliest days of DOS computers. FAT has minimal overhead (less than 1MB) and is the most efficient file system for partitions smaller than 400MB. Since it is the only file system that DOS, Windows 95, and Windows NT have in common, the system partition must be a FAT partition on dual-boot machines. RISC-based computers will boot only from a FAT partition, so all RISC systems must have a small FAT partition to hold boot files.

On the downside, performance decreases as the number of files in a partition increases due to the way files are tracked. Another downside is that the FAT file system has no features to prevent file fragmentation, which can affect performance. As a security feature, Windows NT prevents a deleted file from being undeleted, but on a FAT partition (if the computer is booted to DOS), undelete tools might be able to recover deleted files. Also, there is no file- or directory-level security available on a FAT partition. The only security is that available through directory-level sharing supplied by the operating systems.

The version of the FAT file system included with Windows NT has been enhanced to support long filenames. Filenames adhere to the following criteria:

- Can be up to 255 characters (including the full path)
- Must start with a letter or number, and can include any characters except for quotation marks (""), forward and backward slashes (/\), brackets ([]), semicolons (;), colons (:), equal signs (=), commas (,), carets (^), asterisks (*), and question marks (?)
- Can include multiple spaces
- Can include multiple periods, but the last period denotes the file suffix, which is similar to DOS 8.3 naming conventions (for example, .EXE, .COM)
- Preserve case, but are not case sensitive

TIP As an aid to troubleshooting, many administrators create a FAT partition and place the NT boot files there. In the event of a problem, they can then boot to DOS and access the files on the partition, replacing corrupt files or using DOS-based disk diagnostic tools.

NTFS

NTFS is the file system specifically designed for use on a Windows NT–based computer. NTFS offers many advantages over the older FAT file system:

- File- and directory-level security.

- Larger file and partition sizes. Theoretically, both the maximum file and the maximum partition size is 16 exabytes. Functionally, with today's hardware, the limit is 2 terabytes.

- Built-in file compression.

- A recoverable file system. It uses a transaction log for disk activity. The log file can be used to redo or undo operations that failed.

- Bad-cluster remapping. If a write error occurs, the file system will move the data to another sector of the disk.

- Support for Macintosh files. (You must install Services for Macintosh.)

- Support for POSIX.1-compliant software.

- Reduced file fragmentation.

There are only two, small drawbacks to NTFS—since it has a fairly high overhead (approximately 50MB), floppy disks cannot be formatted with NTFS. Also, NTFS does not support removable media (when using removable media formatted with NTFS, you must restart the computer to change disks).

Managing Hard Disks

The next step in planning your disk drive configuration is to determine how those disks will act together to store your data. NT offers many configuration options—you must be able to determine which option is right for your environment.

Volume Sets

You can add together areas of free space on your hard disks to create one logical drive—thus creating a volume set. This process will be examined later in the "Necessary Procedures" section. Once created, this area must then be formatted with either FAT or NTFS. Once you have created the volume set, it will appear as one drive to the system. When using a volume set, NT will fill each segment, before starting to use the next.

You can also add space to an existing NTFS volume by choosing Extend Volume Set from the Partition menu in Disk Administrator. Once free space has been added to a volume set, you cannot take it back. The only way to reclaim that space is to delete the *entire* volume set (and thus any data stored there).

TIP   If you need to extend a volume set formatted with the FAT file system, first convert it to NTFS using the CONVERT.EXE command-line tool. Remember that this is a one-way operation—once you have converted to NTFS, you cannot go back to FAT.

Stripe Sets

Like a volume set, a stripe set adds free space on two or more hard drives to one logical drive. Unlike a volume set, however, a stripe set must include space on at least 2 drives (up to a maximum of 32 drives). The areas created must be approximately the same size (if they are not, Disk Administrator will adjust the size for you).

When data are placed in a stripe set, the data are written evenly across all physical disks in 64KB "stripes." While a stripe set does not provide fault tolerance, it can improve I/O performance.

Choosing a Fault-Tolerance Method

Because of the critical nature of most data stored on servers, the disk subsystem must be fault tolerant. A *fault-tolerant disk system* can survive the death of a single hard drive, with the data still accessible. The fault-tolerant features of Windows NT are managed through the Disk Administrator tool.

NT provides fault tolerance through software-controlled implementation of redundant array of inexpensive disks (RAID). There are seven primary levels of RAID in the industry; NT Server can implement software versions of three RAID levels—0, 1, and 5. Level 0 (disk striping) is just the ability to create a volume set that spans multiple hard drives. Since this provides no fault tolerance, it will be ignored in this discussion.

Level 1 RAID is commonly referred to as disk mirroring. In a *mirror system,* there is a redundant copy of all data on the partition. With mirroring, if the primary disk dies, the system can switch over to the redundant disk—the users will not notice the hardware failure.

Disk duplexing is a subset of mirroring in which the disks are accessed through separate controllers. In mirroring, if the controller dies, there is no way to access the redundant disk. Since you have multiple controllers in a duplexed system, the server can survive a controller failure—the users will not notice a problem.

Level 5 RAID consists of disk striping (as discussed above) with the addition of a parity set. The *parity set* is a calculation of the contents of the data, placed on another disk in the set. If one disk dies, the RAID system can use the parity information to re-create the missing data on the fly.

Level 1 RAID (mirroring) is an efficient way to provide fault tolerance (especially if you upgrade it to duplexing). Since an entire copy of the data exists on another hard drive, the user will not notice any difference in performance in the event of a hardware failure. However, mirroring is more expensive than level 5 RAID—in mirroring, only 50 percent of the disk space is usable, since the other half is used to maintain redundancy. Mirroring is also the only way to make your system and boot partitions fault tolerant. These two partitions cannot be part of a volume set, stripe set, or stripe set with parity.

Level 5 RAID is very common in today's business environments. It actually increases I/O performance by splitting the work across the hard disks. It is also more cost effective than mirroring. In a level-5 implementation, the more disks involved in the stripe set, the lower the percentage of disk space used for the fault-tolerant information. In mirroring, one-half of the total disk space is used to provide fault tolerance. In a level-5 implementation with the minimum of three disks, only one-third of the space is used to hold the parity information (one-fourth with four disks, one-fifth with five disks, etc.). Level 5 RAID can support up to 32 disk partitions. Keep in mind, though, that level 5 RAID can survive the loss of only one disk. If you lose more than one disk, all the information on the disk array becomes inaccessible and useless.

NOTE Windows NT provides software-controlled RAID. Although this is an inexpensive way to achieve fault tolerance, it is not necessarily the correct choice. Some hardware has been specifically designed to provide RAID functions. In most cases, hardware-based RAID will be faster than software-based RAID.

Necessary Procedures

Most servers act as repositories of data that are accessed by end users. NT administrators must be able to configure and manage the disks on their servers. The procedures for this exam objective concern the skills necessary to manage the disk configuration of an NT server.

Reassigning Drive Letters

You reassign disk drive letters by using the Disk Administrator tool. Click the partition you want to reassign, choose Tools ➤ Assign Drive Letter, and change the letter.

Creating a Volume Set

In Disk Administrator, Ctrl-click all of the partitions that should be included and choose Partition ➤ Create Volume Set.

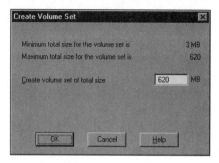

Creating a Stripe Set

In Disk Administrator, Ctrl-click all of the partitions (2–32) that should be included in the set. Remember that the segments must be approximately the same size (Disk Administrator will adjust the size for you if they are not). Choose Partition ➤ Create Stripe Set.

Creating a Mirror Set

In Disk Administrator, Ctrl-click the two partitions that will make up the set (they must be on different hard drives) and choose Fault Tolerance ➤ Establish Mirror.

Creating a Stripe Set with Parity

In Disk Administrator, Ctrl-click the partitions (3–32) that will make up the segments of the set. Remember that these must be approximately the same size (Disk Administrator will adjust the size as appropriate). Choose Fault Tolerance ➤ Create Stripe Set with Parity.

Exam Essentials

Of all the components that can fail on an NT server, the hard disks are the most likely to do so. NT administrators have to understand the options available to minimize the impact of disk failures on their users. Microsoft is quite aware of this, and tests accordingly. Before taking this exam, make sure you are comfortable with Microsoft's disk configuration options.

Know how NT assigns drive letters to partitions. NT will dynamically assign drive letters to each partition using the following procedure:

1. Beginning with disk zero, the first primary partition on each drive is assigned a consecutive letter (starting with the letter C).

2. Beginning with disk zero, each logical drive is assigned a consecutive letter.

3. Beginning with disk zero, all other primary partitions are assigned a letter.

Know how to read an ARC path. An ARC path will look as follows:

multi/scsi(a)disk(b)rdisk(c)partition(d)

Refer back to Table 1.2 for an explanation of an ARC path's components.

Know how to define a volume set. A *volume set* is a collection of partitions combined into one logical drive. The segments do not have to be the same size, and can exist on the same hard drive.

Know how to define a stripe set. A *stripe set* is a collection of 2–32 partitions, from different hard drives, combined into one logical drive. The partitions must be approximately the same size. NT will write data to each of the drives in succession in 64KB stripes. This is also known as level 0 RAID.

Understand mirroring. *Mirroring* is having an exact duplicate of a partition on another hard drive. This is level 1 RAID.

Understand duplexing. *Duplexing* is mirroring, but the two drives must be connected to different controllers. This is another form of level 1 RAID.

Know how to define a stripe set with parity. A *stripe set with parity* is a fault-tolerant disk system that uses 3–32 partitions in a stripe set. Data are written to each of the drives in succession in 64KB stripes. For each stripe, a calculation of parity information is processed and written to a different drive in the set. This allows the system to re-create the data using the parity information in the event that one of the drive partitions in the set fails.

Key Terms and Concepts

ARC path: A path to a particular partition, on a specific disk, on a computer.

FAT (file allocation table):   The file system used by many operating systems to organize and access data on a hard drive. DOS, Windows 95, and Windows NT operating systems can access the FAT file system.

Fault-tolerant disk system: A disk system with redundant data storage that enables it to continue to function in the event of hardware failure.

NTFS (NT file system):   A file system specifically designed for Windows NT. It was designed for larger hard drives and environments that need file- and directory-level security.

Partition: A physical section of a hard drive, set aside for the use of an operating system.

RAID (redundant array of inexpensive disks):   An industry standard definition of fault-tolerant disk subsystems.

RAID level 0/stripe set: A disk system that allows a logical drive to span multiple hard drives.

RAID level 1/disk mirroring: A disk system that has a complete copy of a partition on a separate hard drive.

RAID level 5/disk striping with parity: A disk system that stripes data across multiple drives. In addition, a calculation is performed on each write, which creates parity information that can be used to re-create the data. This information is stored on another drive in the set, which allows the system to continue functioning if one of the drive partitions in the set fails.

Sample Questions

1. Which of the following selections is a valid disk configuration?

   A. Three primary partitions—two set active

   B. Three primary partitions—one set active, one extended partition

   C. Two primary partitions—one set active, one extended partition

   Answer: B—Each disk can have a maximum of four partitions, only one of which can be an extended partition. Since the active partition is the one that the system will use for the boot process, only one primary partition can be set as active.

2. Which of the following selections is a valid configuration for a computer that will dual-boot both Windows 95 and Windows NT?

   A. One large NTFS partition

   B. Two FAT partitions

   C. One FAT32 partition

   D. One large FAT partition

   Answer: B, D—The only file system that both Windows 95 and Windows NT can access is FAT. NTFS is accessible only to NT, and FAT32 is accessible only to Windows 95.

3. When assigning drive letters, in what order does NT perform the following actions?

   A. Starting with drive 0, assign letters to logical drives

   B. Starting with drive 0, assign letters to primary partitions

   C. Starting with drive 0, assign letters to the first primary drive on each disk

   Answer: C, A, B

Choose a protocol for various situations. Protocols include:

- TCP/IP
- NWLink IPX/SPX Compatible Transport
- NetBEUI

In its simplest sense, *protocol* can be defined as a set of rules that govern behavior. Using this definition, one faces, and masters, complex protocols all the time. One of the most common protocols is the one that governs the use of automobiles. Without a set of rules, driving would be a dangerous undertaking (no pun intended).

This analogy can be applied to the protocols that govern the communication between computers. With computers, too, you are controlling traffic on an infrastructure—you need rules that govern right-of-way, how to handle congestion, what types of vehicles are allowed, speed limits, even how to let other drivers know what you are trying to accomplish. If you understand how communication protocols work, it will help you choose the protocols you want to implement in your environment.

You might think that this would be a no-brainer—use all the protocols so that everything can talk to everything else, right? Wrong! Implementing too many protocols on the network is probably the most common cause of slow performance. As a systems engineer, you need to understand when each protocol is appropriate and when it is not. You need to know how you can use a single protocol to provide as many services as possible, and you need to know how to choose that protocol for a given environment. Also, you need to know how to configure each protocol and implement it in the most efficient manner. In other words, you need to understand how computers talk to each other.

NOTE   The objectives in this section are designed to test your ability to choose the right protocols based upon the needs of the network.

Over the course of your MCSE studies, you will be presented with a lot of different protocols. The most important one is probably TCP/IP, because it is the protocol of the Internet. Its strengths and weaknesses will be discussed, as well as two tools to help make implementation a little easier—DHCP and WINS. Microsoft always tests heavily on TCP/IP. This is the protocol of choice—it's one of the three default protocols available when you install NT server.

Some of the other protocols commonly used on NT networks will also be discussed. Each protocol has strengths and weaknesses of which you will need to be aware. (Configuration will be discussed in the next chapter, "Installation and Configuration.")

Critical Information

Of the protocols covered in this objective, the most important one is TCP/IP. Microsoft has made a concerted effort over the last few years to position the NT operating system as Internet-capable. TCP/IP is a key piece of that positioning. Microsoft has also received a bad reputation for its products not integrating well with other operating systems. Microsoft is trying to change that reputation by stressing the various protocol options available in the NT environment.

TCP/IP

TCP/IP is a hot topic in today's networking world. If you pick up any of the industry magazines, you'll find at least one story about the installation, management, or new developments of the TCP/IP suite. TCP is regarded as the future of networking—you will need to understand it to work with the networks of today and tomorrow.

TCP/IP is really a suite of protocols, each piece of which provides a very specific service to the network. The name TCP/IP will be used to refer to the entire suite. If you understand what each piece does, it can greatly increase your ability to solve network-related problems. TCP/IP is also a protocol created, maintained, and advanced by committee. TCP/IP is based upon a complex set of RFCs (requests for comments)—documents that propose additions to the suite and changes to existing protocols. Just about anyone can submit an RFC. It then goes through a series of revisions, until it either gets pushed aside (this happens to most RFCs), gets made an optional piece of a TCP/IP environment, or gets added as part of the standard.

The best way to start when learning TCP/IP is to get a feel for the entire suite. Table 1.3 lists some of the more common protocols in the suite and their functions.

T A B L E 1.3: Common TCP/IP Protocols and Their Functions

Protocol	Function
TCP (transmission control protocol)	Used for connection-oriented, reliable transport of packets
UDP (user datagram protocol)	Used for connectionless, nonreliable transport of packets
IP (Internet protocol)	Provides addressing and routing functions
ICMP (Internet control message protocol)	Used for protocol-level management messages between hosts
ARP (address resolution protocol)	Used to obtain the hardware address of a host. "Resolves" a known IP address to a physical MAC (media access control) address
NetBT (NetBIOS over TCP/IP)	Used by NetBIOS applications to communicate over a TCP/IP-based network
SNMP (simple network management protocol)	An industry standard method of monitoring and configuring hardware or software over a TCP/IP-based network

Windows NT ships with a series of utilities that provide network services on a TCP/IP network. Table 1.4 lists the more commonly used (and tested upon) utilities and their functions.

T A B L E 1.4: Common TCP/IP Utilities and Their Functions

Utility	Function
PING (packet Internet groper)	Tests IP connections
FTP (file transfer protocol)	Bidirectional file transfer services. Requires user to log onto the host providing FTP services, even if anonymous
TFTP (trivial file transfer protocol)	Bidirectional file transfer services. Usually used for UNIX system code files
Telnet	Terminal emulation to a host offering Telnet services
RCP (remote copy protocol)	File transfer services
RSH (remote shell)	Runs commands on a UNIX host
REXEC (remote execution)	Runs a process on a UNIX host
FINGER	Retrieves system information from the host running the finger service
Microsoft Internet Explorer	Browser software
ARP	Displays local ARP cache
IPCONFIG	Displays your current IP configuration
NBTSTAT	Displays cached information for connections using NetBIOS over IP
Netstat	Protocol statistics and connections
ROUTE	Works with the local routing table
Hostname	Displays the host name of your computer
Tracert (trace route)	Displays the route to a remote host

NOTE For this exam, you will not be expected to be an expert in many of these utilities, but you might be expected to know what functions they perform.

Now for the meat of this objective—how does one know if TCP/IP is the right choice? From Microsoft's perspective, that question really should be—why shouldn't one use TCP/IP? TCP/IP is one of the default protocols when you install NT Server, it is discussed in just about every Microsoft course, it is the default protocol used in the classroom for Microsoft-authorized courses, and it is tested upon in just about every MCSE exam. Why? The following bulleted list describes the benefits of TCP/IP.

- TCP/IP was specifically designed to allow diverse computing systems to communicate. No network operating system can hope to make it in the market unless it provides a common protocol that allows communication with existing systems. Most medium- or larger-sized systems are made up of a mixture of hardware and operating systems, and it is not economically feasible to migrate *everything* to NT at once.

- TCP/IP was specifically designed for a routed network. It is the most routable protocol in use today. If you plan on connecting through any type of WAN link, TCP/IP will give you the best performance, the most control, and the least congestion.

- TCP/IP has SNMP (simple network management protocol). This is the industry standard protocol for use in managing routers, bridges, gateways, and all the other components that make up a network. Just about every network-management software package can use the SNMP protocol, and there is no indication that this will change. The bottom line—if you want to manage your network, TCP/IP will be your protocol of choice.

- TCP/IP is the protocol of the Internet. If you plan on connecting to the Internet, creating a Web site, or using e-mail, you will be using TCP/IP.

- A whole slew of tools is available to make TCP/IP more manageable—not only for managing pieces of your network, but for managing the protocol itself. These tools include DHCP (dynamic host configuration protocol), WINS (Windows Internet name service), DNS (domain name service), and others. These tools take the headache out of installing and configuring TCP/IP hosts (more on these tools later in this section).

TCP/IP with DHCP and WINS

As mentioned earlier, numerous tools are available to help manage the TCP/IP protocols. Two of the most commonly implemented tools are DHCP and WINS. Each of these tools is designed to alleviate some of the more common headaches encountered in a TCP/IP network.

DHCP (Dynamic Host Configuration Protocol)

To really appreciate the value of DHCP, you must understand a little more about how TCP/IP works. In an IP network, each host has a unique identifier called an IP address. This address must be unique when compared to all other hosts that are attached to any network with which the local host can communicate. (Stop and think about this—if you are connected to the Internet, your computer must have an address that is different from the addresses of millions of other hosts that can attach to the Internet.)

A discussion of IP addressing is beyond the scope of this book. This knowledge is tested on the exam for the MCSE course "Intranetworking with Microsoft TCP/IP on Microsoft Windows NT 4.0"—thankfully, you won't need to be an expert for the NT Server exam. You do need to know that a unique IP address must be configured on every device that communicates (using TCP/IP) on your network. Along with the IP address, numerous other parameters might also need to be configured. The traditional method for configuring an IP host was to walk to the device, sit down, and start typing. While this was OK for small companies, it had some big drawbacks on most networks.

Traditional IP Headaches

Here is a list of some traditional IP headaches:

- Configuring each host takes time—and lots of it! Each host was configured by hand, which meant that either someone from the IS department went to each device in turn or you trained your users. Neither solution is an efficient use of time and resources.

- Configuration by hand means mistakes! It does not matter how well you type—if you are configuring 500 machines, you are bound to make at least a couple of mistakes. At best, duplicate or invalid addresses will affect only the host where the mistake was made; at worst, they can affect communication across your network.

- Change is problematic. There is a very strict and complicated set of rules for addressing in an IP network. Networks will grow, and sometimes you have to change your addressing scheme. This means changing the configuration at *all* hosts.

- If you add a new IP-based service, you may need to add or change a configuration parameter at each host.

- If you physically move a device within your environment, you may need to change its IP configuration. Usually, when you move a machine, the last thing on your mind is its configuration (you are thinking about what a pain users are, you are griping about a management team that can't leave well enough alone, or you have a list of more important things that you should be doing). Even worse—users occasionally take it upon themselves to move a device without letting you know. In this case, you have addressing problems and don't even know what has changed.

Why DHCP?   Using traditional methods to manage an IP network was a hassle, but it was necessary. DHCP was designed to overcome some of these hassles. The theory behind DHCP is fairly simple—DHCP is a protocol specifically designed to configure IP hosts as they attach to the network. DHCP runs as a service on an NT server. This service manages a pool of IP addresses and configuration parameters. When a DHCP client boots, one of the first things it does is try to find a DHCP server. If it finds one, the DHCP sends it all of the TCP/IP configuration information necessary to function on the network. From a management perspective, this means you have only one place to manage your TCP/IP environment. You assign addresses appropriately, make changes, and add configuration parameters to the "pool"—these changes are reflected every time a client boots on your network.

WINS (Windows Internet Name Service)   Another tool designed to ease the management of a Windows-based network that uses the TCP/IP protocol is WINS. Once again, to really appreciate WINS, you have to delve a little deeper into how IP and NetBIOS work. (NetBIOS is the upper-level protocol that Windows-based networks use to communicate.) WINS adds two basic services to your network—NetBIOS name registration and name resolution.

Name registration   In a NetBIOS-based network (any Windows network), each computer is given a unique name—the NetBIOS name. Since NetBIOS uses this name to communicate between machines, these names *must* be unique. In a traditional NetBIOS network, each machine sends a NetBIOS broadcast that announces its name as it boots. If another host already exists with that name, it will send a message to the new client saying that the name is in use. If it doesn't get a message back, the client assumes that the name is available.

This process works OK on a single-segment network. Unfortunately, most routers do not pass NetBIOS broadcast traffic. This means that there is no mechanism to prevent two computers from having the same name if they are on different network segments. Duplicate names *will* cause communication errors somewhere down the line!

While routers can be set up to pass these broadcasts, there is a more elegant and effective solution—the Windows Internet naming service (WINS). In a WINS environment, each client is configured with the IP address of the WINS server. When the client boots, it sends a message to this server—a request to use a name. The WINS server keeps a database of all the NetBIOS names that are in use—if the name is *not* already in use, it returns an acknowledgement; if the name *is* already in use, it returns a denial. If the name is approved, the WINS server places a record for that client (made up of its NetBIOS name and IP address) in its database.

WINS clients send a name release to the WINS server when they are properly turned off. This allows the WINS server to update its database so that it contains only names for computers that are currently available on the network.

Name resolution Users shouldn't be forced to remember complicated IP addresses for all of the machines with which they need to communicate. Unfortunately, acquiring this address is mandatory before communication can happen. You should give your computers names that are easy to remember so that users can use a "friendly" name to represent a computer.

First, the NetBIOS name (the name you gave the computer when you installed NT) must be resolved into an IP address. Traditionally, this is done by broadcasting a request on the network. Basically, the computer shouts on the wire, "Hey, I'm looking for a computer named XYZ." If computer XYZ receives the request, it will send a message back that contains its IP address. There are two problems with this technique. First, broadcast traffic must be analyzed by *every* computer on the network, adding overhead to machines that are not involved in the communication. Second, most routers are configured *not* to pass broadcast traffic, so your request will be fulfilled only if you are attempting to communicate with a device on your own network segment.

To get around the broadcast problem, you could create a text file named LMHOSTS on every computer. This text file would contain the NetBIOS name and IP address of every computer with which you are going to communicate. What a hassle! Every time you add a new computer to your network, you will have to update the LMHOSTS file on all other computers in your network.

If you have implemented WINS, though, you already have a database that contains the names and IP addresses of all computers available on the network. In a WINS environment, when your computer wants to communicate with another computer, it sends a name-resolution request to the WINS server. This request contains the NetBIOS name of the machine to which you wish to connect. The WINS server looks through its database. If it finds a matching NetBIOS name, it returns the IP address of that machine.

Why WINS? WINS saves time and traffic on your network, therefore helping to keep it efficient. Without WINS, many of the procedures for establishing a connection with another machine are based upon broadcast traffic. Broadcast traffic is the bane of systems engineers. When a packet is broadcast, all computers that receive it must stop what they are doing and waste time reading the packet to determine if they should respond. In a WINS environment, all of this traffic is directed to the WINS server. It is the only computer that will analyze these packets, while all others continue processing without interruption.

NWLink IPX/SPX Compatible Transport

Now that you have a firm grasp of TCP/IP, you can turn your attention to the other protocols supported by NT. These protocols can be called "special case" protocols, because in most cases you will implement them when the situation demands it, but not as your main protocol for communication.

NWLink is Microsoft's implementation of the IPX/SPX protocol suite used by Novell's NetWare products. On most NT networks, you will implement NWLink only if you need to communicate with a NetWare server. As far as the protocol suite goes, IPX/SPX has some advantages and disadvantages of which you will need to be aware. For that reason, NWLink is not installed by default on an NT machine, Server, or Workstation.

IPX/SPX is easy to implement and manage. There are no complex addressing schemes. Each computer gets its unique identifier from its network interface card. This means that you do not have to configure any unique parameters at each computer for communication to occur. Further advantages include:

- IPX/SPX supports routing between networks.

- IPX/SPX allows you to easily connect your NT environment to your NetWare environment. You can slowly integrate NT servers into your network, without having to replace your existing resources.

NOTE   Installing NWLink is only the first step in integration. The rest of the process will be discussed in Chapter 4, "Connectivity."

Although there is no address configuration at each computer, you do have to give unique identification values to each network segment. Unlike TCP/IP, there is no addressing scheme to these addresses. The LAN administrator comes up with a segment-numbering plan and implements it. Other disadvantages include:

- Until recently, there was no way to register your IPX network addresses. This made it difficult to connect to any kind of central network or shared wiring scheme.

- IPX/SPX is not used on the Internet. If you intend to connect to the Internet, you must use TCP/IP.

- IPX/SPX does not support SNMP.

- IPX/SPX uses more broadcast-based traffic to organize the network. Although the process is automatic, it increases the traffic on your network.

NOTE   On the exam, you will implement NWLink only if you need to communicate with Novell NetWare-based file servers.

NetBEUI

NetBIOS extended user interface (NetBEUI) is a protocol that was originally developed for small departmental LANs (with less than 200 computers). It is fast enough for most small networks. Unfortunately, NetBEUI cannot be routed, so it is not suited to any kind of WAN environment. NetBEUI relies on broadcast-based traffic for many of its functions, so it can place more overhead on the network than other protocols. The Windows NT implementation of NetBEUI provides interoperability with Microsoft LAN Manager and Windows for Workgroups networks. NetBEUI provides the following benefits:

- Both connection and connectionless communication

- Self configuration and self timing

- Error protection against corruption on the wire

- Because of its limited function set, requires a very small amount of memory

Exam Essentials

There is no network without connectivity, and there is no connectivity without properly installed and configured protocols. This statement implies that understanding the various protocols that can be used on an NT network is critical to the success of any MCSE in the field. Microsoft is aware of this and tests accordingly.

Know the advantages of TCP/IP. TCP/IP was designed to allow diverse clients to communicate. Every major operating system can use the TCP/IP protocol suite. TCP/IP was designed to be a routable protocol, has many mature tools available for management, includes SNMP, and is the protocol of the Internet.

Understand the major protocols that comprise the TCP/IP suite. These protocols include TCP (transmission control protocol), UDP (user datagram protocol), IP (Internet protocol), ICMP (Internet control message protocol), ARP (address resolution protocol), NetBT (NetBIOS over TCP/IP), and SNMP (simple network management protocol).

Know the tools commonly used on a TCP/IP network. These tools include PING (packet Internet groper), FTP (file transfer protocol), TFTP (trivial file transfer protocol), Telnet, RCP (remote copy protocol), RSH (remote shell), REXEC (remote execution), FINGER,

Microsoft Internet Explorer, ARP, IPCONFIG, NBTSTAT, Netstat, ROUTE, Hostname, and Tracert (trace route).

Understand why DHCP is used.   On a traditional TCP/IP-based network, each host must be configured with a unique IP address and other TCP/IP-based parameters. By using a DHCP server, you can avoid this manual process. DHCP was designed to configure IP clients dynamically from a central server.

Understand why WINS is used.   Traditional NetBIOS networks use broadcast traffic to ensure that computer names are unique and to find the IP address of each host with which they must communicate. A WINS server provides two services:

1. It builds and controls a database of registered names on the network, thus preventing duplication.

2. Clients can access this database to resolve a NetBIOS name into an IP address.

Since the clients are configured with the IP address of the WINS server, any WINS traffic will be directed to it via broadcast. Unlike broadcast packets, these directed packets can cross routers, thus ensuring communication across a routed network.

Know when to install NWLink on an NT server.   You use the NWLink protocol if your NT server must communicate with a Novell NetWare server.

Understand the advantages and disadvantages of NWLink.
NWLink is easy to implement and manage, supports routed networks, and allows easy connection to NetWare servers. However, each network segment must have a unique address, most network addresses are not registered with a managing service (which can make it difficult to connect to a shared wiring system), NWLink is not used on the Internet, it does not support SNMP, and it uses more broadcast traffic to organize the network.

Understand the limitations of the NetBEUI protocol. NetBEUI was originally designed for nonrouted, small networks with less than 200 computers.

Key Terms and Concepts

Dynamic host configuration protocol (DHCP): A service that configures TCP/IP clients automatically as they attach to the network.

LMHOSTS: A text file, stored on each client, used to store NetBIOS names and their associated IP addresses.

Name registration: An action taken by the client as it joins the network. The NetBIOS client queries the WINS server to determine if its name is unique.

Name resolution: Before two NetBIOS computers can communicate, they must acquire each other's IP addresses. Name resolution is the process of asking a WINS server for the IP address of a particular NetBIOS name.

NetBEUI: A nonroutable protocol designed for small networks.

NWLink: Microsoft's implementation of the IPX/SPX protocol suite.

Simple network management protocol (SNMP): One of the protocols in the TCP/IP suite. This protocol was designed to allow remote monitoring and management of resources, and is commonly used by network management tools.

TCP/IP: A suite of protocols designed to provide diverse computing environments with the ability to communicate.

Windows Internet name service (WINS): A service used to build a database of NetBIOS clients and their IP addresses. This database is used to prevent duplicate names on the network and resolve names into IP addresses.

Sample Questions

1. Which of the following tools can be used to automatically con-figure a TCP/IP client?

    A. DHCP

    B. WINS

    C. Client Manager

    Answer: A—DHCP (dynamic host configuration protocol) is a service designed to configure TCP/IP clients as they attach to the network.

2. A network administrator has noticed that network performance has decreased since 20 new workstations were added to the network. Which of the following services might help correct this problem?

    A. DHCP

    B. WINS

    C. RAS

    D. IIS

    Answer: B—By default, name registration and resolution are accomplished by broadcasting packets on the network. These packets can produce heavy traffic in some environments. One way to decrease the amount of broadcast traffic is to implement a WINS server. WINS clients direct their traffic to the WINS server rather than broadcasting on the network.

3. Which of the following statements are correct concerning the NetBEUI protocol?

    A. It is self configuring.

    B. It was developed for small networks.

    C. It uses very little memory.

    D. Routers must be configured to pass NetBEUI packets across a network.

    Answer: A, B, C—Only answer D is incorrect. NetBEUI is a non-routable protocol.

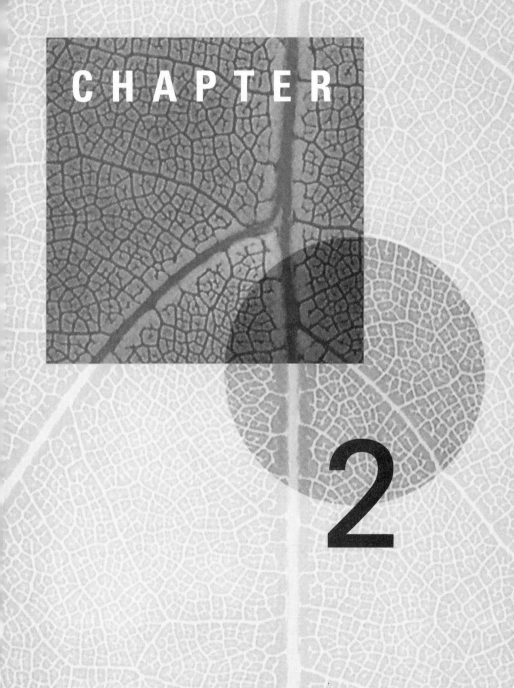

CHAPTER

2

Installation and Configuration

Microsoft Exam Objectives Covered in This Chapter:

▶ **Install Windows NT Server on Intel-based platforms.**
(pages 39 – 47)

▶ **Install Windows NT Server to perform various server roles.
Server roles include:** *(pages 48 – 58)*
- Primary domain controller
- Backup domain controller
- Member server

▶ **Install Windows NT Server by using various methods.
Installation methods include:** *(pages 58 – 76)*
- CD-ROM
- Over the network
- Network Client Administrator
- Express versus custom

▶ **Configure protocols and protocol bindings. Protocols
include:** *(pages 76 – 87)*
- TCP/IP
- NWLink IPX/SPX Compatible Transport
- NetBEUI

▶ **Configure network adapters. Considerations
include:** *(pages 87 – 95)*
- Changing IRQ, I/O base, and memory addresses
- Configuring multiple adapters

▶ **Configure Windows NT Server core services. Services
include:** *(pages 96 – 111)*
- Directory Replicator
- License Manager
- Other services

Configure peripherals and devices. Peripherals and devices include: *(pages 112 – 126)*

- Communication devices
- SCSI devices
- Tape device drivers
- UPS devices and UPS service
- Mouse drivers, display drivers, and keyboard drivers

Configure hard disks to meet various requirements. Requirements include: *(pages 127 – 138)*

- Allocating disk space capacity
- Providing redundancy
- Improving performance
- Providing security
- Formatting

Configure printers. Tasks include: *(pages 139 – 154)*

- Adding and configuring a printer
- Implementing a printer pool
- Setting print priorities

Configure a Windows NT Server computer for various types of client computers. Client computer types include: *(pages 155 – 159)*

- Windows NT Workstation
- Microsoft Windows 95
- Microsoft MS-DOS based

Y ou have made the difficult decisions. Now, it is time to get to the real work—installing the first server on your network. Installation and configuration are not one-time things; they are an ongoing process. As your network grows, your users will demand more and more services. As these demands grow, you will constantly add new hardware to the network.

In Chapter 1, you developed a task list and made decisions on how to implement and provide the basic services your customers will need. By the end of this chapter, you will learn how to update your network to meet the demands of everyday life. Your task list will grow to include the following items:

- Communications

- Adding disk space while allowing for future growth

- Upgrading the tape backup unit

- Adding an uninterruptible power supply

- Upgrading the mouse and video cards

- Putting in a new printer

For a network to be useful, it must provide services to its clients in an easy-to-use format. The company's newest employee should be able to sit down and be productive *now*. The network should be there whenever someone needs to access it. Information and data flow, and services are offered and used. The information in this chapter will help you achieve those goals.

Some of the objectives in this chapter are stressed heavily on the exam. For example, if you know several of the command-line switches used during an installation, it will be more helpful than knowing how to configure certain peripherals and devices. You will need to understand the differences between a PDC, BDC, and member server. Study the objective on hard disk space, and understand the different types of redundancy. Also, questions about minimum requirements for disk striping with parity will pop up in the most unexpected places.

NOTE The objective on printing is crucial. The exam authors must be end users. Experience has shown that end users lose patience more quickly when printing is not available than at any other time.

Install Windows NT Server on Intel-based platforms.

This objective is a behind-the-scenes look at what happens during the installation process. It is not only important to know which and how many pieces to use, but how the pieces will work together to provide the desired results. This section describes how the installation process will work and what NT will do each step along the way. Some installations fail, and it is far easier to troubleshoot problems when you know what was supposed to happen next.

Critical Information

Are you ready to examine the installation process? Is the target computer ready for the installation process? What do you really need for this installation to be successful?

NOTE The "Critical Information" section provides a broad overview, covering only system requirements. The steps involved in the actual installation will be covered in the "Necessary Procedures" section.

NT 4 can be installed on a variety of platforms, including the Intel *x*86, Pentium-based computers, and RISC-based computers. NT 4 will even run on the MIPS R4x00-based microprocessor or higher, the Digital Alpha AXP-based microprocessor, and the PReP-compliant PowerPC-based microprocessor. This book (and the exam) concentrates on the Intel platform.

Microsoft lists minimal hardware requirements that must be met before the installation begins. The official requirements for Windows NT Server 4, as published in Microsoft's TechNet, are as follows:

- 16MB of RAM

- VGA-level video support

- Keyboard

- IDE, EIDE, SCSI, or ESDI hard disk

- 486/33 processor or better

- CD-ROM drive, 1.44MB or 1.2MB floppy disk drive, or active network connection

Because you bought this book rather than one of the others, it implies that you have worked with NT. You *know* that a 486/33 with 16MB of RAM would not cut it in your home lab, much less a production environment. Microsoft agrees, so they have also released a *suggested minimum* list:

- 486DX2/50 processor or better

- 32MB of RAM

- 28.8 v.34 external modem, for remote debugging and troubleshooting

- Windows NT–compatible CD-ROM drive

The folks from Redmond also forgot to mention a network interface card (NIC). You must have one, and it must be on Microsoft's NT hardware compatibility list (HCL). You can find the HCL at Microsoft's NT Web site. How much disk space will an NT installation take? It depends on the accessories that you install, but the minimum space requirements for Windows NT Workstation and Server, as listed on TechNet, are as follows:

- Standard installation: 124MB of free disk space

- WINNT /b: an additional 24MB of free disk space

- Copying I386 folder to hard disk: 223MB more free disk space

---

NOTE Don't worry if you are not familiar with the WINNT /b command. The command-line switches for the NT Installation Wizard will be covered later in this chapter.

These disk space requirements assume that you have a standard hard disk controller, not an enhanced integrated device electronics (EIDE) hard disk controller.

NOTE Some 486 computers operate under the assumption that integrated device electronics (IDE) drives can be a maximum of 504MB. However, translation mode fakes out the system—the inner workings of the computer may think that the new EIDE drive is only 504MB, when in reality it might be 5GB.

Make sure that the disk is partitioned and formatted. Here are the recommendations from Microsoft on the disk configurations:

- The root folder (the folder to which you will install NT 4) should be on a disk formatted with either the original FAT 16 format (translated to NTFS during installation) or NTFS from NT version 3.51 or 4. If you are using NTFS, the drive can be compressed. NT will not install on a hard drive that has been compressed with any other utility.

- If your target drive uses address translation, it should use:
  - Logical block addressing (LBA)
  - ONTrack Disk Manager
  - EZDrive
  - Extended cylinder head sector

If you make sure that your BIOS and hard drive support these translations, you should be in good shape.

NOTE If you are unsure of the translation method used for your drive, try to find the manual for the disk. If you are unsuccessful, check the drive maker's Web site or do an Internet search on the make and model number. As a last resort, buy a new large drive that will act as your root drive. As cheap as these drives are, it's worth it to avoid spending time in subsequent troubleshooting.

Keep in mind that these are the recommended *minimum* requirements. NT will make use of all of the tools you give it, so give it as much as you can. The more advanced the processor and the more memory you give the server, the better.

Necessary Procedures

Now that you know what NT demands in the way of hardware, it is time to examine what will happen during the installation process.

If you have installed NT Workstation, you know that you can install the operating system in several ways. Microsoft provides three pre-configured setup scenarios, as well as a Custom option. If you select the Custom option, it gives you the right to install NT Workstation just the way you want it.

With NT Server, there are no preconfigured methods of installation—you will perform a custom installation. Most of the decisions that you will need to make were covered in Chapter 1 and are available in your working papers.

The installation is really quite elegant and is carried out in four easily definable steps, each with its own set of tasks to accomplish. Working together, these tasks lay the foundation on which your network will be built. The four steps are as follows:

- Initializing installation
- Gathering information
- Installing NT networking
- Finishing setup

Initializing Installation

A complete installation will be covered later in this chapter. For now, it is important to know what you will face as you go through the installation. During the initialization phase:

- NT checks for previous versions of NT. Will this be a new install or an upgrade? If it is an upgrade, NT will ask you some pointed questions about the directory into which you will put the operating system. NT 4's default root folder is WINNT (this is a change from previous versions).

- NT examines your computer to see what hardware it recognizes. It will then check whether what it found corresponds to what you think it should have found.

- NT looks for a formatted disk partition. If you plan to dual boot between DOS and NT, you must have at least 200MB of free disk space in the DOS partition so that NT can use it for temporary file storage. The Installation Wizard will copy files to the DOS partition before the installation process continues.

- The Installation Wizard will ask you which file system you will use—NTFS or FAT. NTFS is more effective for drives over 400MB.

- The initialization phase completes when NT asks you where you want to put the program files.

Gathering Information

This phase is as simple as it sounds. The progressive information screens will ask for the following items:

- Name and organization of the person to whom the copy of NT is licensed. At this point, do you enter your own name, or the name of the MIS director, the CEO, or the CIO?

- Licensing mode: Per Server or Per Seat.

  - Per Server licensing—With Per Server licensing, each client access license (CAL) is assigned to a specific server for the basic file and print services. Once a CAL has been assigned to a server, that user can access any file or share on that server. The number of CALs must equal the maximum number of clients that will connect to that server at the same time. If your server reaches the maximum number of licensed connections and another client attempts to connect, NT will issue an error message and not allow the connection.

- Per Seat licensing—With Per Seat licensing, a CAL applies to a specific seat or client. With this licensing mode selected, an unlimited number of clients can attach to your server, as long as each of the clients has a license. This is an NT Server CAL. A Windows 95 workstation does not necessarily have the right to attach to the server.

NOTE If you are not sure which licensing mode to choose, use Per Server. You can convert from Per Server to Per Seat one time only at no cost. It is not possible to convert from Per Seat to Per Server. Be sure to look over the section on licensing carefully and understand the differences between Per Seat and Per Server, and when to use each.

- Computer name. This name must be 15 characters or less and unique among all computers, workgroups, and domain names on the network. You can change it later.

- The type of server to install: primary domain controller (PDC), backup domain controller (BDC), or member server.

- A password for the administrator account.

- Optional components to install. Here, you will have to make some decisions. For the most part, though, these are not installation-critical decisions—if you decide to skip this phase, you can always install the optional components later. Optional components include:

  - Accessibility options—These options make running your server easier for the physically challenged.

  - Accessories such as WordPad, Paint, Clock, and Calculator.

  - Communications programs for rudimentary modem communications.

  - Games, such as FreeCell and Solitaire.

  - Windows messaging, which will give you an e-mail client.

  - Multimedia programs.

Also, have a 3.5-inch floppy disk handy. You may want to create an emergency repair diskette, which can come in handy in times of crisis.

Installing NT Networking

The purpose of buying and installing NT Server is to enable users to share information and resources. To make that happen, you have to install NT networking. This piece of the puzzle provides the communication link between the server and all of the resources on the network. It is a subsystem that can consist of NICs, modems, software services, and protocols. You will have to provide information about the following items:

- Whether the computer will be on LAN, dialed into remotely, or both.

- Which network adapter cards are installed and the configuration parameters for each.

- Which protocols to install—for example, TCP/IP, NetBEUI, or NWLink.

- Whether any additional network services need to be installed—for example, Internet Information Server, proxy services, or DHCP.

- Which domain the computer will join. You have already chosen the role that the server will play in the domain.

Finishing Setup

To finish setup, you need to provide the following information to the new NT server:

- The date, time, and time zone in which the server will reside.

NOTE   Be sure that the date, time, and time zone reflect where the server will "live," not where you are when you install it.

- Statistics about the video card driver and its configuration. Be aware of the optimum resolution of the card/monitor combination.

Exam Essentials

As mentioned in the chapter introduction, parts of this section are stressed on the exam. Be sure to look over this material carefully.

Know the differences between licensing modes. Microsoft is famous for providing you with situational questions on the exam. Be prepared—the licensing information lends itself to this type of question.

Key Terms and Concepts

\WINNT: Default root folder for the installation of Windows NT 4.

BDC: Backup domain controller.

CAL (client access license): License that allows a workstation to access an NT server.

EIDE (enhanced integrated device electronics): Allows for drives of higher capacity. An EIDE paddleboard can handle a maximum of four devices.

Emergency repair diskette: A set of critical data that can help boot an NT server and repair system files in the event of a catastrophic server failure.

FAT (file allocation table): The original DOS-based format method of saving and accessing disk files. In an NT server, drives under 400MB should be formatted as FAT.

HCL: Windows NT hardware compatibility list.

IDE: A hardware disk technology in which the controller hardware is placed on a circuit board attached to the drive itself. IDE devices can be disk drives or CD-ROM drives. You can configure and control these devices as a single device or in pairs.

Member server: An application or resource server in an NT domain that has no NT domain administrative responsibilities.

NIC: Network interface card.

NTFS (NT file system):   NTFS is most efficient in drives greater than 400MB. In addition to other capabilities, NTFS allows for local file system security.

PDC: Primary domain controller.

Per Seat licensing: NT server licensing method. In Per Seat licensing, the CAL is assigned to the workstation. Each server can handle an unlimited number of clients, as long as each workstation has a CAL.

Per Server licensing: NT server licensing method. In Per Server licensing, the CALs are assigned to the server. Each server will have a maximum number of connections.

Sample Questions

1. Suppose that your network consists of an NT 4 primary domain controller. It is configured with 50 CALs and set to use Per Server licensing. Your users continue to access the resources provided by your network, and it has become necessary to add a second server to provide BDC capabilities. Your client workstations include 35 NT 4 workstations, 5 Windows 95 workstations, and 5 Windows for Workgroups workstations. What would be the most cost-effective way to license the servers?

   Answer—Since the scenario did not mention network growth, you can convert the PDC to Per Seat licensing and configure the new server to use the Per Seat mode as well. In this case, if you switch the PDC to Per Seat mode and configure the BDC to Per Seat mode, you would meet the objectives of the scenario.

Install Windows NT Server to perform various server roles. Server roles include:

- Primary domain controller
- Backup domain controller
- Member server

When you install an NT server, you should have a clear idea of the services that it will provide to your network clients. An NT server can provide numerous services—from DHCP and WINS to acting as a domain controller and your e-mail server. Each of these services will add overhead to a server. This overhead will be characterized in Chapter 5, "Monitoring and Optimization." For now, the discussion will be limited to the first service-related decision you have to make during the installation—whether a server should be a domain controller? In Chapter 1, a domain controller was defined as a server that holds a copy of the domain accounts database (SAM). However, as you'll see in this section, that definition is not complete.

Critical Information

One of the first things that you do when planning a network is determine the role each server will perform. This decision will influence your purchase plans, network design, and long-term management.

Primary and Backup Domain Controllers

Primary and backup domain controllers are similar—they both hold a copy of the SAM and are used for authentication during the logon process. Since they are alike in their duties, their hardware needs are similar. Before their function is examined, hardware will be discussed.

Necessary Hardware

The process of choosing hardware for a domain controller is not as easy as it would seem. Sure, you *could* just buy the best computer that you can afford—but how do you know whether that will be enough? Before you buy your server, you need to know the load.

Load is mainly determined on a domain controller by the size of the SAM. The bigger the SAM, the bigger the load. A big SAM indicates a large number of users, and the more users there are, the more logons the server will have to authenticate and the more changes there will be to the database. Before you can determine the minimum requirements for a domain controller, you need to approximate the size of the SAM it will support.

If you took the Microsoft-authorized Course 689, "Supporting Microsoft Windows NT 4.0 Enterprise Technologies," you have a piece of software to help you. From your class CD-ROM, install the Job Aid and follow the directions. If not, you'll have to use math.

The number of objects you define determines the size of the SAM. Each object represents a record in the database; each type of object has a record of a different size. Table 2.1 describes the sizes of the various records in the SAM.

T A B L E 2.1: Objects in the SAM

Object Class	Size
User account	1KB
Computer account	.5KB
Global group account	512 bytes plus 12 bytes for every member
Local group account	512 bytes plus 36 bytes for every member

You need to estimate the number of user and computer accounts that you will create. This *should* be easy—determine how many users and NT-based servers and workstations are in your company. Next, you need to estimate the number of groups that you will create. Analyze the resources you will share, then come up with a plan for sharing each resource. This will tell you approximately how many groups you will need to create. Once you have the number of groups, estimate how many users will be members of each group. Take the numbers and do a little math.

Once you've calculated the size of the database, use the information in Table 2.2 to determine the minimum hardware needed to support it.

T A B L E 2.2: Hardware Requirements Based upon SAM Size

Number of Users	SAM Size (MB)	CPU Needed	RAM Needed (MB)
3,000	5	486DX/33	16
7,500	10	486DX/66	32
10,000	15	Pentium, MIPS, or Alpha	48
15,000	20	Pentium, MIPS, or Alpha	64
30–40,000	40	Pentium, MIPS, or Alpha	128

WARNING These numbers were obtained from Microsoft's TechNet Technical Information Network (Article Q130914). They are probably a little low for most installations, because Microsoft assumes that the server will be dedicated to the task of acting as a domain controller—in other words, that you will not use the server to provide any other network services.

When planning your domain, you should compare the estimated size of the SAM with the hardware you will have available as a server. If the hardware won't support the SAM, buy a more robust server. The only other option is to split the domain into multiple domains, until the hardware *will* support the SAM, which can make for a long-term administrative headache.

Now that you have chosen your hardware, the functions of domain controllers can be discussed. The primary responsibility of domain controllers is user authentication. Since domain controllers are the only computers that hold the accounts database, all users must access them when logging onto the network. When the user logs onto the network, their name and password are compared to information in the SAM. If the name and password match an existing account, the domain controller creates the SID (system identification) for that user. The SID contains the identification and the access control elements of the user and any groups of which the user is a member. This information will be used when the user tries to access a resource, so copies of the accounts database must be synchronized on a regular basis. If it isn't, information about the user might not be current at the domain controller to which the user attaches during the logon process.

Synchronizing Primary and Backup Domain Controllers

The primary domain controller holds the main copy of the accounts database. All changes to the SAM must be made on the primary domain controller (PDC), which then updates the copies stored on the backup domain controllers (BDC). This is known as a *single master model,* because all changes are made to the master copy and then synchronized with all other copies. The process of synchronization is fairly simple. Every time a backup domain controller comes online, one of the first things it does is try to find the primary domain controller (PDC) to verify that its user accounts database is up to date. The PDC keeps a log of all changes to the database. Each change that has been made is given a version ID—think of this as a counter. When the PDC updates a BDC, it records the highest version ID (counter) on the updated records. The next time the PDC checks for changes, it compares the highest version ID of the last synchronization with the version IDs in the change log. If anything in the change log has a higher value than the last recorded update of the BDC, that change has not been synchronized on the BDC. The PDC will then synchronize the changes on the BDC.

By default, the PDC checks the BDC version IDs against the change log every five minutes. This time period is referred to as the pulse. There are two types of updates—partial and complete. In a partial update, only the changed information is synchronized. In a complete update, the entire database is sent to the BDC. From an optimization perspective, it is preferable to do a partial update rather than send the entire database.

A complete update might occur for various reasons:

- Every time a new BDC is brought online.

- When the change log fills up (it has a specific size), the PDC starts writing over the oldest change records. If there are enough changes in a pulse, the last known version ID for a BDC will no longer be in the change log. In this case, the PDC can no longer be sure of exactly which changes have been synchronized and which have not. At this point, a complete update must occur.

- When an error occurs during a partial update.

- When the administrator forces a complete update. (Use Server Manager to accomplish this task.)

This synchronization traffic can have an impact on where you physically place domain controllers on the network backbone. If you place a backup domain controller on the other side of a WAN link, the synchronization traffic will have to cross that link—this could affect the link's ability to support other types of traffic. On the other hand, if you don't place a BDC across the wire, all logon traffic will have to cross the link to find a domain controller for authentication.

Microsoft expects you to understand the trade-off between synchronization traffic and logon traffic. For faster synchronization, put all domain controllers in a central location. For faster logons, put the domain controllers near the users so that logons can be done locally.

WARNING Most consultants consider synchronization traffic to be a reasonable cost of business. You don't optimize for background traffic—you optimize for your users. If you force users to cross a WAN link every time they log on, it is not a good design. The logon process will take too long, and if the link is down, users cannot log onto local resources. Distributed design adds significant redundancy and insulates your network somewhat from data-pipeline outages that can be beyond your control.

Most of the time, you will distribute domain controllers across your network so that users don't have to cross any slow links to log on, which means that the synchronization traffic *will* have to cross those links. If you are short on bandwidth, you can change a couple of registry parameters to control the amount and frequency of traffic generated.

Synchronization Parameters in the Registry

There are two ways to control synchronization traffic—controlling how often it happens and/or controlling how much traffic is generated. Both of these methods are accomplished through a parameter called the ReplicationGovernor. This parameter is set to a percentage. By default, it is set to 100 percent, which means that the PDC can take up to 100 percent of the available bandwidth and buffer 128KB of data at a time. This can greatly affect a slow link where users are also competing for a limited amount of bandwidth. If you set the ReplicationGovernor to 50 percent, the NetLogon service can buffer only 50 percent as much data (64KB) for each transmission and can have synchronization messages on the network only 50 percent of the time. This will spread out the traffic over twice as much time.

WARNING If you set this value too low, it can prevent synchronization from completing. It can also make more complete updates (rather than partials) occur because it takes longer for changes to be synchronized.

You can also change the timing of the pulse. By default, the PDC checks for changes every five minutes. You can increase this time by increasing the pulse parameter—to a maximum value of 48 hours. (Once again, though, if you check for changes less frequently, it is more likely that you will be forced to do a complete update.)

To increase the odds of being able to do partial updates, increase the size of the change log by changing the ChangeLogSize parameter. By default, the change log is 64KB, which is enough room to record approximately 2,000 changes. You should make changes to the pulse and the ChangeLogSize in parallel.

Member Server

A *member server* is any NT server that was not installed as a domain controller. Unlike domain controllers, member servers are not involved in the management of the domain accounts database, which means that the processing power and memory will be more fully utilized by functions other than domain administration. You might install a server as a member server for three reasons:

- You already have enough domain controllers for your environment. Microsoft recommends that you have at least one backup domain controller for fault tolerance. After that, though, they recommend one backup domain controller for every 2,000 users. If you have 5,000 users and 10 servers, Microsoft would recommend one PDC (mandatory for each domain) and three backup domain controllers, for a total of four domain controllers.

- A server performs a function that is so processor or memory intensive that no resources are left for the overhead of acting as a domain controller. Perhaps the server will act as an SQL or Exchange server. In this case, you might choose to limit any other services that it provides.

- Member servers can be moved from domain to domain. Domain controllers, on the other hand, cannot be moved from the domain into which they were installed. If a server might be moved from domain to domain, it would be better to install it as a member server.

Exam Essentials

As discussed in Chapter 1, planning is critical if you want to create an NT-based network that is manageable. You must understand the role of your NT servers. This objective concerns the various roles that NT servers can take in your network. For this exam, you must be comfortable with the various services that an NT server can provide.

Understand domain controllers.   A domain controller is an NT server that holds the domain security accounts manager (SAM) database. Because it holds the database, the server can perform authentication functions during the logon process.

Know the difference between a primary domain controller (PDC) and a backup domain controller (BDC).   The PDC holds the master copy of the domain accounts database. All changes and additions to the database must be made to this copy first. The PDC then synchronizes those changes to all of the BDCs in the domain. BDCs hold a copy of the domain accounts database. They receive all changes made to the master copy from the PDC on a regular basis.

Understand member servers.   A member server is any NT server that was not installed as a domain controller. Member servers cannot be used to authenticate a user to the domain. Unlike domain controllers, member servers can be moved from one domain to another.

Understand the process for determining the hardware needed at a domain controller.   First, estimate the size of the SAM. Then, check Table 2.2 to determine the hardware that will be necessary for a SAM of that size. If your hardware will not support the SAM, upgrade as needed. Otherwise, partition the database until you reach an estimated size that your hardware will support.

Understand the synchronization process between the PDC and a BDC.   Every five minutes (the default pulse value), the PDC checks its SAM for changes. It compares the version ID for the last changes sent to the BDC with the version ID of changes in the change log. It will synchronize all changes in the change log that have version IDs greater than that of the last change updated to the BDC.

Understand how the ReplicationGovernor works. The ReplicationGovernor is a registry setting that controls the synchronization process between domain controllers. It controls how often the synchronization process will occur and how much data can be transferred. By default, it is set to 100 percent, which means that 128KB of data can be buffered for updates and the PDC can utilize 100 percent of the available bandwidth to accomplish this task. If you change the value to 50 percent, the PDC can buffer only 64KB for transfer and can have synchronization messages active only 50 percent of the time. If you set this value too low, the BDCs may never fully synchronize.

Key Terms and Concepts

Backup domain controller (BDC): An NT server that performs authentication functions using a copy of the domain accounts database.

Change log: A log of the changes made to the domain accounts database. Used to determine which records need to be updated on the BDCs.

Domain controller: An NT server that holds a copy of the domain accounts database.

Primary domain controller (PDC): An NT server that performs authentication functions using the master copy of the domain accounts database.

ReplicationGovernor: A registry setting that controls the frequency of synchronization and the amount of data transferred.

Synchronization: The PDC holds the master copy of the SAM. When changes are made to the database, the process of synchronization updates the copies stored on the BDCs.

Version ID: Each change in the change log is given a version ID (counter). The PDC compares the version ID of the last change replicated to the BDC with the version ID of changes in the log file. Changes with higher values need to be replicated.

Sample Questions

1. When the change log fills up, which of the following things will occur?

   A. A new log will be created.

   B. Records will be overwritten.

   C. A complete update will occur in the next pulse.

   D. An administrative alert will be sent to members of the administrators group.

   Answer: B, C—The change log records transactions to the domain SAM. If it fills up between synchronization pulses, the oldest records will be overwritten. Since this means that certain changes might not have been synchronized to the BDCs, a complete update will occur.

2. If you are placing domain controllers to facilitate the logon process, which of the following statements would be correct?

   A. Place all domain controllers on the same side of a WAN link.

   B. Place domain controllers near the users that will need them.

   C. The placement of domain controllers will have no effect on the logon process.

   Answer: B—Users must access a domain controller each time they log onto the network. If all domain controllers are across a WAN link (from the users), authentication traffic will have to cross that WAN link every time a user logs on.

3. To update a member server to a domain controller, what would you do?

   A. Use the PROMOTE.EXE command-line utility.

   B. Reinstall Windows NT, choosing to make the server a domain controller during the installation process.

   C. Use Server Manager.

   D. Install the domain controller service in the Network control panel.

Answer: B—There is no convenient way to promote a member server to a domain controller. The only method would be to back up all data, install NT Server, and then restore your data from the backup.

Install Windows NT Server by using various methods. Installation methods include:

- CD-ROM
- Over the network
- Network Client Administrator
- Express versus custom

Before you can start working on the rest of your wish list, you have to install NT on the first computer. To do this, you will perform a CD-ROM installation. You can install from it directly or copy the directory to a network share and make sure that the installation files are always available. NT installation files, like those for Windows 95, should be available on the network. When something new is added to an NT server, it needs to access information on the installation CD. If you make these files available on the network, you won't have to carry around a CD.

You will also need to configure the system to handle communication with workstations. This is done through management of the agent software. Once the installation has been completed, examine closely the "Exam Essentials" section. This objective includes several key areas that are favorites of exam writers everywhere.

Critical Information

Before you begin the installation process, look very closely at your new server and make sure that every component is on the NT hardware compatibility list (HCL). If you aren't sure what you have in your computer, NT can help—with a handy utility called the NTHQ tool. This tool is stored on the NT Server CD-ROM in \Support\ HQTool. Put a formatted floppy disk in drive A: and run the MAKE-DISK tool. Once MAKEDISK has finished, restart the computer with the diskette in the drive. Keep in mind that this is not the most sophisticated diagnostic tool. For example, if you have 128MB of RAM in your system, the tool will report it as >=64MB. When you run the tool, it will show you only what is in your computer that NT recognizes and cares about.

If you know that there are SCSI devices in your system, try running SCSITOOL, which is in the \Support\SCSITool folder of the NT Server CD-ROM. Insert a floppy disk in drive A:, run the MAKE-DISK utility, and reboot with the floppy disk still in the drive. SCSI-TOOL will check your system and report on any SCSI controllers that it finds.

It is now time to start the actual installation of your first NT server. You have already located the CD-ROM that contains NT Server. The NT installation program works fastest from an NT environment, which presents an interesting dilemma—how do you install from an NT environment without having NT installed? Microsoft has provided a simple solution. Use the three 3.5-inch diskettes that came with NT Server to boot the computer. As part of the boot process, the system hardware is analyzed and the CD-ROM is recognized, providing the medium for the installation program.

CD-ROM

Some of you are installing NT for the second, third, or fourth time—you have the licenses and the CD-ROM, but seem to have misplaced the diskettes. Don't worry. These diskettes can be re-created by doing as follows:

1. Put the NT Server CD-ROM in a CD-ROM drive and open a command prompt. The type of operating system on the computer you are using for this procedure does not matter. You need to have a computer with working CD-ROM and 3.5-inch disk drives.

2. Select the drive that contains the CD-ROM. For example, the D: drive.

3. Select the i386 directory. You will see a file called WINNT.EXE.

4. Type **WINNT /?** at the command prompt and then press Enter.

When you press Enter, you will be presented with a list of all the command-line switches for the NT installation program. The proper syntax for utilizing these switches is as follows:

```
WINNT.EXE [/S[:]sourcepath] [/T[:]tempdrive]
[/I[:]inffile] [/X | [/F] [/C] [/D[:]winntpath]]
```

Table 2.3 describes the functionalities of the command-line switches.

T A B L E 2.3: Command-Line Switches and Their Functionalities

Switch	Functionality
/S[:] source path	Specifies where the NT files are located.
/T[:] temp drive	Specifies where NT stores temp files during the installation.
/I[:]inf file	Tells NT where the information files (.INF) are located. If you are really creative, you can automate this process.
/OX	Creates boot floppy disks for CD-ROM installation.
/X	Specifies to not create the boot floppy disks, because you already have them.
/F	Specifies that you will create the boot floppy disks, but will not verify the files that are being copied to those floppy disks.
/C	Skips the free-space check on those floppy disks, because you know that they are empty and formatted.
/B	Provides floppy disk-less operation. Requires the /S parameter.
/U:script file	Provides unattended operation. Also requires /S.

T A B L E 2.3:   Command-Line Switches and Their Functionalities *(cont.)*

Switch	Functionality
/R:directory	Specifies optional directory to be installed.
/RX:directory	Specifies optional directory to be copied.
/E:command	Specifies command to run at the end of the GUI setup.

To create a set of installation diskettes, your command-line syntax will be WINNT /OX (that's "o" as in "orange").

If you have created the diskettes or have the originals from Microsoft, put the first diskette in the A: drive of your computer. Turn on the machine—the system will boot, using at least two of the diskettes. The Installation Wizard will also load the drivers to access the computer's CD-ROM drive. You must have the NT Server CD-ROM in that drive.

You can also install NT in other ways. Once the first server has been installed, you can configure it to be a distribution server for further installs.

Over the Network

The concept is simple—to perform an over-the-network installation, you access files normally stored on the NT 4 CD-ROM from the potential server and start the installation. However, before you can access files stored on the distribution server, you have to do some work.

You can provide access to the files from the NT 4 CD-ROM in two ways. First, you can put the NT CD-ROM into a CD tower or shared CD-ROM drive, and share various folders. Another method, if you have the available disk space, is to use XCOPY to copy the NT CD-ROM to a drive and share the various folders. If you choose this method, be sure to use the /S parameter with the XCOPY command to copy all of those pesky subfolders. In reality, though, you don't have to copy over the whole CD, just the \i386 and \Drvlib folders.

TIP You can also use NT Explorer to copy the folders to the disk. Be sure that the default settings are changed to allow files with extensions such as .DLL, .SYS, and .VXD to be displayed and copied. Select View ➤ Options, and then in the Hidden Files list, click Show All Files.

Why go to the trouble of copying all the folders to a drive, when you can just share the CD-ROM? In a word, speed. The shared CD-ROM method is much slower than accessing the files from a server's hard disk. However, by sharing the CD-ROM, you are not taking up as much disk space. Furthermore, you can run multiple installations in parallel if needed.

Network Client Administrator

As discussed, if you access the installation files from the server's hard disk, your installation will be faster than if you share a CD. However, in either case, your computer must be able to access the share point on an NT server somewhere on the network. To connect to that share point, the new computer must have a configured network client or redirector to communicate with the server. How do you configure the network client? Use the Network Client Administrator, which is located in the Network Administration group on an existing NT server.

You can use the Network Client Administrator for four tasks:

- To make installation startup disks to download network client software

- To make the setup disks for the client software

- To copy administration tools to a server and create a share

- To view remote-boot client information

To use the Network Client Administrator, you must first copy and share the tools. Start the Administrator, select Copy Client-Based Tools, and specify a path to the server files. You can either choose to share those files or create a new folder, copy the files to the folder, and then share the folder.

NOTE   You will find more information on the setup of the Network Client Administrator in the "Necessary Procedures" section.

Express versus Custom

Sometimes, Microsoft throws in objectives to make your life more interesting. This is one of those objectives. When you look through NT Server 4 installation and configuration information, you will never see something called Express Setup. As a matter of fact, the documentation makes it clear that during an NT Server installation, there is only one installation choice—Custom installation.

So what is this objective about? If you have to perform multiple NT Server installations on a corporate-standard file server that is always configured exactly the same way, you can simplify your life by automating the installation process.

You can configure two files to make the automated installation process work really well. You can also automate the installation process to perform an *unattended* installation. If your servers are configured exactly the same way, you can create an unattended answer file to mirror the setup configurations in your organization. These files are just text files with section names and keys that can be edited. You can access these files from any text editor. There is a sample unattended .TXT file in the NT Server Resource Kit; or, use the Setup Manager utility on the NT CD-ROM.

The other file is called a uniqueness database file (UDF). While the UNATTEND.TXT file is generic and relates to several computers, the UDF is unique and provides answers for a specific computer.

SEE ALSO   There are 14 different sections and dozens of selections that can be made in the UDF, which is far beyond the scope of this book. If you want more information on what a UDF can do for you, check Appendix A of the Microsoft Windows NT Workstation Resource Kit.

Miscellaneous NT Upgrade Paths

Microsoft exams, at times, stretch the boundaries of the objectives, which makes it challenging for the exam taker. For example, the objectives say nothing about upgrading various operating systems (MS-DOS, Windows 95, NT 3.51) to NT 4. Although this is not covered in the objectives, it is covered on the exam.

How do you upgrade DOS to NT Server? This is straightforward—perform a complete installation.

NOTE For information on performing a complete installation, see the "Necessary Procedures" section of this objective.

You have probably heard that there isn't an upgrade path from Windows 95 to Windows NT. Well, the people from Redmond partly tricked you again. There is a pseudo-upgrade path—installing Windows NT into a separate directory on your Windows 95 machine. In other words, don't put the program files in the \Windows directory. Reinstall all applications so that the information gets written to the NT registry. The lack of a true upgrade path is due to fundamental structural differences between the Windows 95 and Windows NT registries.

To upgrade from NT 3.51 to NT 4 (assuming you followed all of the defaults in your 3.51 installation), start the upgrade process by putting the NT 4 CD-ROM in the 3.51 server CD-ROM drive. In the \i386 directory of the Windows NT 4 CD-ROM, you will find a file named WINNT32.EXE. Run this executable instead of WINNT. Place the NT 4 server files in the \WinNT35 directory instead of the default \WinNT directory. If you place the files in any other directory, you will have a dual-boot situation, not an upgrade situation.

Necessary Procedures

Now that you have a broad overview of what happens, let's examine the step-by-step process.

Installing NT Server 4

The system is booting, it's using the three diskettes you created, the NT installation CD-ROM is in the CD-ROM drive, and the drivers necessary to access the CD-ROM are loading.

1. Watch the screen while the system is booting from the three diskettes. The setup program does a cursory investigation of your computer before starting to load the NT Executive and creating the hardware abstraction layer.

2. Insert setup disk number two when prompted. The second disk starts with Windows NT setup, and provides support for PCMCIA, SCSI, keyboard, and video drivers, and the FAT/NTFS file systems. A setup screen will give you four options:

   - Learn more about NT setup

   - Set up NT now

   - Repair a damaged NT installation

   - Quit without installing

3. Press Enter to continue with the installation. At this point, NT setup is looking for drives. It looks for only ESDI and IDE drives. If you have SCSI controllers and devices in your system, be sure to RTFS (read the fine screen), because you can bypass this section by typing S and make manual selections later. If you have IDE drives in your system, press Enter and let the setup program take care of things for you.

4. Once you make your selection, the Wizard prompts you to put in setup disk number three and then looks for all of the different adapters. Do not get impatient at this point. Just let NT do its thing.

5. After NT is finished searching the system, it presents you with a list of the adapters—PCI, IDE, and SCSI—it has found. The designers of the Installation Wizard recognized that there would be hardware NT could not recognize, so you also have the opportunity to make further selections. If there is a card in your system that does not show up on the drop-down list and you have the driver diskettes provided by the hardware manufacturer, you can choose to install

support now. To install support for a special mass-storage device, type S and make your selection, or provide the appropriate diskette. Otherwise, hit Enter to proceed.

6. The system loads the disk drivers and the device driver for the NT file system (NTFS). It also has to go through other device drivers before letting you know what it found.

7. Type C to continue.

8. Page down through the license agreement—you are prompted to press F8 to continue.

9. Once you press F8, the standard hardware summary screen appears. Make sure it matches your computer (or at least comes close—you can make changes later). You will see the phrase, "The above list matches my computer." If it does, press Enter to go to the next screen.

10. If you are installing NT on a computer that already has a hard drive installed and partitioned, the next screen shows the current drive partitions for all devices located. Highlight the partition where you will install NT and press Enter to continue.

11. The system asks whether you want to use the FAT file system or the NTFS. The features of these two files systems are reviewed in Table 2.4.

T A B L E 2.4: Features of the FAT File System and the NTFS

FAT 16 File System	NTFS
Accessible through NT, Windows 95, MS-DOS, and OS/2	Accessible through NT
Does not support file compression	Supports file compression
Does not support local security	Supports local security
Maximum file/partition size of 4GB	Maximum file/partition size of 16 exabytes—2 terabytes actual

---

NOTE FAT has minimal file system overhead and is most efficient for file system partitions under 400MB.

---

12. After the drives have been formatted, NT is ready to begin the most time-consuming part of the process—copying the files. First, it needs to know where to put them. The default is C:\WINNT. This is called the root directory. The partition in which this directory is located is known in NT terminology as the system partition.

13. Before NT copies files, it wants to check your drive for corruption. Press Enter to continue with the check or Esc to skip it. After the check, the copying begins.

14. Once the copying has been completed, it is time to pull the NT setup disk from the floppy disk drive and the NT CD-ROM from the CD-ROM drive, and press Enter to restart the computer. When the system finally boots, NT is now actually running in a reduced configuration. The operating system says that it wants to check things over. In addition, you have to start entering some system-unique information. First, enter your name and company.

15. Enter the CD key number from your CD-ROM case.

16. Review the first section of this chapter—about licensing modes—and choose the appropriate mode.

TIP When in doubt, choose Per Server. Per Server can be changed once to Per Seat, but Per Seat can never be changed to Per Server.

---

17. NT wants to know what you will name this server. The name must be unique on the network. If you are not sure what name to enter, be sure to ask someone.

18. Grab your notes from Chapter 1—it is time to tell NT what you want it to do. Will it be a primary domain controller (PDC), a backup domain controller (BDC), or a stand-alone member server?

19. Enter the administrator password. It can have a maximum of 14 characters, and like most passwords, you have to reenter it once you've typed it the first time. Don't forget that unlike other NT data, the password is case sensitive.

20. Now that the system knows who the administrator is and what the password is, you can begin to select components to install, such as the accessibility components for the keyboard layout, sound cards, etc. You can choose to install the calculator, wallpapers, mouse pointers, screen savers, and all of the items that will personalize your server so that it reflects your tastes. You will also be able to select communications for some rudimentary dial-up tools, games so that you can play FreeCell while waiting for the backups to finish, multimedia drivers, and MAPI (mail application programming interface) tools for Windows messaging.

NOTE   If you choose to install all of the accessories, it will take up another 26MB of disk space.

---

21. It is time to start installing networking. Select whether your server will be wired to the network or need remote access to the network.

NOTE   You will find a discussion of the various protocols supported by NT as well as how to install and configure a network adapter later in this chapter.

---

22. The next screen asks whether you want to install Microsoft Internet Information Server. Unless this server will be a Web or FTP server on the Internet or an intranet, clear the Default Install checkbox. (A different exam covers IIS, so this screen will not be discussed here.)

23. The system now needs to find out whether it can talk to the network. This is a physical-layer task that requires a network interface card. NT will now try to find your network card, or you can choose to select it from a list.

24. After the network card has been discovered, it is time to select protocols. By default, NT selects TCP/IP and NWLink IPX/SPX Compatible Transport. The defaults will work with the Internet and Novell networks. You can also choose to install NetBEUI.

25. The next choice you are given concerns the services, such as server or workstation, that you want your server to start. Stay with the defaults.

NOTE   NT services will be discussed later in this chapter.

---

26. After you choose the services, you can select the protocol bindings and the order in which the system will access them.

27. At this point, NT is ready to start the network so that the rest of the installation can be completed. However, before that, if you have chosen to install a PDC, NT wants to know the name of the domain. Be really careful when entering the domain name. You can change it later, but if too much time passes before you do, the ramifications can be significant.

28. The next choice is the date, time, and time zone. This should be set to where the server will actually reside. If you are in Minneapolis and prepping a server for Reno, choose PST. After you figure out the date and time, choose OK.

29. The final choice is your display properties. Pick the one that is right for you and be sure to test it, because NT will not let you get by with just a wild guess. Even if you know for sure what display you will use, NT will still make you test it, just to be sure.

Once you have done all of this, click OK—NT finally starts to configure itself. When it restarts, it will come up as a happy server, with the default operating system (in the case of a computer with multiple operating systems) as NT Server. If not, check Chapter 6, "Troubleshooting."

Installing NT Server over the Network

How does the installation process vary if the files are being accessed from a share point rather than a CD-ROM? In reality, there are not many differences. You configure the potential server to access the network. Once you have accessed the network, you can authenticate and access the share where WINNT.EXE is located. Run WINNT.EXE from the share—it will install the OS to the new server. In effect, you are using a share point on another server as the NT Server installation server.

You can also automate the installation process to perform an unattended installation, as discussed in the "Express versus Custom" section earlier in the chapter. When you save the answer file, it does not have to bear a special name. The command syntax to run a setup using an answer file is as follows:

```
WINNT /U:AnswerFilename
```

Your potential server must be able to access the network to get to the share point. To communicate with the server, the potential server (and all workstations) must be running a network client.

Creating Network Client Diskettes

Once your original NT server is installed, you can create a set of network client diskettes. This will provide the basic communications to the network. Choose Administrative Tools ➤ Network Client Administrator to bring up the menu shown below.

To create the diskette:

1. Select Make Network Installation Startup Disk and click Continue. This brings up the Share Network Client Installation Files dialog box.

```
┌─────────────────────────────────────────────────┐
│ Share Network Client Installation Files    □ ▣ □ │
│                                                   │
│  Path: [                        ] [..]  [  OK  ]  │
│  ◇ Use Existing Path                    [ Cancel] │
│  ● Share Files                          [  Help ] │
│         (No server hard disk space required)      │
│            Share Name: [Clients    ]              │
│  ◇ Copy Files to a New Directory, and then Share  │
│              0 MB  server hard disk space required │
│          Destination Path:  [            ]        │
│             Share Name:     [            ]        │
│  ◇ Use Existing Shared Directory                  │
│             Server Name:    [            ]        │
│             Share Name:     [            ]        │
└─────────────────────────────────────────────────┘
```

2. Enter the path to the client files. If you are using the CD-ROM, as shown in the screen shot above, the path will point to the \Clients directory. This is where the system will copy files *from*.

3. Now, you have to make a decision. Are you going to leave the CD-ROM on the server and share the CD, are you going to copy the client files to a folder on the server hard drive and then create a share pointing to the folder, or do you already have a folder set up? Make your decision. As you can see from the screen shot above, the client folder on the target server will be located at C:\Clients. A share name called Clients will be created, and it will take up to 64MB of disk space to accomplish this task. After you have made your decision, click OK.

4. Now that the server is configured to work with the clients, you need a diskette to use on all of the workstations. After all the information is copied to your server folder, you will see a handy message that tells you 254 directories were just added and 1,141 files have been copied. Click OK to continue.

5. The Target Workstation Configuration dialog box comes up and offers another set of pretty obvious choices—the size of the diskette, the network client to install (either Network Client 3 for DOS/Windows or the Windows 95 client). The final section asks about the NIC that is installed in your workstations. Once you have made your choices from the drop-down menu, click OK to continue.

NOTE A quick perusal of the list of NICs failed to turn up a selection for the PCMCIA card for laptops. Also, there is no Browse feature to supply your own driver. So, if you have a NIC that isn't listed, you should not attempt this method of installation. Use the Installation Disk Set method.

---

6. A dialog box appears with the Network Startup Disk Configuration selections. This allows you to enter a computer name, user name, domain, and network protocol. You can specify whether this computer will use DHCP to acquire its IP address or have a static IP address. You can also specify the destination for the new diskette. After filling in the appropriate selections, click OK.

7. The confirmation screen appears, reiterating all of the information you have just entered. Before clicking OK, make sure the diskette in the A: drive has been formatted with the appropriate version of DOS and is a system diskette. If all of the above criteria are met, click OK to continue. This will create the startup disk.

It might be easier to create a set of diskettes to carry around with you, especially if you need only one or two clients. In that case, select Make Installation Disk Set from the Network Client Administrator screen. You will be prompted for the client or service and the drive on which to create the diskettes. Once you have provided that information, you will be told how many diskettes you really need. Click OK to continue.

If you choose the third selection from the Network Client Administrator screen, it will allow you to copy administration tools to a client workstation. The tools you can copy depend on the operating system your client is configured to use. For example, between NT and Windows 95, tools such as Server Manager and User Manager for Domains are shared. With NT Workstation, you can manage DHCP, DNS, and WINS; from Windows 95, you can look at the event viewer, and check file and print security.

Exam Essentials

This section contained information on startup switches, root directories, and procedures. All of these topics are prime targets for exam writers.

Know the command-line switches for \i386\WINNT.EXE.   You may see the /OX switch on the exam. This switch creates the startup floppy disks. Another popular switch is the /u switch for unattended installation. This is a rather common switch among Microsoft products, so you may see it on other exams as well.

Know how to start the over-the-network installation.   Before you attempt an over-the-network installation, configure the distribution server. The \i386 directory and the \Drvlibs directory must be shared. Connect to a \i386 share point and execute either WINNT.EXE or WINNT32.EXE (if upgrading from a true 32-bit environment, NT 3.51).

Know the syntax for WINNT /U: *Answer Filename* **and when to use it.**   Use the /u parameter for an unattended installation.

Know the upgrade paths.   For a DOS workstation, the upgrade is a new NT 4 installation. For a Windows NT 3.51 upgrade, put the NT 4 files in the \WINNT folder instead of the default WINNT35 folder. For a Windows 95 upgrade, install NT into a folder other than \Windows, such as the default WINNT, and then reinstall all of the applications.

Know when to use NTFS and when to use FAT.   In general, NTFS is used when the disk is 400MB or larger. FAT is more efficient when the disk is under 400MB.

Know when to use Per Seat and Per Server licensing.   Per Seat licenses allow the client to access any server on the network. Per Server licenses allow only *x* number of clients to access that server. You can change from Per Server to Per Seat once.

Key Terms and Concepts

\DRVLIB folder: A folder on the NT installation CD-ROM in which drivers are located. This is an optional folder that can be XCOPIED to the distribution server.

\i386 folder: A folder on the NT installation CD-ROM in which WINNT.EXE can be found. Should be XCOPIED to the distribution server.

Distribution server: An NT server configured to provide network access to the files normally found on the NT installation CD-ROM.

HAL (hardware abstraction layer): A set of hardware specific DLLs that allows the operating system to be independent of the system hardware.

Network client: Software services run at the client workstation to provide communication with a server.

NT Explorer: Operating system graphical-based utility that can be used to copy files and subdirectories. If you are using NT Explorer to copy folders and subfolders to a distribution server, change the default settings to allow the utility to show hidden files.

NTHQ: A software tool provided on the NT Server installation CD-ROM that determines the NT compliance of the hardware on the potential server that is being run. Available from the \Support\HQTool folder on the CD.

NWLink IPX/SPX Compatible Transport: Communication protocol installed by NT as a default protocol. NWLink provides communication between NT servers and Novell servers.

PCMCIA (personal computer memory international association): A set of devices used generally in laptop computers to provide peripheral support. Usually a network card or SCSI adapter.

SCSI (small computer system interface): A technology to allow a chain of devices to be accessed by a single computer. These devices are primarily storage and scanning devices.

SCSITOOL: A tool provided on the NT Server installation CD-ROM that will return a list of the SCSI hardware in the potential server. Available from the \Support\SCSITool folder on the CD.

TCP/IP (transmission control protocol/Internet protocol): Suite of communication protocols installed by NT as a default protocol.

UDF (uniqueness database file): While the UNATTEND.TXT file provides generic answers to questions, the UDF provides answers to questions that require unique settings. For example, the UNATTEND.TXT file would contain information on the standard network interface card (NIC), while the UDF would provide an individual computer name.

Unattended installation: Allows a generic automated installation of NT Server. Answers are provided from a file called UNATTEND.TXT. There is a sample UNATTEND.TXT file on the NT Server Resource Kit; or, you can generate the file using the Setup Manager utility on the NT Server installation CD-ROM.

WINNT.EXE: The executable that starts the Windows NT Installation Wizard from a non-NT operating system environment.

XCOPY: Operating system command-line utility that can be used to copy files and subdirectories. Used with the /S parameter to copy directories from the NT installation CD-ROM to the distribution server.

Sample Questions

1. The /OX switch, when used in conjunction with the WINNT.EXE file, will do what?

   A. Start an unattended installation

   B. Point to the unattended installation file

   C. Run the installation without creating three startup diskettes

   D. Create three startup diskettes

   Answer: D—The /OX switch will create three startup diskettes.

2. Suppose that you are charged with creating a distribution server. Which two subdirectories do you need to XCOPY from the NT installation CD to the distribution server?

   A. Windows

   B. i386

   C. Tools

   D. DRVLIB

   Answer: B, D—The two directories that should be copied to the distribution server are the i386 and DRVLIB directories.

3. What does HAL stand for?

   A. It's Microsoft's homage to the computer in *2001: A Space Odyssey.*

   B. Hardware and layout

   C. Hardware abstraction layer

   D. Hardware adherence layer

   Answer: C—HAL stands for the Windows NT hardware abstraction layer.

Configure protocols and protocol bindings. Protocols include:

- TCP/IP
- NWLink IPX/SPX Compatible Transport
- NetBEUI

In this section, the installation and configuration of the protocols discussed in Chapter 1 will be examined. For each protocol, the tools used for installation and the configuration parameters available will be discussed.

Critical Information

Unfortunately, you will probably encounter a number of questions on the exam in which the answers are a list of menu choices. This is why you will see a lot of lists and screen captures in this chapter.

TPC/IP

Numerous configuration options are available with the TCP/IP protocol. Fortunately, only a few are absolutely necessary for communication. The first choice you will have to make is whether this machine should get its IP configuration from a DHCP server. In most cases, you will want to manually configure the IP information at NT servers just in case the DHCP server goes off-line.

WARNING   If you configure your servers as DHCP clients, you could be asking for a big problem. Suppose that a storm knocks out power at your office. When the power comes back on, all of your servers will power up and boot. (Of course, if you have a proper UPS, this wouldn't be an issue.) When they boot, they will look for the DHCP server to configure them. If that server either didn't boot properly or booted slow, your other servers won't get IP addresses. However, don't take this to mean that DHCP isn't the right tool for client workstations.

You can set three IP addressing parameters: the IP address, the subnet mask, and the default gateway.

If this server is to be a DHCP client, click Obtain IP Address from DHCP Server on the Properties page for the TCP/IP protocol; if not, you need to configure the parameters described in Table 2.5.

T A B L E 2.5: IP Parameters

Parameter	Description
IP address	A 32-bit unique identifier for each host on an IP network. The four-octet address is made up of two parts—a network address and a host or node address.
Subnet mask	Used to identify which portion of the IP address represents the network and which portion represents the host. Most IP networks are divided into subnets to help control traffic on the wire.
Default gateway	Identifies a router address to send all packets that are not local (the destination is not on the local subnet).

If your environment includes WINS servers, your server needs the IP address of your WINS servers.

If you use DNS (domain name service) on your network, you will need to configure the DNS information for this server. DNS will be discussed in Chapter 4, "Connectivity."

NWLink IPX/SPX Compatible Transport

As discussed in Chapter 1, NWLink is usually used to communicate with Novell NetWare environments. You will need to configure only two parameters: internal network number and frame type.

The internal network number is used to identify servers on an IPX/SPX network. In the case of NT, you might set this if your server is running a program that can be directly accessed by clients. (In an NT environment, this would probably be SQL Server or Microsoft SNA Server.) In other words, the program can be accessed *without* logging onto the NT domain. This allows Novell clients to access the service without loading Microsoft Windows client software. The internal network number is a hexadecimal value that must be unique across your entire IPX/SPX network.

The frame type defines how IPX/SPX packets will be formed for transmission on the physical wiring of the network. Each packet transmitted on the network has a series of headers attached to the data. These headers identify items such as the sender of the packet, its intended recipient, a checksum (calculation against the contents that can be recreated at the destination to see whether the packet has been corrupted in transit), or other information defined by the protocol. The definition of how these headers are organized is called the frame type. Many frame types are defined to be used in an IPX/SPX network.

The nice thing about NT is that it will pick a packet off the network and determine its frame type for you. To configure this, click Auto Frame Type Detection on the Properties page for the NWLink protocol. Unfortunately, NT will detect only one packet type in the automatic mode. So, if you are using multiple frame types on your network, you will have to manually configure them. On the same page, click the Add button and pick the frame type(s) in use from the drop-down list.

That's it for configuring the NWLink protocol. Of course, it is only half the story. To actually communicate with a NetWare server from a Windows NT domain client, other services must be installed and configured. These will be discussed in Chapter 4, "Connectivity."

NetBEUI

No configurable options are associated with the NetBEUI protocol. Once it is installed the only thing you can do to it is uninstall it. Just remember that NetBEUI is fast and efficient, but not routable.

Protocol Bindings

In the most generic sense, to *bind* is to link components at different levels to enable communication. The architecture of NT is made up of various layers—each layer provides a certain type of service. Some of these services will need to communicate with the services on another layer. The process of binding enables this communication. In the discussion of protocols, binding referred to establishing a communication channel between the network adapter card driver and a protocol.

On a simple server, you don't need to worry too much about protocol bindings. By default, each protocol you install will be bound to all network adapters installed in the computer. In a more complex environment, though, you can control the use of the binding of protocols to increase security or performance.

Increasing Security

Binding enables communication between the adapter's driver and a protocol. If you do *not* bind a protocol to an adapter, that card cannot communicate using that protocol. You can use binding to control traffic on your network and provide increased security.

To increase security, first consider your environment. Which protocols are needed, and where are they needed? Suppose that you work for the following company:

> King Technologies, LLC, is a small company made up of less than 10 employees. The owner of the company has decided that the company should be represented on the Internet. You have been assigned the task of implementing a Web server and ensuring security. After discussing the project, you decide that:

> - You want to ensure that no traffic from the Internet can make it to your internal Web.

> - None of your employees need to access the Internet at this time.

> - You will host the Web server on your own machine so that you have total control.

After analyzing your needs, you determine that you really don't need TCP/IP on your internal network. You will use NetBEUI instead, because it is fast and easy to configure. Your server will have two network adapters installed—one attached to the internal network, one with access to the Internet. You can use the protocol bindings to ensure security by disabling the TCP/IP binding to the adapter attached to your internal network. This configuration would ensure that no TCP/IP traffic can be routed from the Internet to your internal network.

Increasing Performance

In the Network applet on the Binding tab, you can manage the protocol bindings. The protocols are bound to both server and workstation services. The order in the list of bindings affects the efficiency of network communication. When an NT-based computer attempts to communicate with another device on the network, it will try to communicate using the protocols in the binding list—in the order that they are listed. If you have multiple protocols in the list, make sure that the most commonly used protocol is listed first.

As an example, assume that you have a TCP/IP-based network. Because of a few legacy NetWare servers, you added the NWLink protocol to your NT servers. If NWLink is listed first in your binding list, all communication attempts will try to use IPX/SPX first, and switch to TCP/IP only after IPX fails. You can decrease connection time to most hosts by moving TCP/IP to the head of the list.

Necessary Procedures

The MCSE exams are designed to determine a candidate's ability to perform administrative tasks associated with an NT network. Protocol management is a big part of those tasks. Be comfortable with the various procedures listed for this objective before you take the exam.

Installing a Protocol

You install all of the protocols discussed in this chapter from the same location. To install a protocol, do as follows:

1. Right-click the Network Neighborhood icon on your desktop and choose Properties (or open the Network control panel).

2. Click the Protocols tab.

3. Click the Add button. You will see the following list:

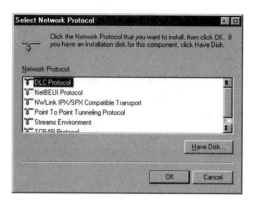

Installing a Service

The network services discussed in this section are installed in a similar manner:

1. Right-click the Network Neighborhood icon on your desktop and choose Properties (or open the Network control panel).

2. Click the Services tab.

3. Click the Add button. You will see the following list:

Setting the IP Addressing Information

You can configure the following addressing parameters: IP address, subnet mask, and default gateway.

Setting the WINS Server Address

Access the configuration screen by clicking the WINS Address tab on the protocol's Properties page. Add the primary (and secondary) WINS server IP addresses.

Setting the DNS Client Information

Enter the host name for this computer (in most cases, it will be the same as the NetBIOS name) and the IP addresses of your DNS servers.

Configuring NWLink

Open the Network control panel. On the Protocols tab, highlight NWLink IPX/SPX Compatible Transport and click the Properties button. Unless you need to change the default values, leave the Internal Network Number set to 00000000 and Auto Frame Type Detection selected.

Exam Essentials

While you are not expected to be an expert in each of the protocols listed in this objective, you are required to be comfortable with them.

Know the three main TCP/IP parameters and what they represent.   The parameters are IP address, subnet mask, and default gateway. See Table 2.5 for details.

Understand what the IPX network number is used for.   The IPX network number uniquely identifies a server on an IPX/SPX network.

Understand what a frame type is.   A frame type is a definition of how the data within a packet should be organized.

Understand how to use protocol bindings to increase security. You can increase security by using a different protocol on each side of a router. By not binding each protocol to both network interface boards, traffic cannot be routed between them.

Understand how to use protocol bindings to increase performance. When a packet is received, NDIS (network driver interface specification) passes that packet to each protocol until one of them accepts it. By placing the most efficient or frequently used protocols early in the list, you can reduce the amount of time involved in processing each packet.

Key Terms and Concepts

Binding: To link components at different layers of the operating system so that they can communicate. More specifically, to link the NDIS NIC driver to a communication protocol.

Default gateway: The IP address of the device to which a client will send packets destined for a host on another IP subnet.

Domain name service (DNS): A TCP/IP service used to resolve an IP address from a host name.

Dynamic host configuration protocol (DHCP): A service used to configure IP clients as they attach to the network.

Frame type: The definition of the industry standard way to organize data and headers within a packet. On an IPX network, two computers cannot communicate unless they are using the same frame type.

IP address: A unique identifier for each host on an IP network.

Subnet mask: An IP parameter that identifies which portion of the IP address represents the network address.

Sample Questions

1. Which of the following TCP/IP configuration parameters are mandatory for clients on a routed network?

   A. IP address

   B. Subnet mask

C. Default gateway

D. DNS server address

Answer: A, B, C—The DNS server address would be important for the process of finding resources using fully qualified domain names, but is not critical to the functioning of TCP/IP.

2. Which of the following parameters should be configured for the IPX/SPX protocol?

A. Frame type

B. Packet size

C. Network number

D. NetWare server name

Answer: A, C—The frame type defines how packets are formed—what headers will be included and in what order they will appear in each packet. The network number identifies the network segment.

3. On a network where TCP/IP, NWLink, and NetBEUI are all configured, but NWLink is the main protocol, which of the following binding orders would be appropriate at most clients?

A. TCP/IP, NWLink, NetBEUI

B. NWLink, TCP/IP, NetBEUI

C. NetBEUI, TCP/IP, NWLink

D. TCP/IP, NetBEUI, NWLink

Answer: B—Order the protocol bindings list so that the most-used protocol is listed first.

Configure network adapters. Considerations include:

- Changing IRQ, I/O base, and memory addresses
- Configuring multiple adapters

Essentially, there are only three ways to configure network adapters: put one in during NT installation, put several in during installation, or put a card in after installation. With the advent of multipurpose cards, not to mention the ever-expanding needs of your network, it can be challenging to find the hardware resources.

Critical Information

The configuration of the computer's current network cards is usually readily available. If the PC is up and working, and already configured with Windows 95 or Windows 3.1, you can get this information from the Network Tools control panel or Windows setup. If it is a DOS machine, check whether the card came with a diskette. If it did, the card is probably software configurable and has a utility to read the settings. Once you have the settings, write them down.

Changing IRQ, I/O base, and memory addresses

The settings that you wrote down for your current network card look pretty cryptic— IRQ 3, I/O address 0x300h, 10BT. These are the resources that this card uses, and they cannot conflict with anything else in the computer.

In the Network control panel, there are lots of choices for each setting on a network card. Figure 2.1 shows the settings available for a Xircom CreditCard 10/100 network card.

F I G U R E 2.1: PC card setup

The large number of settings implies that there may be a right or a wrong setting. However, that is not the case. There is no right or wrong, just used and unused. Computers of all shapes and sizes can be really stupid. If you configure peripherals within your computer to use some of the same resources, strange things happen. The quick and easy resolution to this problem is to make sure that the new piece of hardware has the interrupt set to something that is not currently being used.

NOTE You should identify the available resources and make changes to the IRQ setting before installation. This is usually done with a software program provided by the card manufacturer. When you change the settings, make sure everything is unique. I/O ports and the memory address also need to be unique.

Pentium-based computers now come equipped with several peripheral component interconnect (PCI) slots. The slots are designed to provide faster throughput to the CPU. As computer people, we all know that faster is *always* better. By purchasing a network card that is a PCI card, you eliminate the interrupt problem. Each PCI slot has the intelligence to assign an unused interrupt and address. The card takes its settings from the slot, not the other way around. Since the slot manages the address and interrupt, there should be no conflicts.

Configuring Multiple Adapters

As networks grow, a server will occasionally need to participate on more than one network segment, which involves adding multiple adapters to the system. NT, as an operating system, can handle an unlimited number of adapters. Your server hardware may not be as flexible.

Each time you add a new adapter to the system, you must adhere to the basics. Adapters cannot share resources. When you install the adapter, it must have a unique IRQ, I/O base, and memory address. It is challenging to choose a set of unique settings in a computer full of components. Remember to read your system documentation and the information on the utilities discussed in the objective on installations, such as the NTHQ tool and SCSITOOL.

Necessary Procedures

Suppose that you have to install a new piece of hardware into a server. Sometimes, one piece of hardware has a more extensive set of resources than another piece. At that time, you may have to change settings on an existing card. If you are adding additional network cards to your server, you will have to configure each card to take advantage of unused resources.

Changing IRQ, I/O base, and memory addresses

To change settings on an existing network card:

1. Open the Network control panel. Click the Adapters tab and high-light the adapter. Click Properties.

2. From the Properties page, select the drop-down menu for the setting you need to change.

3. Click the new selection.

4. Make any other necessary changes (IRQ, memory address, etc.).

5. Click OK.

6. Click Close to shut the Network window.

7. Select Yes to restart the computer.

WARNING When you change the settings on cards that are currently installed and configured, it can lead to unexpected network problems. This should be attempted only by a competent hardware technician and then, only as a last resort.

Configuring Multiple Adapters

If you are installing multiple cards as part of the installation process, once NT finds the first card, you can click a button to tell it to look for more. NT will continue looking for cards until it doesn't find any-more or you run out of manufacturer's diskettes. What if you want to add a new NIC to an existing system?

If you are installing a new PCI card into an available slot:

1. Shut down the server.
2. Install the hardware per the manufacturer's directions.
3. Open the Network control panel.
4. Click the Adapters tab.
5. Click Add.
6. From the Select Network Adapter window, select the appropriate network card and click OK, or click Have Disk. If you clicked Have Disk, insert the disk in drive A:, or provide the appropriate path, and click OK.
7. When you choose a network card, you will be prompted for the path to Windows NT system files—from either the CD-ROM or a location to which the files have been copied. After providing the path, click Continue.
8. The files will be copied, and a default binding will be provided.
9. Close the dialog boxes and restart the system when prompted.

If you do not have an open PCI slot, you will have to install an ISA-compatible card. Each card has its own installation routine. So, before you begin any installation, be sure to RTFM (read the fine manual). As an example of installing a card, the steps necessary to install a plug and play–compatible LinkSys 16-bit ISA-compatible Ethernet card are listed below.

To install the card:

1. Turn off the PC.
2. Remove the cover.
3. Physically install the card.
4. Cable the card to the concentrator.
5. Turn the server back on and log on as administrator.

The card is now physically installed. The next step is to configure the card to work in your server. Because the card in the example went into an ISA slot, you have to run the setup utility. Boot your server to DOS and run setup, which shows the default parameters—an IRQ setting of 3 and memory address of 300. If you choose to let the final IRQ and memory address be plug and play compatible, the operating system should handle the actual settings.

To install the new card and driver for NT:

1. Open the Network control panel.

2. Click the Adapters tab.

3. Click Add, which will bring up the Select Network Adapter dialog box.

4. Choose Have Disk.

5. In the Insert Disk window, add the path to the software drivers—A:\WINNT, in this case.

6. Select the card by highlighting the card name and click OK.

7. Enter an open I/O port or choose Auto, depending on the capabilities of the card.

8. Enter an open IRQ number or choose Auto, depending on the capabilities of the card.

9. Enter a network address, if necessary.

10. Click OK. The system begins to examine the network subsystem to make sure that everything is just the way it is supposed to be.

11. Since IP is loaded by default, the first glitch the system will find is that the new card does not have a working IP address. The Microsoft TCP/IP Properties dialog box is displayed—you can choose to receive your IP address from a DHCP server or static address. Since this is a server, you opt for a static address.

12. Enter DNS and WINS information, if necessary. Click OK.

13. Restart the computer.

Exam Essentials

This information is great for general knowledge, but the exam writers did not spend much time here.

Know what an IRQ does and how to change the settings.   Prior to installation of NT, use the NTHQ software configuration program to search your system. Make a note of the settings that the program returns. Remember to save the settings and update the documentation when you add a new device.

Match the network settings in the installation to the Network Settings screen.   You will be asked for the LAN adapter settings during the installation procedure. You should have that information written down.

Know the I/O port address in its various forms.   Algebra does not play a part—300 can equal 0x300 or 300h. From the drop-down menu, select the down arrow and pick the number that looks like the one from your notes.

Know the different transceiver types. You will also be presented with choices as to how your network cable attaches to the card. For Ethernet, some settings are Thin Net (BNC/COAX) or 10BaseT (RJ45). A BNC connector is a small *T* connector with coax running to both sides. A 10BaseT connector looks like the end of the telephone cable that plugs into the wall, except that it is bigger. Make sure that you select the right one.

NOTE There are a few questions about installing and configuring NICs in the exam-question pool, but not enough to worry seriously about.

Key Terms and Concepts

I/O port: The base input/output (I/O) port specifies a channel through which information is transferred between your computer's hardware (such as your network card) and the CPU. The port appears to the CPU as an address.

Interrupt: Calls to the CPU for action or attention.

IRQ (interrupt request lines):   Sixteen hardware lines, numbered 0 to 15, over which I/O devices, keyboards, and disk drives can send interrupts to the CPU. The IRQs are built into the hardware, with preassigned priority levels.

Memory address: The base memory address defines the address of the location in your computer's memory (RAM) that will be used by the network card to exchange information between your computer and the other computers to which you are connected. This setting is sometimes called the *RAM start address*.

WINS (Windows Internet name service):   A name resolution service that resolves Windows networking computer names to IP addresses in a routed environment. A WINS server handles name registrations, queries, and releases.

Sample Questions

1. Which software tool do you use to check currently used interrupts?

   A. SCSITOOL

   B. WINNT32 /OX

   C. NTHQ

   D. HQ-NT

   Answer: C—NT hardware qualifier.

2. IRQ is the same as:

   A. Port address

   B. I/O port

   C. DMA channel

   D. Interrupt

   Answer: D—An IRQ is also described as an interrupt.

3. When you install a network interface card, if you are using a 16-bit AT bus slot, what must the interrupt setting on the card be?

   A. Unique

   B. Shared

   C. Assigned to the slot

   D. The same for every card

   Answer: A—If you are using a 16-bit AT bus slot, interrupts must be unique.

Configure Windows NT Server core services. Services include:

- Directory Replicator
- License Manager
- Other services

NT can be configured to work on a small scale, but it is also flexible enough to expand to an enterprise. Microsoft knows that you don't want to work any harder than necessary, so they have provided core services to alleviate some of the pain of routine and mundane tasks. Windows NT Server core services are as follows:

Directory Replicator—Provides the ability to automatically move logon scripts, policies, folders, and files from one server to another.

License Manager—Provides a way to manage and track NT licenses and BackOffice application licenses.

Computer Browser Services—Makes it possible to see network resources from the Network Neighborhood utility. Computer Browser Services establishes the hierarchy of how search tasks are divided and which domain controller will fill which role.

NOTE If you are operating a small network with a single domain containing one or two servers, this objective will not have much impact on your world. As you study for the MCSE exam, however, you will need to understand this material.

Critical Information

It is time to figure out what information is passed from one server to another, how many applications you have on the network and where the licenses are kept, and how many of your domain controllers are overworked. It is now up to you to configure (tweak) the network. You can assign the server that will keep track of information and replicate it. The replicating server can service several other servers. Not every server needs to receive the same information—you can be selective. Backup domain controllers can either participate in the browser election process or wait for the results to determine their place in life.

Directory Replicator

Directory replication is a method of copying files and folders containing commonly used information from one NT server to another. This can also be referred to as an update. The most common items that need to be replicated are logon scripts, system policies, and information commonly shared across the network. In addition, you can use replication for load balancing by choosing which information to send to a server at a certain time of day or night.

Directory replication has several components. You must have an export server, an import computer, and export and import directories.

Export server—This is the single point of administration for the shared files, but a network can have as many exporters as they have servers. Changes you make to this server will be replicated throughout the system, as you designate. The export server must be running NT Server.

Import computer—You can't export without something willing to import. The import computer can be running NT Server, NT Workstation, or Microsoft LAN Manager OS/2 servers. These machines receive the information from the export servers. An import computer can receive updates from more than one export server, just like an export server can export to multiple import servers.

Export and import directories—How does the export server know what to export to each import computer? This is done through a series of folders and subfolders that each of the computers knows about and agrees on. For example, by default, information to be exported will be placed in subfolders of the \Winnt\System32\ Repl\Export folder. As a system administrator, you will create subfolders and files under this folder for each group of files that need to be exported.

Each import computer will have a directory that corresponds to the export server's export directory. For example, suppose that your network is the backbone of a company that is growing rapidly. It is necessary to export and import information to servers at each of the regional offices. Take a look at the directory structure below. The system will be configured to export/import this spreadsheet.

On the export server, you have the following directory:

    \Winnt\System32\Repl\Export\INF

On the import computer, you have the following directory:

    \Winnt\System32\Repl\Import\INF

TIP If you want to set a default import and export path, use Server Manager. These folders must be manually configured. Files stored directly under the export directory will not be exported.

Now that the folders are in place, here is a broad overview of how the system works:

- Information that needs to be passed to other servers is saved to the Export folder on Server-1. The replication service on Server-1 checks occasionally to determine whether there is anything that needs to be replicated. When it finds new information, it sends an update notice to all the computers or domains that are configured to import from the INF folder.

- Once the import computer has received the update notice, it checks the export server's directory structure.

- The import computer will now copy any new or changed files to its import directory. In addition, it will do some house cleaning—it will delete any files or subfolders that are no longer present in the export directory.

License Manager

Every client connection to an NT server needs a client access license (CAL), a license to run the client operating system, and a license to run any of dozens of applications. For example, if a computer boots and runs Windows NT Workstation, it needs a valid license to run NT Workstation. When that client attaches to the server, it must also have a CAL to have a legal client connection. Then, when the user opens Word, the user needs a valid license to use that application.

There are two types of NT Server CALs: Per Server and Per Seat. The client workstation receives the CAL, not the person using the workstation.

Per Server Licensing

In Per Server licensing, CALs are associated with a specific server. If Server-1 is configured to 50 connections, it may maintain 50 simultaneous connections. When you configure an NT server to use Per Server mode, you must take into account the maximum number of concurrent connections that will be made to that server, and purchase the appropriate number of licenses.

When should you use Per Server mode? Per Server mode is ideal for special-use servers, such as a remote access server (RAS) or Internet Information Server (IIS). In both cases, clients will attach to the server for a relatively short period of time and then disconnect. If you have the Per Server license mode selected, it also serves as a kind of heavy-handed approach to load balancing. If you feel this server can adequately handle 25 connections and you have 25 CALs allocated, when user number 26 tries to connect, the connection is refused.

Per Seat Licensing

When you license your network on a Per Seat basis, you walk around the office counting computers. If you come up with 500 computers, you should buy 500 CALs. Every time you buy a new computer, you need to buy a new CAL. With the Per Seat licensing mode, a client can access any resource on the network and may be connected to multiple servers at the same time.

Choosing the Right Licensing Method

How do you decide which system is best for your organization? If there is only one server on your network, select the Per Server mode and specify the maximum number of client connections. If the company grows to the point that Per Seat mode becomes more economical, a one-time change from Per Server to Per Seat is allowed.

Suppose that your network grows. You add an Exchange server to the mix. You still have the same 50 users, but now they each need to connect to two servers. You have a choice: You can keep both servers running in Per Server mode, with 50 licenses each (a total of 100 CALs), or you can switch to Per Seat mode on each server and get by with just 50 CALs.

Tracking Licenses

How do you keep track of all these licenses? NT Server provides two tools to help in that effort. The first is the Licensing program in Control Panel; the other is the License Manager program on the Administrative Tools (Common) menu. By using these tools, licensing information will be replicated from the PDC to a centralized database on a server that you designate.

Using the Licensing program to track licenses   If you go into Control Panel and select Licensing, you will bring up the Choose Licensing Mode screen. At this point, you choose between Per Server and Per Seat; if you have designated Per Server, you can add or remove licenses. There is also a Replication selection. When you choose Replication, you will be allowed to designate whether the master server to hold the database will be a domain controller or one of the servers in the enterprise. If you select the Enterprise radio button, it gives you the opportunity to specify the server. This server will then act as a master license replication server for two or more domains.

The Licensing program also gives you the opportunity to specify how often the replication takes place. You can specify whether you want the replication to start at a certain time every day or after so many hours. The range of hours is between 1 and 72. How many times a day do you add licenses to the network?

Using License Manager to track licenses   The other option is go into Administrative Tools (Common) and select License Manager (see Figure 2.2).

F I G U R E 2.2: License Manager

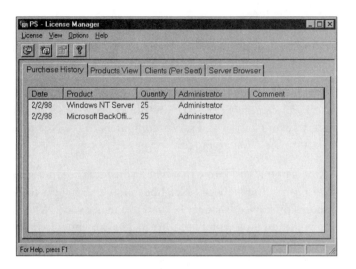

This utility will allow you to track a purchase history of licenses needed on your network—not just for NT Server, but for things such as BackOffice and some third-party applications. You can also keep track of Per Seat or Per Server licensing. You can browse the servers in your domain. Double-click a server to bring up the Licensing Mode screen for that server. You can add or remove licenses, and switch between Per Seat and Per Server licensing.

Other Services

NT offers several other services that may be of use to your network.

DHCP Service

By starting the dynamic host control protocol (DHCP) service, you can choose to make your NT server either a DHCP client or a DHCP server. As a DHCP client, your server will be dynamically assigned an IP address by a DHCP server. The DHCP server service will allow your NT server to manage and assign IP addresses.

DNS Service

When you start the domain name service (DNS), it allows you to configure your server to resolve DNS names to IP addresses. As a DNS resolver, it will take the DNS name www.microsoft.com and resolve it to an IP address.

WINS Service

Windows Internet name service (WINS) resolves NetBIOS computer names to IP addresses. WINS resolution specifies that computer name WS1, for example, is at a specific IP address.

Browser Service

You will definitely need to know about browser service. This service allows workstation and server computers to use Network Neighborhood to see other resources.

At this point, you know that when you add a computer to a domain, people can use Network Neighborhood or Explorer to browse for shares or services that are offered to the network. What keeps track of where all those computers are located and how to find the services that are offered? Computer Browser Services provides this service. There are five types of browsers:

Domain master browser—The computer on your desk is part of a massive computer network. Your WAN could have hundreds or thousands of servers, services, and shares available to users. What keeps track of all that information? The primary domain controller (PDC) is not just for authentication and management. It has several other responsibilities, including maintaining a master list of services available for the entire domain. That makes it the domain master browser. The PDC delegates some of its chores. The first delegation goes to the master browser.

Master browser—In any network, there is at least one workgroup. If you have a larger network, you may have several workgroups. If you have several network cards in your file server and are using the TCP/IP protocol, you will have several subnets in your network. Each of these workgroups or subnets must have a master browser. If there is another NT server on the subnet or in the workgroup, when that server comes up, it will check in with the master browser and tell it what services the newcomer has to offer. When you open your Network Neighborhood, the new server and its services will magically appear. What does the master browser do with the list of all services available in its workgroups or on its subnet? It passes that list up to the domain master browser so that the domain master browser knows where everything is in the domain.

Backup browser—The backup browser acts as a kind of backstop for the master browser. The master browser is always trying to keep track of all the services on the subnet or in the workgroup. While the master browser is gathering and sorting all of that information, the backup browser answers all of the "where is" requests floating around the network. The backup browser gets its list from the master browser.

Potential browser—The potential browser is otherwise known as the browser wanna-be. This computer just hangs out while waiting to become a browser.

Nonbrowser—The name says it all. This computer cannot act as a browser. Actually, it is probably too busy doing other things to be bothered with answering browser requests.

How does a master browser get to be a master browser while a potential browser waits around with all of its potential going to waste? Computer networking is really much more democratic than you may have thought—the systems can call for an election.

For example, suppose that you boot your workstation and go into Network Neighborhood looking for the Joke Repository share. Your computer first looks to the master browser and asks for a list of backup browsers. Once your computer has the list of backup browsers, it will ask the backup browser for the location of the share. If the master browser fails, a browser election is held. The election is somewhat weighted. For example, if a computer is running NT Server, it gets more votes than a computer running NT Workstation. If a computer is just running Windows 95—you get the picture.

Now that all of the computers with NT Server have checked in, there is still a deadlock—NT 4 is higher than NT 3.51, so it gets more votes. If there is still a tie, the backup browser will get a higher vote than the potential browser.

You can rig the election by tweaking the HKEY_Local_Machine\ System\CurrentControlSet\Services\Browser\Parameter setting. If you set the parameter to Yes, the system will always try to become a browser. If you set the parameter to No, the system will sit on the sidelines and watch the elections go by. If you set the parameter to Auto (the default), it ensures that the server is at least a potential browser.

Necessary Procedures

This objective covers a lot of really useful material, even if it were not on the exam. The fact that most of this material is covered on the exam makes this section even more critical.

Configuring the Replication Service

Before you start configuring directory replication, review the basics:

- You need something to share.

- You must configure the replication service.

- You must configure an export server.

- You must configure an import server.

- Information stored in the \Winnt\System32\Repl\Export root folder will not be exported. You must manually create subfolders to share information.

To configure directory replication:

1. The replication service needs a user account. This account is set up just like any other user account—using User Manager for Domains. The account must meet the following criteria:

   - All logon hours are allowed.

- The User Must Change Password at Next Logon checkbox must be cleared.

- The user must be a member of Backup Operators and the Replicator group for the domain.

- The Password Never Expires checkbox must be selected.

2. Open the Services control panel. Click Directory Replicator Service to open the Directory Replicator Service window.

```
┌─────────────────────────────────────────────┐
│ Service                                  [X]  │
├─────────────────────────────────────────────┤
│  Service:    Directory Replicator             │
│  ┌─ Startup Type ──────────┐   ┌─────────┐   │
│  │  ○ Automatic            │   │   OK    │   │
│  │  ● Manual               │   └─────────┘   │
│  │  ○ Disabled             │   ┌─────────┐   │
│  │                         │   │ Cancel  │   │
│  └─────────────────────────┘   └─────────┘   │
│  ┌─ Log On As: ───────────────┐ ┌─────────┐  │
│  │  ● System Account          │ │  Help   │  │
│  │   □ Allow Service to Interact with Desktop │
│  │                            │              │
│  │  ○ This Account:  [        ] [..]         │
│  │     Password:     [        ]              │
│  │     Confirm       [        ]              │
│  │     Password:                             │
│  └────────────────────────────┘             │
└─────────────────────────────────────────────┘
```

3. The Directory Replicator Service window is used to configure Directory Replicator to start automatically and to log on using the account you just created. You will have to enter the password and a confirmation for the password.

Configuring the Export Server

To configure the export server:

1. Create the folders that will be replicated. These folders must be created in the folder \Winnt\System32\Repl\Export.

2. Start Server Manager by selecting Start ➤ Programs ➤ Administrative Tools ➤ Server Manager.

3. Highlight the Export Server and press Enter.

4. Choose Replication.

5. Select Export Directories and click Manage.

6. Click Add.

7. Type in the name of the subdirectory and click OK to call up the Manage Exported Directories window.

You will notice several checkboxes at the bottom of the window and selections to add or remove a lock.

- Add Lock prevents the directory from being exported.

- Wait Until Stabilized makes the file remain in the subdirectory for a set period of time before being exported.

After clicking OK, you can choose to which computers you want to export these files:

1. Select Add (located under To List:).

2. Highlight and select the computers to which you want the information copied.

3. Click OK.

4. Click OK again—replication services will start.

Configuring the Import Computer

To configure the import computer:

1. Open the Services control panel. Configure the Directory Replicator to start automatically and log on using the account you just created.

2. From Server Manager, configure the import computer to import files from other computers or domains.

To manage the import process:

1. Start Server Manager.

2. Highlight the import computer and press Enter.

3. Choose Replication, which will bring up the Directory Replication window.

4. Select Import Directories and click Manage.

5. Click Add.

6. Type in the name of the subdirectory and click OK.

After clicking OK, you can choose the computers from which you want to import:

1. Click the Add button under From List:.

2. Highlight and select the computers from which you want the information copied.

3. If you click Manage, it will allow you to enter specific subdirectories from which you will be importing. You will also be given information on whether the subdirectory is locked, the status of the master file, when the last update has been received, and how long the folder has been locked. You can also use the Manage screen to lock the receiving folder.

4. Click OK.

5. Click OK again—replication services will start.

All information that is placed in these subfolders will be replicated to other servers. Policies and logon scripts will be covered in more detail later in the book.

Running License Manager

To start License Manager:

1. Choose Start ➤ Programs ➤ Administrative Tools (Common) ➤ License Manager.

2. From the menu, select License.

3. Select New License—this will bring up a dialog box. Select Windows NT Server in the Product dialog box within the New Client Access License dialog box.

4. Enter the appropriate quantity.

5. Click OK.

6. Check that you understand the Microsoft licensing agreement. Click OK.

7. Verify that the licenses showed up under the Product History tab.

NOTE Not every application works with License Manager. Not even every Microsoft application works with License Manager. Currently, the short list contains NT and BackOffice products. When you install new BackOffice applications, the licenses will magically appear in License Manager.

Configuring a Computer to Participate in Browser Elections

To configure a computer to participate in the browser elections, you must modify the \HKEY_LOCAL_MACHINE\SYSTEM\CurrentControlSet\ Services\Browser\Parameters\MaintainServerList parameter:

1. Start \WINNT\System32\Regedt32.EXE.

2. Select the HKEY_LOCAL_MACHINE hive.

3. Double-click SYSTEM.

4. Double-click CurrentControlSet.

5. Double-click Services.

6. Double-click Browser.

7. Double-click Parameters.

8. Click MaintainServerList. At this point, you can enter three values: Yes, No, or Auto.

   - Yes—Computer will be a master or backup browser.

   - No—Computer will not be a browser.

   - Auto—Computer can be a master, backup, or potential browser.

If your computer is on a network that does not have a PDC (such as a workgroup), you can force a computer to be the master browser by changing the key \HKEY_LOCAL_MACHINE\SYSTEM\Current-ControlSet\Services\Browser\Parameters\IsDomainMaster to True. It is set to False by default, even on a PDC.

Exam Essentials

Exam writers really like parts of this section. You will see questions on licensing modes and the different types of browsers.

Know the default directory path.   Anytime there are mandatory directory structures involved, it is a good idea to memorize them. In this case, remember the \WINNT\System32\Repl\Export and \WINNT\System32\Repl\Import directories.

Know where to put information to be replicated.   You must manually create subfolders on both the export server and the import server before any replication can take place.

Know which licenses can be managed.   License Manager can manage NT Server licenses and BackOffice product licenses.

Know the difference between Per Seat and Per Server licensing.
Per Seat licensing licenses the workstation. Workstations can log onto multiple servers and access resources from each. There is no limit to the number of workstations that can attach to a server.

Per Server licensing allows a certain number of connections to the server. If that number is exceeded, connections will be refused.

Know the difference between a domain master browser, master browser, and backup browser.   The domain master browser is always the PDC. It maintains the domain master list. Each workgroup or subnet must have a master browser. It gathers information on services for the domain or subnet, gives the list to the PDC to include in the domain master list, and passes the list to the backup browser. The backup browser answers all the browsing inquiries and gets the browser list from the master browser.

Key Terms and Concepts

Backup browser: Answers all the browsing inquiries and gets the browser list from the master browser.

Domain master browser: Always the PDC. Maintains the domain master list.

Hive: A part of the registry made up of keys, subkeys, and values. A hive is stored in its own file, \\WINNT\System32\Config.

Logon scripts: Batch files, executables, or another form of command structure attached to a user account to configure the environment after logon.

Master browser: Each workgroup or subnet must have one. Gathers information on services for the domain or subnet, gives the list to the PDC to include in the domain master list, and passes the list to the backup browser.

System policy files: Another way of controlling the user's work environment or system configuration.

Sample Questions

1. WINS provides what kind of name resolution?

  A. DNS name to IP address

  B. IP address to DNS name

  C. NetBIOS name to IP address

  D. IP address to NetBIOS name

  Answer: C—WINS resolves NetBIOS computer names to IP addresses, even if the computers are not on the same subnet.

2. The types of browser computers include:

  A. Domain master browser

  B. Backup browser

  C. Potential browser

  D. BDC browser

  Answer: A, B, C—Computers can be a domain master browser, backup browser, or potential browser.

3. Which types of licenses will License Manager track?

  A. NT Server client access licenses

  B. Number of licenses purchased for Microsoft Office

  C. Number of licenses purchased for Microsoft Word

  D. Any license for any product

  Answer: A—License Manager will track NT client access licenses. It does not track application licenses at this time.

Configure peripherals and devices. Peripherals and devices include:

- Communication devices
- SCSI devices
- Tape device drivers
- UPS devices and UPS service
- Mouse drivers, display drivers, and keyboard drivers

This objective returns to the realm of hardware. As your network grows, you can add certain devices to provide services and peace of mind for the administrator.

First, you will install and configure a communication device. This is your basic modem. A modem comes in handy not only so that users can dial in and access the network, but so that many utilities have the ability to dial out. If a problem is detected, you can configure third-party utilities to page the administrator, which gives the administrator the ability to be proactive instead of reactive. A modem makes this possible.

Next, the backup subsystem is discussed. This subsystem consists of the tape backup device and the software that actually archives the data. This book (and the objectives) was not designed to sell tape backup devices or software, so the discussion will be limited to the installation and configuration of tape device drivers. If your storage devices are large enough, the backup components that you will install will utilize small computer system interface (SCSI) technology.

What constitutes the biggest routine threat to your network? Even if you are safe from floods, tornadoes, and hurricanes, your system can still be affected by thunderstorms. The average human may not even notice these effects, but power fluctuations and power spikes caused by thunderstorms, brownouts, blackouts, power outages, or other everyday problems can reek havoc with your network. Many people look at a UPS as a method for users to save their data before the server has to go down because of a power outage. A good UPS is much more than that. A good UPS conditions your power as it comes in from the power company to provide your server with a stable source of electricity. The ability to keep the server up for a polite shutdown is just a nice side benefit.

Finally, there are the routine, mundane tasks such as driver upgrades. Many of the devices used daily are driven by software drivers. The manufacturers of these devices know that updates will be released occasionally—so does Microsoft. This objective covers how to install new drivers or update old drivers.

The utilities that you use to configure these devices are utilities that you use regularly. If you have ever added or removed a disk drive, tape backup unit, or modem to or from an NT server, you have accomplished many of these tasks.

Critical Information

Installing and configuring peripherals can be rather tricky topics to discuss. The answer to many of these questions is the same—it depends. The best way to be sure about the installation of any device is to read the manual.

Communication Devices

Modem installation and configuration can be a big job if you are installing a system that works with multiple COM ports and processors. Some manufacturers make systems that will integrate with NT and handle up to 256 ports, each with its own CPU. If you don't have the problem of remote users who need to dial into your system, you may be able to get by with a single modem.

NOTE   For this objective, it is necessary to know the basics. Remote access service will be covered in Chapter 4. At that point, what happens after you connect with the modem will be discussed.

Modem selection has gotten more complicated in recent years—you have to make some difficult decisions. Will it be a "regular" modem to handle dial-up features over everyday phone lines, or will it be a modem designed to work with the latest and greatest ISDN lines? If it is ISDN compatible, will it work with a single channel or dual channel? Once you have answered these questions and purchased the modem, most of the hard work is completed.

SCSI Devices

SCSI (pronounced scuzzy) stands for *small computer system interface*, which is a standard high-speed parallel interface defined by the American National Standards Institute (ANSI). A SCSI interface is used for connecting microcomputers to peripheral devices such as hard disks.

All sorts of devices—plotters, scanners, tape devices, and manufacturing devices—use SCSI interfaces, because SCSI is a very flexible technology.

SCSI technology is more flexible than others, such as IDE. SCSI can address anything from disk and tape drives to CD-ROMs, scanners, printers, and even other computers. However, with flexibility and intelligence, there comes a price—that price can be steep. While the price of disk space has quickly fallen in recent years, you still will not find SCSI devices at the same price point as an IDE drive.

Windows NT works well with many SCSI devices—it works with the industry standards, and recognizes their presence and function during installation. Since not every SCSI device and SCSI driver is written to the defacto industry standard, be careful when making out that purchase order. Be sure to check the HCL. If you will use your new SCSI controller with some specialty software, be sure that the software likes the SCSI controller as much as NT likes the SCSI controller. Many administrators have installed a controller, plugged in the tape backup device, and had the controller recognize and talk to the device, only to have the software ignore the whole subsystem.

Tape Device Drivers

It has been said that all good administrators are COPS—Compulsive, Obsessive, Paranoid, and Suspicious. Keeping in that vein, it is not a question of *if* your storage devices will fail, it is a question of *when* your storage devices will fail.

Windows NT comes with a utility called NT Backup that will allow you to archive your data to an off-line device such as a tape storage unit. Before NT Backup can send the data to that tape, you must add a tape backup device and drivers.

All configuration of tape devices and the associated drivers is handled through the Tape Devices control panel. Discovery methods will be discussed in the "Necessary Procedures" section.

UPS Devices and UPS Service

UPS stands for uninterruptible power supply. If you live and work in an area where the power can go out, a UPS can be the difference between a nice, clean shutdown and a long night trying to recover data from a tape backup unit.

UPSs come in a variety of shapes, sizes, and configurations. (However, the $3.95 power strip from the local hardware store is not a UPS.) Some UPSs will keep the server up for only 10 to 15 minutes after the power goes out. Some can keep it up for hours. Others will not only ensure that the system will not crash due to a power outage, but will condition the power that comes into your place of business. This provides a constant flow of even current, without the spikes and valleys that can ruin even the best servers.

How important is buying a good UPS? Well, how important is the data on your server? Next to a tape backup unit, a UPS can be all that separates you from the unemployment line.

UPS technology varies. UPSs with more features are more costly. Some UPSs will shut down the system. Some will send out broadcast messages saying that the system is coming down. Others will page you before the system goes down. When it is time to configure your new UPS, you do it through the UPS control panel.

Mouse Drivers

While most people view the mouse as a useful device, many people don't realize that it is configurable. The Mouse control panel gives you the opportunity to configure the mouse to meet your specifications. Users who are left handed can swap the buttons on the mouse. You can even choose the time between clicks that constitutes a double-click.

Display Drivers

Display drivers drive your video display. Depending on the type of video card in your computer and the amount of memory it has, you can configure your monitor to display millions of different colors, with clarity that will surpass your television set.

The display driver gives you all sorts of options to personalize your computer, from wallpapers to screen savers that deliver a message for the day.

Keyboard Drivers

Keyboard drivers are used to customize the keyboard so that it meets the individual user's preferences. Some users are very fast typists and need to alter the repeat rate for keys. The keyboard driver also customizes the keyboard layout for languages other than English.

For systems with multiple users who speak multiple languages, you can configure the keyboard for several different languages, as long as one is the default.

Necessary Procedures

There is a lot to do to configure all of these peripherals. If you paid close attention to the section above, you would have noticed a theme running through all of the discussions—in each case, the configuration is handled by a control panel.

Installing Communication Devices

Since communication devices are the first selection on the objectives list, installing a modem will be the first priority:

1. Physically install the modem. If you have a problem with your internal modem, check the interrupt and COM port settings (how they are set on the modem compared to what you have available). COM1 and COM3 share an interrupt, COM2 and COM4 share an interrupt, and interrupt 3 is a common choice among network cards. When in doubt, read the manual.

2. Once the modem is installed, open the Modems control panel.

3. If this is the first modem in the system, the Installation Wizard will open. The Installation Wizard will search for the modem and return the brand and type of the modem. If the brand and type don't match what you have, use the Change button—a drop-down menu with a long list of modem manufacturers and models will appear. Choose the one that matches your needs. If your modem still does not show up, check the modem's manual for a compatible model.

4. Once the hardware is recognized, you will be presented with a Modems Properties screen. This screen lists the modems that are installed. Highlight a specific modem and choose Properties to bring up a rather generic screen. The General tab allows you to select the volume of the modem speaker and the speed of the modem.

5. The Connection tab will allow you to change the connection preferences, if necessary, and determine how to handle outgoing calls. There are several checkboxes at the bottom of the screen—Wait for Dial Tone before Dialing, Cancel the Call If Not Connected within x Seconds, and Disconnect a Call If Idle for More Than x Minutes. The interesting options appear when you click the Advanced button on the Connection tab.

6. The Advanced Connection Settings screen (shown above) allows the administrator to choose how to handle error control and flow control, and the type of modulation. For error control, you can require error control to connect, you can choose to compress data, and you can use the cellular protocol for users dialing in with cell phones.

NOTE You may have to remember the Compress Data tab, not for testing purposes, but for real life. Some software communications programs compress the data before they get to the modem. If the modem tries to compress them again, data corruption can occur.

---

7. Use Flow Control tells the modem how to determine the speed at which data are sent. Your two choices are Hardware and Software.

TIP Unless you are told otherwise, keep modems set to the defaults. The basic rule of telecommunications between computing devices is that both modems must agree on certain parameters. If these parameters don't match, there will be no communication. Modem speed is usually not an issue—the modems will negotiate a common speed. To get the best speed out of your communication link, make sure that both ends of the link use the same make and model of modem. This is especially critical if you are trying to reach the 56KB limit (download only) advertised by some modem manufacturers. There are currently two competing standards in the 56K world. So, while the market slugs it out to determine the eventual champion, you get speeds that are slower than advertised.

Installing SCSI Devices

Before the computer can access SCSI devices, you must install a controller. The installation varies with manufacturer and type, but some common threads run through the process:

1. Install the SCSI adapter and driver as instructed by the manufacturer.

2. Open the SCSI Adapters control panel. Each SCSI controller system will look different. The following screen is a sample of all of the installed devices.

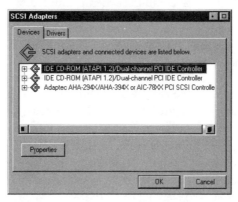

On this screen, there are two entries for the Dual-Channel PCI IDE Controller, which say that these devices are ATAPI compliant. The ATAPI standard is a subset of SCSI drivers. When the designers of NT needed a place to put them, this is where the designers decided they should go.

The Dual-Channel PCI IDE Controller was installed as part of the NT installation process. NT found the controller and loaded the drivers, and everything worked. The other driver listed is the Adaptec AHA-294X/AHA-394X driver. This card was installed after the server was configured. The installation went as follows:

1. Shut down the server.

2. Install the controller card and the SCSI device (in this case, an external CD-ROM), ensuring that SCSI IDs are properly set and cable termination requirements are met.

3. Restart NT and log in as administrator.

4. Open the SCSI Adapters control panel.

5. Choose the Drivers tab.

6. Click Add.

7. Choose the controller manufacturer and select Have Disk.

8. Put the disk in the A: drive.

9. Click OK.

10. Restart the computer when prompted.

11. Open My Computer to observe the new CD-ROM device. Create a share so that the second CD-ROM can be shared throughout the network.

Other than the Add/Remove button on the Drivers tab, there is not much to configure here. If you highlight a driver under the Devices tab and click Properties, you will get an information screen on the card. You will also be able to see an information screen on the driver. If you are curious, open the Resources tab of the Properties screen to see which IRQ and memory settings the card is using. Since the demonstration card is a PCI card, there are no changeable settings on this screen.

Configuring Tape Device Drivers

Configuring a tape drive is a two-step process. You configure the driver and then make NT discover the tape device. There are default drivers for some of the more common tape devices, but you might want to have any software drivers that came with the controller and tape drive handy, just in case. To install a tape backup unit:

1. Install the necessary hardware, as described by the hardware vendor.

2. Once the hardware has been installed and the computer has been restarted, log on as an administrator.

3. Open the Tape Devices control panel.

4. Select the Drivers tab and click Add.

5. Choose from the list of manufacturers and tape devices, or select Have Disk.

6. Click OK. At this point, the Installation Wizard will copy and install the device drivers. You will be prompted to restart your computer.

7. After the computer restarts, reenter the Tape Devices control panel.

8. With the Device tab selected, choose Detect to have NT find and configure the tape device.

Installing UPS Devices and Services

To install UPS devices and services:

1. Install the hardware according to the vendor's specifications.

2. Make sure that you attach a serial cable (usually nine pin) from the UPS to an available COM port. Make note of the port.

3. Open the UPS control panel.

4. Select the Uninterruptible Power Supply Is Installed On: checkbox and add the appropriate COM port.

5. You can now configure your UPS to recognize the loss of power. The configuration is accomplished by selecting one or more checkboxes.

NOTE When power is lost, an event is logged and no new connections can be made to the server. However, existing connections can continue. Warning messages will be broadcast according to the parameters you specify.

6. When the Power Failure checkbox is selected, you can choose how you want NT to react to a loss of power. By selecting Execute a Command File, you can write a series of commands for the system to carry out before shutting down.

- If you opt not to write a command file, you can manually configure the UPS characteristics. Service characteristics include the time between power failure and initial warning message. The default is five seconds. If you live in an area with frequent storms that cause power outtages, you may want to change that setting. You can also specify how often you want the message to be rebroadcasted. The default is every two minutes.

- The other manually configured options revolve around what happens when the power comes back on. The first is the Expected Battery Life. This tells NT how long the UPS is rated to keep the computer up and working before shutting things down. You can also provide an informational selection, showing how long the battery must be recharged for each minute it is run. The default is 100 minutes per minute of downtime.

- You can configure NT to issue a Low Battery Signal warning at least two minutes before shutdown. After the server runs on batteries for a while, the system will signal when it is two minutes away from shutdown. If the administrator decides to select the Low Battery Signal option, the UPS characteristics remain grayed out.

- The final configuration is remote UPS shutdown. This signals NT to start shutting itself down.

You can also configure a command file to execute before shutdown. You can design this command file to shut down services and send out notifications to end users of the pending shutdown.

Changing or Updating a Mouse Driver

To change or update a mouse driver:

1. Log onto the computer as an administrator.

2. Open the Mouse control panel.

3. Select the General tab.

4. Click Change.

5. Choose the appropriate driver, or select Have Disk.

6. Click OK after the file copy and installation has been completed.

7. Restart the computer when prompted.

Changing or Updating a Display Driver

To change or update a display driver:

1. Log onto the computer as an administrator.

2. Open the Display control panel.

3. Select the Settings tab.

4. Click Display Type. If you know the type of adapter you are using and have the diskettes, click Change. Otherwise, click Detect.

5. Highlight the appropriate manufacturer and model number of your video card.

6. Click OK.

7. Click OK again.

8. When you return to the Settings tab, click Test. If the test is completed successfully, click OK and restart the computer if prompted.

Changing or Updating Keyboard Drivers

Keyboard drivers are also configured through the control panel.

1. Log on as administrator.

2. Open the Keyboard control panel.

3. Click General.

4. Click Change.

5. Choose the appropriate driver, or select Have Disk. Click OK.

6. When you return to the Select Device screen, click OK.

7. Click OK at the Keyboard General screen and restart the computer when prompted.

Exam Essentials

There is a lot of information in this objective, but not too many exam questions. The questions that do show up are of the off-the-wall variety.

Know what utility is used to configure the modem. You configure the modem using the Modem control panel.

Know how to install and configure SCSI adapters and drivers. If you get an exam question on this objective, it will likely revolve around installation of the drivers, which is accomplished by choosing Control Panel ➢ SCSI Adapters ➢ Drivers ➢ Add.

Know what the NT Backup Utility can back up. The objectives imply that you need to study how to install and configure the drivers, but the exam writers took a different approach. As you study, it is important to remember the hardware requirements to perform tape backups. By installing a tape backup unit (TBU) on your NT server, you can use that TBU to back up the server and remote workstations. The NT Backup Utility will back up both the NTFS and the FAT file system.

Know where and how to configure the UPS. The UPS is configured in the UPS control panel.

Know that there must be a serial cable between the UPS and the server. The nine-pin cable must be connected to one of the computer COM ports.

Know how to change the mouse driver. Be familiar with the tabs in the Mouse control panel.

Know which menu is used to set the display adapter type. Choose Control Panel ➤ Display ➤ Settings ➤ Display.

Know what the Keyboard control panel has to offer and what changes can be made from it. This topic is more for your personal information than for the exam.

Key Terms and Concepts

ATAPI (AT application programming interface): A subset of the SCSI standard drivers.

Error control: Can be required at connection. The two modems will agree on an error-checking protocol. Any packet that is received by either modem will be checked to determine whether it has been corrupted during the transmission process. The agreed-upon protocol will be used to determine whether the information received is the information sent.

Flow control: How the modem will control the flow of information. Either Software or Hardware.

NT Backup Utility: Utility provided with NT 4 that can back up local and remote computers. Backup will back up NTFS and FAT volumes.

TBU (tape backup unit): A device used to archive data currently stored on a hard disk to a tape. The tape can then be stored away from the computer. This is called off-site storage.

UPS (uninterruptible power supply): Supplies power during a power failure. May also condition power when the power is on.

Sample Questions

1. An uninterruptible power supply will keep a computer running how many minutes after a power failure?

   A. 15

   B. 10

   C. 5

   D. It depends

   Answer: D—It depends on the UPS. Generally, the more expensive the UPS is, the longer the system will stay up.

2. Configuring a modem in NT can be done through:

   A. Control Panel

   B. Rocker switches on the bottom of the modem

   C. Buttons on the front of the modem

   D. User Manager for Domains

   Answer: A—Modem configuration can be done by using the Modems control panel.

3. Which item is not an example of a device that can use a SCSI interface?

   A. Disk drive

   B. CD-ROM

   C. Tape drive

   D. Monitor

   Answer: D—A monitor is not a SCSI device.

Configure hard disks to meet various requirements. Requirements include:

- Allocating disk space capacity
- Providing redundancy
- Improving performance
- Providing security
- Formatting

In Chapter 1, choosing your disk subsystem hardware and picking a file system were discussed. Once you have made these choices, you must configure the disks for use.

Critical Information

Before you can make any decisions regarding the configuration of your disk storage environment, you need to know the options that are available. This objective walks through the various choices you can make once the disks are physically installed on your server.

Allocating Disk Space Capacity

Before a hard disk can be used by an operating system, it must be partitioned. When you partition a hard disk, you define the boundaries of a physical area on the disk. You can then format this area for use by an operating system such as Microsoft Windows NT.

You can use partitioning as a method of organizing your data by creating a boot partition that contains only NT system files, and another partition to hold your data. On a dual-boot computer, you could create separate partitions for each operating system so that each system file has its own physical space.

If you make proper choices, it will be easy to manage your disk space. If you make poor choices, it won't kill you, but upgrading may be difficult—or you might end up with two operating systems that just don't get along on one partition.

On the physical level, you must partition a disk before an operating system can use its storage space. A partition is made up of unused space on the drive. That free space will be used to form either a primary or an extended partition. You can create a maximum of four partitions on each disk.

A primary partition has the necessary configuration to be used by an operating system for the boot process. You can create up to four primary partitions on a single disk. A primary partition allows you to isolate the system files from multiple operating systems on a single drive. One of the primary partitions will be marked as active—this is the partition that will be booted from.

You can set up a computer to dual boot NT and Windows 95. To accomplish this, the partition must be formatted with the FAT file system. It is important to note that NT cannot read a partition formatted with FAT32 (a file system available as an option in Windows 95), so do not use this file system on machines on which you intend to dual boot NT and Windows 95.

Primary partitions cannot be further subdivided. One way to get around the four-partition limit is to use an extended partition. There can be one extended partition on each disk (it *does* count against the four-partition limit). You can subdivide the extended partition into multiple logical disks, each of which will be given a drive letter by the system.

Like a primary partition, an extended partition is created from unused space on the drive. Since there can be only one extended partition, you usually create it last and use all of the remaining space on the drive. You can then divide into logical drives for management purposes.

NT will dynamically assign drive letters to each partition using the procedure shown in Figure 2.3.

F I G U R E 2.3: Assigning drive letters

1. Beginning with disk 0, the first primary partition on each drive is assigned a consecutive letter (starting with the letter C).

2. Beginning with disk 0, each logical drive is assigned a consecutive letter.

3. Beginning with disk 0, all other primary partitions are assigned a letter.

You can override these default assignments in the Disk Administration tool, by choosing Tools ➤ Assign Drive Letter. A screen capture of this process will be shown in the "Necessary Procedures" section that follows.

Understanding Partition Numbering and ARC Paths

Windows NT assigns each partition an identification number, as described below. NT uses the partition number in an ARC path (defined later in this section) to locate the area on a disk needed for read and write operations. For troubleshooting purposes, you need to know how NT assigns partition numbers.

NT assigns a number to all primary partitions first, starting with the number *1*, and then assigns an ID to each logical drive in the extended partition if one exists.

NT uses the partition numbers in an ARC (advanced RISC computing) path to find the partition. You must understand ARC paths, for the exam and real-life troubleshooting. An ARC path will look as follows:

multi/scsi(a)disk(b)rdisk(c)partition(d)

Each *a*, *b*, *c*, and *d* will have a value, as described in the Table 2.6.

T A B L E 2.6: ARC Path Components

ARC Convention	Definition
multi/scsi	Identifies the type of controller. If the controller is a SCSI device with the BIOS *not* enabled, this value will be scsi; for all others, it will be multi.
(a)	The ordinal value of the controller. As each controller initializes, it is given a value; the first controller will be given a value of 0, the next 1, etc.
disk(b)	The SCSI bus number; for *multi*, this value is always 0.
rdisk(c)	For non-SCSI disks, the ordinal value of the disk. It is assigned in the same way as (a).
partition(d)	The ordinal value of the partition (it starts at 1 instead of 0).

ARC paths will be reexamined in Chapter 6, "Troubleshooting."

The next step in planning your disk drive configuration is to determine how those disks will act together to store your data. NT offers many configuration options—you will have to determine which is right for your environment.

Volume Sets

You can add together areas of free space on your hard disks to create one logical drive—thus creating a volume set. The process will be discussed later in this section. Once created, you must format this area with either FAT or NTFS. Once you have created the volume set, it will appear as one drive to the system. When using a volume set, NT will fill each segment before starting to use the next.

You can also add space to an existing NTFS volume by choosing Partition ➤ Extend Volume Set in Disk Administrator. Once you have added free space to a volume set, you cannot take it back. The only way to reclaim that space is to delete the *entire* volume set (and thus any data stored there but not backed up).

TIP If you need to extend a volume set formatted with the FAT file system, first convert it to NTFS using the CONVERT.EXE command-line tool. Remember that this is a one-way operation—once you have converted to NTFS, you cannot go back to FAT.

Stripe Sets

Like a volume set, a stripe set combines free space on two or more hard drives into one logical drive. Unlike a volume set, however, a stripe set must include space on at least 2 drives (up to a maximum of 32 drives). The areas created must be approximately the same size (if they are not, Disk Administrator will do this for you).

When you place data in a stripe set, the data are written evenly across all physical disks in 64KB stripes. While a stripe set does not provide fault tolerance, it can improve I/O performance, especially if the drives are on separate controllers.

Providing Redundancy

Because of the critical nature of most data stored on servers, it is important that the disk subsystem be fault tolerant. A fault-tolerant disk system is one in which the system can survive the death of a hard drive, while the data remain accessible. You manage the fault-tolerant features of Windows NT through Disk Administrator.

NT provides fault tolerance through software-controlled RAID. There are many levels of RAID in the industry—NT supports internal software implementations of RAID levels 0, 1, and 5. Level 0 is the ability to create a volume set that spans multiple hard drives. Since this provides no fault tolerance, it will be ignored in this discussion.

RAID level 1 is commonly referred to as disk mirroring. A mirror system is one in which there is a redundant copy of all data on the partition. The point of mirroring is that if the primary disk dies, the system can switch over to the redundant disk so that the users will not notice the hardware failure.

Disk duplexing is a subset of mirroring in which the disks are accessed through separate controllers. In mirroring, if the controller dies, there is no way to access the redundant disk. Since you have multiple controllers in a duplexed system, the server can survive a controller failure without the users noticing a problem.

RAID level 5 consists of disk striping (as discussed above), with the addition of a parity set. The parity set is a calculation of the contents of the data, placed on another disk in the set. If one disk dies, the system can use the parity information to re-create the data on the fly.

RAID level 1 (mirroring) is an efficient way to provide fault tolerance (especially if you upgrade it to duplexing). Since an entire copy of the data exists on another hard drive, the user will not notice a difference in performance in the event of a hardware failure. However, mirroring is more expensive than RAID level 5—in mirroring, one-half of the disk space is redundant. Mirroring is also the only way to make your system and boot partitions fault tolerant. These two partitions cannot be part of a volume set, stripe set, or stripe set with parity.

RAID level 5 is very common in today's business environments. It increases I/O performance by splitting the work across hard disks. It is also more cost effective than mirroring. In a level-5 implementation, if more disks are involved in the stripe set, the percentage of disk space used for the fault-tolerant information will be lower. In mirroring, one-half of the total disk space is used to provide fault tolerance. In a level-5 implementation with three disks, only one-third of the space is used to hold the parity information (one-quarter for four disks, one-fifth for five disks, etc.). Keep in mind, though, that RAID level 5 can survive the loss of only one disk. If you lose more than one, the parity information becomes useless. However, the likelihood of more than one drive failing simultaneously is much more remote than that of just one, making RAID level 5 an effective insurance policy.

NOTE Windows NT provides software-controlled RAID. Although this is an inexpensive way to achieve fault tolerance, it is not necessarily the correct choice. Some hardware has been specifically designed to provide RAID functions. In most cases, hardware-based RAID will be faster than software-based RAID.

Improving Performance

The first step in improving the performance of your disk subsystem was covered in Chapter 1—knowing the hardware technologies available and purchasing equipment that will be fast enough to meet your needs. However, once the disks have been installed, you can use a few optimization techniques to get the most performance from your hardware.

First, you need to analyze your disk storage trends. If you have multiple disk controllers, try to place heavily used data on separate drives. You should try to split the load equally across all of the physical devices.

If you have two heavily used databases and two disk controllers, give each one its own path to a hard drive. In other words, split them across drives attached to the different controllers. When you plan your disk storage strategy around this philosophy, it can dramatically affect disk drive performance.

Another suggestion is to watch the placement of the paging file (PAGEFILE.SYS). The paging file is used as virtual memory—effectively allowing your NT server to allocate more memory than there is physical RAM in the computer. When the operating system detects a need for more memory, but there is no RAM available, it will move portions of RAM into the paging file until they are needed again. A small amount of paging is normal on an NT server. However, this process is disk intensive. If you place the paging file on a disk that is busy performing other functions, you will notice a decline in overall server performance. Microsoft suggests that you move the paging file off the disk that contains the NT system files. If possible, you should create paging files on multiple disks to spread the workload.

Providing Security

In the discussion of file systems in Chapter 1, the benefits and drawbacks of the FAT file system and NTFS were discussed. If security is a major concern in your environment, you should probably use NTFS. NTFS provides file- and directory-level security—FAT does not.

To put it another way, any user who can log in at a computer can access any files on that computer that are stored on a FAT partition. Files stored on an NTFS can be secured using NT permissions.

NOTE You can secure files on a FAT partition if those files are being accessed remotely. When you create a share point, you can assign permissions to the data stored there. Security is an issue on FAT partitions only when the user logs onto the computer locally—not from across the network.

Formatting

Before you can use a partition to store data, it must be formatted. In NT, you can format a partition in two ways—through Disk Administrator or using the command-line utility FORMAT. Both of these techniques will be discussed in the "Necessary Procedures" section.

Necessary Procedures

Most servers act as repositories of data that are to be accessed by end users. NT administrators must be able to configure and manage the disks on their servers. The procedures covered for this exam objective concern the skills necessary to manage the disk configuration of an NT server.

Reassigning Drive Letters

You reassign disk drive letters using the Disk Administrator tool. Click the partition you want to reassign, choose Tools ➤ Assign Drive Letter, and change the letter.

Creating a Volume Set

In Disk Administrator, Ctrl-click all of the partitions that should be included and choose Partition ➢ Create Volume Set.

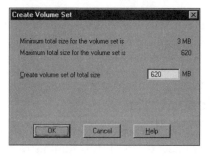

Creating a Stripe Set

In Disk Administrator, Ctrl-click all of the partitions that should be included in the set. Remember that the segments must be approximately the same size (Disk Administrator will adjust the size for you if they are not). Choose Partition ➢ Create Stripe Set.

Creating a Mirror Set

In Disk Administrator, Ctrl-click the two partitions that will make up the set (they must be on different hard drives) and choose Fault Tolerance ➢ Establish Mirror.

Creating a Stripe Set with Parity

In Disk Administrator, Ctrl-click the partitions that will make up the segments of the set. Remember that they must be approximately the same size (Disk Administrator will adjust the size as appropriate). Choose Fault Tolerance ➢ Create Stripe Set with Parity.

Formatting a Partition

In NT, you can format a partition in two ways—both ways can format the partition with either the FAT file system or NTFS.

From a command prompt, you can use the FORMAT command. The syntax is as follows:

```
FORMAT Drive: [fs:file-system] [/v:label]
```

The other option is to use Disk Administrator. Highlight the partition to be formatted and choose Tools ➤ Format.

Exam Essentials

Of all the components that can fail on an NT server, the hard disks are the most likely to do so. NT administrators must understand the options available to minimize the impact of disk failures on their users. Microsoft is aware of this and tests accordingly. Before taking this exam, make sure you are comfortable with the Microsoft disk configuration options.

Know how NT assigns drive letters to partitions. NT starts by assigning a letter to the first primary partition on each drive, beginning with drive 0. It then assigns drive letters to all logical drives, again beginning with drive 0. Finally, it assigns letters to all of the remaining primary partitions.

Know how to read an ARC path. An ARC path will look as follows:

multi/scsi(a)disk(b)rdisk(c)partition(d)

Each *a*, *b*, *c*, and *d* will have a value, as described in Table 2.6.

Know how to define volume set. A volume set is a collection of partitions combined into one logical drive. The segments do not have to be the same size, and can exist on the same hard drive. This is also know as RAID level 0 (spanning).

Know how to define stripe set. A stripe set is a collection of 2 to 32 partitions, from different hard drives, combined into one logical drive. The partitions must be approximately the same size. NT will write data to each of the drives in succession in 64KB stripes.

Understand mirroring. Mirroring is having an exact duplicate of a partition on another hard drive.

Understand duplexing. Duplexing is mirroring, except that the two drives must be connected to different controllers for additional redundancy.

Be able to explain a stripe set with parity. A stripe set with parity is a fault-tolerant disk system that uses 3 to 32 drives in a stripe set. Data are written to each of the drives in succession in 64KB stripes. For each stripe, a calculation of parity information is processed and written to a different drive in the set. This allows the system to re-create the data using the parity information if one of the drives in the set fails.

Explain the difference between security on a FAT and an NTFS partition. NTFS partitions offer directory- and file-level security that can affect the local user; FAT partitions do not.

Key Terms and Concepts

ARC path: A path to a particular partition on a specific disk on a computer.

Fault-tolerant disk system: A disk system with redundant data storage, which enables it to continue to function in the event of hardware failure.

Log on locally: To access a computer directly rather than remotely across the network.

Paging file: A file, named PAGEFILE.SYS in NT, that is used as virtual memory.

Partition: A physical section of a hard drive set aside for the use of an operating system.

RAID (redundant array of inexpensive disks): An industry standard definition of fault-tolerant disk subsystems.

RAID level 0/volume set: A disk system that allows a logical drive to span multiple hard drives.

RAID level 1/disk mirroring: A disk system that has a complete copy of a partition on a separate hard drive.

RAID level 5/disk striping with parity: A disk system that stripes data across multiple drive. In addition, a calculation is performed on each write, which creates parity information that can be used to re-create the data. This information is stored on another drive in the set, which allows the system to continue functioning if one of the drives in the set fails.

Sample Questions

1. Which of the following items are true for a volume set?

   A. Adds together multiple sections of free space.

   B. Data are written to each partition until that partition is full before moving to the next partition.

   C. Data are written to each partition in sequence so that all are used equally.

   D. Can hold the system and boot partition for Windows NT.

   Answer: A, B—Answer C describes the process used by a stripe set. Neither a volume set nor a stripe set can hold NT's system or boot partition.

2. Which of the following items are fault-tolerant disk configurations?

   A. Volume set

   B. Stripe set

   C. Mirroring

   D. Duplexing

   E. Stripe set with parity

   Answer: C, D, E—Neither a volume set nor a stripe set provide any automatic recovery in the event of a disk failure.

Configure printers. Tasks include:

- Adding and configuring a printer
- Implementing a printer pool
- Setting print priorities

What is the name of the device that actually puts the ink/ toner to paper? In the real world, you go out and buy an XYZ laser *printer.* In MicroSpeak, the object you load paper into is called a *printing device.* However, don't let the name change fool you—a printing device is still connected to a computer by way of a parallel or serial cable. Printing devices can also be connected directly to the network or through an infrared port.

If a printing device is the object that puts ink to paper, what is a printer? A *printer* is the software interface that takes the information from your application and redirects it to a printing device.

Another term that requires definition is print driver. A *print driver* is the piece of software that translates application information into the printer-specific commands that are passed to the actual print device. The printing objective receives *lots* of attention on the exam. This objective and the objective on configuring hard disks to meet various requirements are probably the hardest hit. You have been warned— read carefully.

Critical Information

In the NT print architecture, the application that you use to generate the output does not care about the kind of printer you are using. It just sends the job off to the printer and the print job magically appears. This magic is made up of many processes that work together to give your users the desired results.

Adding and Configuring a Printer

Printing is an ever-evolving process. You will constantly add or upgrade printers to make sure that your users have access to the appropriate resource. For example, you don't want to provide the CEO's administrative assistant with a high-speed dot matrix printer to send out the boss' correspondence, when a laser printer would do a better job.

Printer configuration has many aspects, depending on the driver that is supplied with the printer. Usually, you will be able to configure paper size, input trays, duplexing, fonts, and paper layout. You can also specify default settings for specialty printers. To understand the complexities of printing, you must understand the entire printing process—from the selection of Print to the final output.

To make this workflow more understandable, suppose that you need to print a copy of last week's expense report. You open the file in Excel, click Print, and your workstation goes to work. It first attaches to the printer device to which you will print. This is more complicated than it seems. For example, the workstation client can obtain a software print driver from the server, which means the print driver does not have to be stored locally (on the workstation) or updated at the workstation if a new driver comes out. It can be upgraded at the print server—the print server will update everything else.

Excel has no idea what kind of printer your report will go to, nor does it care. It simply creates an application print request and passes that request to the graphics device interface (GDI). The GDI is the first of several "translation" pieces. The GDI takes the application print request and translates it into device driver interface (DDI) calls.

Next, the print request begins to move from the generic to the specific. The DDI calls apply specific printing characteristics to the document. Notice that the term used was *printing* characteristics, not *printer* characteristics—the job has not gotten far enough to worry about a specific printer. When the DDI gets done with the file, it can now be called a print job. There are two types of print jobs:

Raw print job—A set of commands that the printer will understand to produce the final product.

Journal file print job—A list of DDI calls that can be used to come up with a raw print job. This is used when the printer is directly attached to the workstation printing the job.

The print job still isn't printer specific. Now that the DDI calls have been stored in the print job, the print driver comes into play. It takes these generic calls and turns them into printer-specific commands.

The print job is basically complete. It just needs to find its way to the right printer. So, the printer router takes over. It looks at the print job and figures out the best way to get it to its destination printer. The printer router does not look for the actual printer—it looks for the print spooler. The print spooler (also called a provider) is the holding area where the job waits until the printing device is ready to print the job. When the printing device is ready, a print monitor takes the job from the print spooler and feeds it to the printing device.

NOTE   The print monitor is actually three DLL files. One handles local printing devices through the parallel and serial ports. This is the LOCALMON.DLL. The HPMON.DLL sends jobs to HP printers hooked directly to the network rather than to a computer. The LPRMON.DLL (LPR stands for line printer) sends jobs to Unix print daemons.

Printing devices come in several categories:

- Network printing device—A printing device hooked directly to the network cable.

- Local printing device—To be local, the printing device must be hooked directly to the server computer.

- Remote printing device—Any printing device hooked to another computer on the network.

In this book, connecting a network printing device to the system will not be discussed. If you are configuring a network printing device, you are using a third-party printing solution. Follow the manufacturer's installation instructions.

Implementing a Printer Pool

Every network administrator reaches the time in their professional life when the amount of paper to be generated by a specific department is greater than the capacity of a single print device. A decision must be made—upgrade to a bigger, faster print device, or just add another print device of the same type to take up the slack. If you decide to add another printer of the same type, you can create a printer pool to double your output. With a printer pool, one printer controls multiple printing devices. This is beneficial to the administrator, because print jobs are spread across multiple printers, balancing the load and decreasing the time an end user must wait for their output. A particular printing device will not sit around without printing, while jobs are stacking up for another device.

While this concept sounds appealing, there are some catches. First, the printing devices in the printer pool must be the same type—they must use the same driver. For the sake of logistics, it is also a good idea to have all of the devices located in the same area, because the print job will be given to the next available printer in the pool. Users get really finicky when they show up to collect a print job at one printer and the job has printed to a printer on the other side of the room.

Setting Print Priorities

To set a print priority, you must first configure two printers for the printing device in question. One of the printers is granted a higher priority. When two print jobs hit the printers at the same time, the printer with the higher priority will print and the other job will wait.

NOTE Print priorities are set from 1 to 99. A printer with a priority of 99 has a higher priority than a printer with a priority of 1. Higher numbers print first.

Necessary Procedures

There is much to do in this objective. You will install several different kinds of printers and printing devices, create a printer pool, and set up print priorities.

Creating a Local Printer

Here, you are creating a local *printer*. Before you can send tasks to a local *print device*, you have to configure a local printer.

To create the local printer:

1. Log on as an administrator on the computer.

2. Choose Start ➤ Settings ➤ Printers.

3. Double-click the Add Printer icon.

4. Because you are creating a local printer, check the My Computer radio button. Click Next.

5. Choose the port to which the printer will be attached. Click Next.

6. You will see two lists. The one on the left allows you to select the manufacturer of your printer. The one on the right lets you pick the model of your printer. Make your choices and click Next.

7. Give your printer a name. If it will be the default printer (the one you usually print to), select the Yes checkbox; otherwise, select No. Click Next.

8. If you want to share the printer, enter a share name. What if you want the printer to be shared by something other than a Windows product? Hold down the Ctrl key and click all of those other operating systems with which you want to work. Then, click Next to continue.

9. The Wizard will let you print a test page. This is usually a good idea, because it helps in troubleshooting. If there is a problem, it is good to find it early.

10. Make sure that you have your NT Server installation CD-ROM handy. NT may ask for it to copy some files.

11. If you look closely at the Printer window, you should notice a new icon for your printer. You can use the icon to make changes to the printer.

12. Click OK to exit the Install a Printer Wizard.

Configuring a Local Printing Device

Now that the printing device is installed, it is time to configure it. Configuration is done from the Printers control panel. Choose the printer you want to configure, highlight it, right-click, and select Properties.

As you can see, there is plenty to play with on this page. The properties shown here are a function of the particular print driver, so your Properties page may not look like the one shown.

General Tab

Under the General tab, you will see the New Driver button. If you click it, the first screen will warn you that changing the drivers may change the Properties screen. If you agree to the warning, the system reopens the Add Printer Wizard to the driver's page. Make your selection here, or use the Have Disk function.

Back to the General tab. If you click Separator Page, it will allow you to put a page between each document or switch printing modes from PCL to PostScript. You can create a document for this purpose and browse to it. Once you have found the document you want, click OK. This option is important in the following situations:

- In a busy office where many people share the same printer. The separator page will let your end users know when they have grabbed someone else's document.

- If you are using a laser printer that can handle both PostScript and PCL languages, but cannot automatically sense the change. This was the case in early versions of the HP III SI. Most printers that can use both PCL and PostScript can automatically sense—the printing device recognizes the PostScript header and switches to PostScript mode automatically.

The Print Processor button allows you to choose the way you want jobs processed. The print processor is the rendering piece of the printing puzzle—it is where the print job is completed before being sent to the print monitor. NT provides two generic processors, with selections for each.

- Windows print processor:

    - RAW—Set of instructions that will result in a printed document.

    - RAW (FF Appended)—Puts a form feed at the end of the job, if one is not already there.

    - RAW (FF Auto)—Automatically puts a form feed at the end of a print job.

    - NT EMF 1.003—When you print a document that contains a read-only embedded font not listed as an installed font in the Fonts folder, Windows NT uses a substitute font if the printer is set to use NT EMF 1.003 mode. Windows NT prints the font correctly in RAW mode.

    - Text—Prints documents in Text mode.

- Macintosh print processor:

    - Handles jobs sent from a Macintosh workstation to a non-PostScript printer attached to an NT computer. In other words, this processor translates PostScript code into something the designated printer can understand.

The last selection on the General tab is self explanatory—Print Test Page. This is a great place to start troubleshooting.

Ports Tab

While looking at the Ports tab, you will notice all of the standard ports that any good computer should have. There is LPT1 to LPT3 for your parallel printing devices, COM1 to COM4 for serial printing devices, and the FILE selection so that you can print to a file rather than a real printing device. If this does not give you enough choices, you can always add your own port by clicking the Add Port button. If you click Add Port, you can add specialty ports, such as a digital network port, DLC ports, TCP/IP ports, or a local port. When you configure the port, it will set the Transmission Retry parameter. The Transmission Retry parameter sets the amount of time the user must wait before NT reports that the printer is not available. This setting not only affects the specific printer, but all printers using the same driver.

Don't overlook the two checkboxes at the bottom of the screen. The top checkbox allows you to enable or disable bidirectional support. The bottom checkbox allows you to enable printer pooling.

NOTE A printer pool is defined as multiple print devices of the exact same type that work together. For example, you may have six HP LaserJet 5Ps combined into a printer pool to provide printing services for the Word Processing area of your company.

Scheduling Tab

On the Scheduling tab, you determine when this printing device will be available to actually print. You can choose to have the printing device always available, or you can specify certain hours when the print device will be available. You can also use this tab to specify a priority to jobs going to the printing device.

NOTE   The default priority is set to Lowest.

Once you decide whether this device will have a special schedule or priority, you can decide how you want it to handle print jobs. It can spool documents so that the program finishes faster or print directly to the printer. If you choose to spool documents, you can make the system wait to start printing until the last page is spooled, or you can start printing immediately.

The checkboxes at the bottom of the screen are as follows:

Hold Mismatched Documents—Suppose that the Accounting department has only one printer. That printer can be used to print both checks and memos. You have mismatched documents when checks and memos are sent to the printer at the same time. In this case, the printer will expect you to manually change the paper.

Print Spooled Documents First—This option groups the documents together by type. In the case mentioned above, all checks would be printed, and then all memos would be printed.

Keep Documents After They Have Printed—When a job moves through the printing process and is finally outputted on the printing device, the print job is deleted. Usually, this is not a problem, because you have a copy of the document stored somewhere on the system. However, some applications will generate a report, send it to the printer, and then delete the report. This option allows you to keep the print job in the spooler until you are sure it has printed correctly, and then you must manually delete it.

Sharing Tab

The next tab available on the Properties screen is the Sharing tab. It is a fallback to the Sharing tab from the Install Wizard. Here, you can select the drivers that you want the printer to make available. You can choose from a variety of alternate drivers, depending on the operating systems your clients are running.

Security Tab

The Security tab will allow you to manage who can use the printer. By clicking Permissions, you can grant users the right to use or manage the printer, or take away their right to even see the printer.

From the Security tab, you can select from Permissions, Auditing, and Ownership.

Permissions—This button is for user permissions. User permissions define who can print to this printer and who can manage the documents submitted to this printer. By default:

- Administrators have full control.

- The creator or owner of the document has the permission to manage documents.

- Everyone can print.

- Print operators have full control.

- Server operators have full control.

Auditing—This button allows the administrator to track the success or failure of various print functions.

Ownership—This button allows a user to take ownership of a printer.

Device Settings Tab

The final tab is the Device Settings tab. This tab is driver/printing device specific. It lets you define which paper tray will be used for which form, how much memory is installed in the printer, if there are any font cartridges installed, and what soft fonts are accessible.

Installing a Remote Printer

A remote printer is a printing device that is attached to another computer on the network. It is not physically attached to your NT server. When the print job is sent to the remote printer, the job is first sent to the remote printer, where it is spooled for the printer.

A remote printer leads a double life. Not only is it shared with other computers, but it is still a local printing device. You begin the installation process by going to the computer that the printing device will be attached to and configuring the printer as a local printer for that computer. Once that is done, you can share the printer with others. After that, for everyone you have just shared the printer with, it is a remote printer.

For your users to share the printer, do as follows at the workstation that needs access to the printer:

1. Choose Start ➤ Settings ➤ Printers.

2. Click Add Printer. This will begin the Add Printer Wizard.

3. Choose Network Printer instead of Local Printer.

4. Browse the network to find the appropriate printer.

5. Select the printer you want and click OK in the Connect to Printer dialog box. You may be asked to install a print driver if one is not available from your operating system.

6. You will be asked whether this printing device will be your default printer. This is your call—it is a Yes or No decision.

7. Click Finish.

Implementing a Printer Pool

To create a printer pool:

1. Open the Printers control panel.

2. Highlight the printer that will be part of the pool and right-click.

3. Select Properties and then choose the Ports tab.

4. Check the Enable Printer Pooling option.

5. Select the ports that also have printing devices of the same type attached to them.

   - If the printing devices are attached to physical ports (LPT2 and LPT3 as well as LPT1), select those ports.

   - If the printing devices are remote printers, connected through an LPR port, select each network printer port. Use this selection if you are using TCP/IP printing.

6. Select OK.

Setting Print Priorities

Once you have put the pieces together, you can change the priority of one printer to a higher setting:

1. Create two printers connected to the same printing device.

2. In the Printers control panel, highlight the printer that will receive the higher priority, right-click, and choose Properties. Select the Scheduling tab.

3. Change the priority to the highest setting.

NOTE The default priority setting is Lowest. So, when you simply change the priority on one printing device, it accomplishes the task as outlined.

---

4. Click OK.

Exam Essentials

Printing is hit hard on the exam—each of the three subobjectives will be addressed.

Know how to install print drivers. If a print driver needs to be updated, update it only on the print server. Once that has been accomplished, the driver will be passed to all workstations using the printing device.

Know which print drivers to install. Windows 95, NT 3.51, and NT 4 approach printing differently. If you have a mix of workstation operating systems, including OS/2, you will have to install the drivers for each OS.

Know about the use of a separator page. A separator page can be used to switch printing devices between PostScript and PCL modes. If you look in the \Winnt\System32 folder, you will see a file called PCL.SEP provided for this purpose.

Know how to share a printer. Printer sharing can be accomplished during the printer installation process or from the individual printer's Properties page. If you share the printer, it makes it available to other network users.

Know how to create a "hidden" shared printer that will be shared between several coworkers, but not with everyone in the office. To do this, put $ in the share name.

Know how to attach to a shared printer. If you are using a Windows NT– or Windows 95–based application, this is not a difficult task. You can map a UNC path to the printer. If you are trying to print from a DOS-based application, you need to map a physical port to the network printer.

Know how to manage printer security for operating systems other than Windows NT. If you are working from a Windows 95 workstation, you can load and run Windows NT Server Tools for Windows 95, which gives you the User Manager for Domains and Server Manager utilities. However, neither of these tools will allow you to manage printer permissions. A little known fact is that the Server Tools utilities also change Windows Explorer—you can manage file permissions and printer permissions from Explorer.

Know scheduling. For large print jobs, you can create and configure a printer to be available during after-hours. All large jobs must be sent to this printer. When print jobs are sent to this printer during the day, they will be stored in the print spooler.

Know how to create a printer pool. All printers in the printer pool must be connected to the same print server. All printers should be identical or use the same print driver. To add a new printer to an existing printer pool, enter the port for the new print device. Printers in the pool share the same printer name and print driver.

Know how a printer pool is used. A printer pool is used to balance the load of printing across several printers. This provides increased redundancy and a more responsive printing environment.

Know why print priorities are used. Print priorities are used to give one printer quicker access to the printing device than another printer. A priority of 99 is a higher priority than a priority of 1—the higher the number, the higher the priority.

Know how to configure print priorities. Configure two printers for the same printing device. Give one printer a higher priority by choosing the Scheduling tab on the Properties page and setting the priority to High. Print jobs will be handled from the high-priority printer before print jobs are handled from the low-priority printer.

Key Terms and Concepts

Local printer: A printer that sends the print jobs it receives to disk. It then processes the jobs and forwards them to a printing device.

LPR printer port: A printer port configured to use TCP/IP print properties.

Network-attached printing device: A physical device that connects parallel or serial printing devices to the network, or a printing device that has an internal network interface card.

Print priorities: Provide the scheduling opportunities for one set of print jobs to print routinely before another.

Print server: A computer that shares its printers with network clients.

Printer: A software device to which applications send print jobs. A Windows NT printer matches a name with a printer driver, an output port, and various configuration settings. (Often referred to in other operating systems, such as Novell, as a *queue*.)

Printer pool: A collection of similar printers attached to the same print server. The printers must use the same printer driver. Ideally, the printers will be in the same physical location.

Printing device: The device that physically produces printed output.

Queue: A holding area for print jobs received by a print server but not yet sent to the target printing device.

Remote printer: A printer that does not save the print jobs it receives to disk. Instead, it redirects its jobs directly to a print server.

TIP For more information on printing, check out *MCSE: NT Server 4 Study Guide, Second Edition,* by Matthew Strebe and Charles Perkins with James Chellis, published by Sybex. It is a great resource.

Sample Questions

1. In the world of NT, what is an HP Laserjet 5P?

   A. A printer

   B. A print device

   C. A print server

   D. A print spooler

   Answer: B—When taking a Microsoft exam, read each question carefully. In printing, an HP Laserjet 5P is a print device. A printer is a software tool that operates at the client or workstation.

2. In the NT printing subsystem, what is a printer?

   A. Hardware

   B. Software

   C. Hardware and software

   D. Virtual

   Answer: B—A printer is a software device that operates at the start of the printing process.

3. What is a queue?

   A. A line to a movie in London

   B. A physical connection between a print device and a computer

   C. A print job in waiting

   D. A holding area for print jobs

   Answer: D—A queue is a holding area for print jobs.

Configure a Windows NT Server computer for various types of client computers. Client computer types include:

- Windows NT Workstation
- Microsoft Windows 95
- Microsoft MS-DOS based

Now that the network is configured, you can tweak the configuration to make the server more accessible to various client types. If you work in a mixed environment (and most people do), this section can help alleviate the complaint that the network is slow on a given day. When you take the exam, if you know the information in this section, it will put your mind at ease when you see questions that start out as follows: "You have a network comprised of 45 Windows 95 clients, 100 Windows NT Workstation machines, and 37 Windows-based systems…"

Critical Information

In Chapter 1, there was a section devoted to protocols. In that section, you were shown how to configure your server to communicate with different clients utilizing different protocols. Depending on the client computers that your network is servicing, it is important to provide the right protocol. As you saw in Chapter 1, some of the protocols supported by NT Server are NetBEUI, TCP/IP, IPX/SPX, DLC, and Apple-Talk (also DHCP, WINS, and DNS, but these are really services). Not all of the clients that you attach to the network will have the flexibility to connect using each of these protocols. Table 2.7 lists the protocols or services that can be used with various operating systems.

T A B L E 2.7: Operating System Protocols and Services

Client	NetBEUI	NWLink IPX/SPX	TCP/IP	DLC	DHCP	WINS	DNS	AppleTalk
MS-DOS	Yes	Yes	Yes	Yes				
LAN MAN for DOS	Yes	Yes	Yes	Yes				
LAN MAN for OS/2	Yes		Yes					
Windows 95	Yes	Yes	Yes		Yes	Yes	Yes	
Macintosh					Yes	Yes	Yes	Yes
NT Workstation	Yes	Yes	Yes	Yes	Yes	Yes	Yes	

Once you have configured the server to support the protocols, you can enhance client operation by changing the binding order on client machines—it is the client that chooses the protocol it will use to "talk" with the server. If you place the more frequently used protocols at the top of the binding order, performance will increase.

Necessary Procedures

Working with binding order at the workstation machine may affect how quickly it communicates over the network.

Changing the Binding Order of Protocols

To change the binding order of protocols for a client machine using Windows NT Workstation:

1. Highlight Network Neighborhood.

2. Right-click and select Properties.

3. On the Network screen, select the Bindings tab.

4. Expand Workstation.

5. Highlight the chosen protocol and use the Move Up or Move Down button.

Exam Essentials

There isn't much in this section, but the material is tested.

Know how binding order affects system performance. Make sure that the most frequently used protocols are at the top of the binding order.

Key Terms and Concepts

AppleTalk: The set of network protocols on which AppleTalk network architecture is based. When you set up Services for Macintosh, it installs the AppleTalk protocol stack on a computer running Windows NT Server so that Macintosh clients can connect to it.

DLC (data link control): An older network transport protocol that allows PCs to connect to IBM mainframes and some HP printers.

DNS (domain name system): Sometimes referred to as the BIND service in BSD UNIX. Offers a static, hierarchical name service for TCP/IP hosts. The network administrator configures the DNS with a list of host names and IP addresses, allowing users of workstations configured to query the DNS to specify remote systems by host names rather than IP addresses. DNS domains should not be confused with Windows NT networking domains.

NetBEUI: A network protocol usually used in small, department-sized local area networks of 1 to 200 clients.

NetBIOS (network basic input/output system): An application program interface (API) that can be used by application programs on a local area network. NetBIOS provides application programs with a uniform set of commands for requesting the lower-level services required to conduct sessions between nodes on a network and transmit information back and forth. Can be driven on NetBEUI or TCP/IP transport protocols.

NWLink IPX/SPX Compatible Transport: A standard network protocol that supports routing and can support NetWare client-server applications, in which NetWare-aware sockets-based applications communicate with IPX\SPX sockets-based applications.

Protocol: A set of rules and conventions for sending information over a network. These rules govern the content, format, timing, sequencing, and error control of messages exchanged among network devices.

TCP/IP (transmission control protocol/Internet protocol): A set of networking protocols that provides communications across interconnected networks made up of computers with diverse hardware architectures and various operating systems. TCP/IP includes standards for how computers communicate and conventions for connecting networks and routing traffic.

WINS (Windows Internet name service): A network service for Microsoft networks that provides Windows computers with Internet addresses for specified NetBIOS names, facilitating browsing and intercommunications over TCP/IP networks.

Sample Questions

1. You notice that the NT workstation you are using communicates slowly on the network. What can you do to speed up communications?

    A. Change the Ethernet card to a Token Ring card

    B. Change the Token Ring card to an Ethernet card

    C. Change the binding order of the protocols

    D. Add another network card to the workstation

    Answer: C—Changing the binding order at the workstation may affect the speed of communications. NT workstation uses the different protocols in the order they were bound.

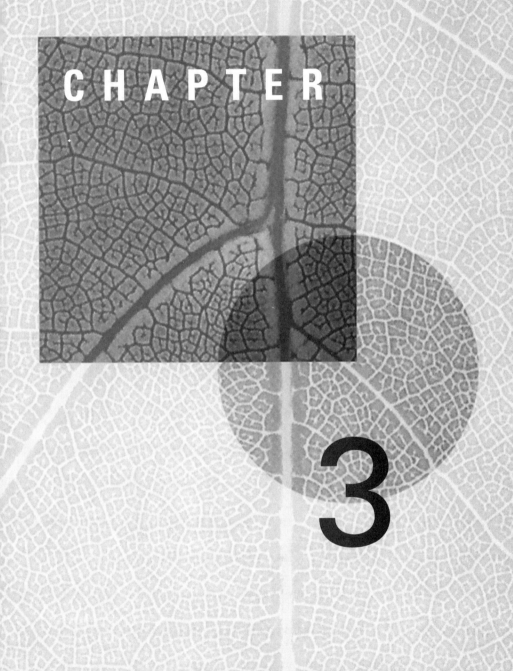

CHAPTER

3

Managing Resources

Microsoft Exam Objectives Covered in This Chapter:

Manage user and group accounts. Considerations include: *(pages 164 – 182)*

- Managing Windows NT user accounts
- Managing Windows NT user rights
- Managing Windows NT groups
- Administering account policies
- Auditing changes to the user account database

Create and manage policies and profiles for various situations. Policies and profiles include: *(pages 182 – 192)*

- Local user profiles
- Roaming user profiles
- System policies

Administer remote servers from various types of client computers. Client computer types include: *(pages 193 – 197)*

- Windows 95
- Windows NT Workstation

Manage disk resources. Tasks include: *(pages 198 – 226)*

- Copying and moving files between file systems
- Creating and sharing resources
- Implementing permissions and security
- Establishing file auditing

One of the best definitions of a network is having two or more people with information to share, a communication medium to send the information, and rules to govern the communication. The whole reason for having a computer network is sharing—sharing information, sharing resources, and sharing applications. That very broad overview is great for discussions over your favorite frosty, cold beverage, but it tends to get complicated really quickly when the amount of people with something to share grows to 50, 100, 1000, or more. It is especially complicated when *you* have to provide others with the opportunity to share files and peripherals throughout the entire company. It can be a daunting task. However, it doesn't have to be that way. As you study this chapter, you will find ways to cut that task down to size.

The first objective involves how to create user accounts, and then how to group those accounts together and control them. What rights does a particular group or individual need to gain access to a network resource? Is there a way to set up a basic set of rights for each user when the account is created? Is there a way to monitor the network to see that the users are not abusing the rights you have given them? These are the questions that will be answered with the first objective.

While the first objective groups users together and handles them *en masse*, the second objective starts to give the user some human characteristics. Now, the user is a person who actually uses this specific computer. The user is not only someone who works on the network, but roams from office to office, desk to desk, and still needs to access the same resources in the same way, no matter where they are. System policies let the administrator control the way users "see" their desktops. The third objective pertains to remote server administration. If you are administering a network of 500 people or more, that network will almost certainly contain more than one server computer. Those servers may not be in the same building or the same state as your desk. However, you still have to make changes to the servers, even if you can't sit down in front of the monitor and move the server's local mouse. There are utilities that will allow you to administer an NT server remotely from a Windows 95 workstation or a Windows NT workstation. The tools are similar. By the end of the section, you will know which utilities you can use based on the operating system installed on your next desktop or laptop.

The fourth objective on managing disk resources is not a rehash of Chapter 2. It shows how to manage the information stored on the disks. In this section, some of the subtle touches that you must be aware of when making rights and policies decisions will be examined. This section also delves into security. Impressive chapter, isn't it? Lots of exam questions will be asked about the material covered in this chapter—be sure to pay close attention to the concepts of local groups and global groups. Questions on groups will haunt you during the NT Server test, the NT Enterprise test, and beyond.

Manage user and group accounts. Considerations include:

- Managing Windows NT user accounts
- Managing Windows NT user rights
- Managing Windows NT groups
- Administering account policies
- Auditing changes to the user account database

To break down this objective, remember one of the commandments of LAN administration—do unto many. Anytime you can group users together as one entity, it will make your life much easier.

Critical Information

As you try to see the "big picture" of your network, you look around at all those users, running all those applications, printing to all those printers, and you have to wonder how you can manage all of that. The more you look, the more you realize these people can be grouped by the tasks they perform and the resources they require.

Managing Windows NT User Accounts

The more users you group together, the less work for the administrator or Information Services team. Who wants to work harder? The NT domain model provides security for the files and resources on your network. This security is implemented by assigning permissions to four types of objects: the local user, the global user, the global group, and the local group. Are you wondering how each is used?

NOTE Make sure you pay close attention to this discussion, because you need to know what can go where. Questions about which users can go in which groups and which default user can do what will keep showing up in exam after exam.

Let's start the discussion small—with the user. With Windows NT, there are two kinds of users, local users and global users. Each has separate roles to fill. In addition, NT creates a set of default users that you can use as templates or role models.

Local User Account

Sometimes, naming can be tricky. This is one of those times. A local user account is created on an NT computer via an NT domain, and its purpose is to serve a single user on just that server. That user account can enable access for local users in addition to those from other NT domains. For example, assume that you have a diverse network made up of NT servers and Windows 95 clients. A user who primarily logs on and uses the services of the NT network could have direct server login authentication provided through a local user account—without a local account, they would not.

NOTE Local accounts can access services only from within the NT server (or workstation) where they reside, since they are in the local (via domain) SAM. They are created in the individual computer SAM by using the User Manager utility as opposed to the User Manager for Domains utility.

Global User Account

Because global user accounts are the most commonly created, they are generally referred to as just "user accounts." A global user account differs from a local account in that it can provide permissions to access resources in any domain, beginning with the domain in which it was created. As long as there is a trust relationship between domains, these accounts can utilize resources in any trusting domains. Global user accounts can receive these permissions either individually or through membership in a group. A global user account is created with User Manager for Domains.

As mentioned, two default user types are created with the NT installation:

- Administrator—user account for administering the computer and/or domain

- Guest—user account for providing guest access to the computer and/or domain

A local user account is designed for the user who will log onto the computer itself. A global user is someone who is allowed to log on and access resources from the domain. Local accounts are created using User Manager if the NT computer is designed as a part of a peer-to-peer network or standalone system. Local users can be implemented regardless of whether the server is being used in an NT domain environment. Otherwise, global users are created using User Manager for Domains.

User accounts can be created two ways—you can create a new user account or you can copy an existing user account. No matter which way you choose to create the account, you can still make changes in three key areas—user account information, group membership information, and user account profile information.

The New User dialog box is shown in Figure 3.1.

The procedures for creating each account type will be discussed in the "Necessary Procedures" section of this objective.

What do you do with the users once they have been created?

FIGURE 3.1: New User dialog box

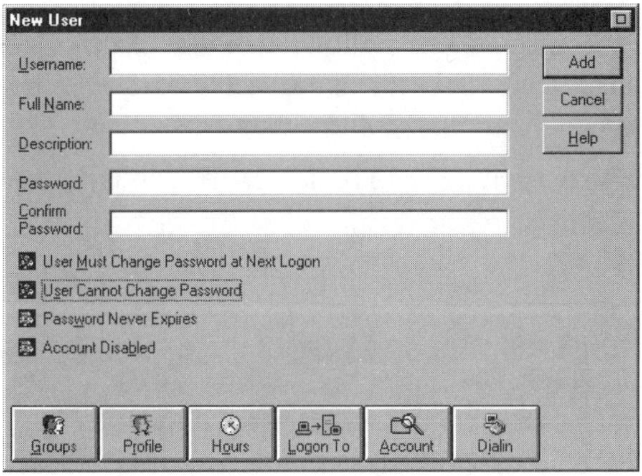

Managing Windows NT User Rights

Now that the users have been created, you have to give them permission to do something. If you remember the beginning of this chapter, it was mentioned that the assignment of rights and permissions is a democratic thing—the majority rules. If you can do unto many, you probably won't have to do unto the individual.

Usually, you will plan for your groups first. In most cases, rights and permissions can be assigned at the group level, leaving user accounts to be assigned to global groups.

Even if you have laid out a security plan in which all rights and permissions are assigned to groups, there are still some universal settings you may want to set for all users, such as using the corporate logo as wallpaper or making sure the network hookup is just the way you want it. You can make these edits on the User Environment Profile screen. Microsoft's TechNet defines a *user profile* as follows:

> Configuration information that can be retained on a user-by-user basis, and is saved in user profiles. This information includes all the per-user settings of the Windows NT environment, such as the

desktop arrangement, personal program groups and the program items in those groups, screen colors, screen savers, network connections, printer connections, mouse settings, window size and position, and more. When a user logs on, the user's profile is loaded and the user's Windows NT environment is configured according to that profile.

The User Environment Profile screen is shown in Figure 3.2.

FIGURE 3.2: User Environment Profile

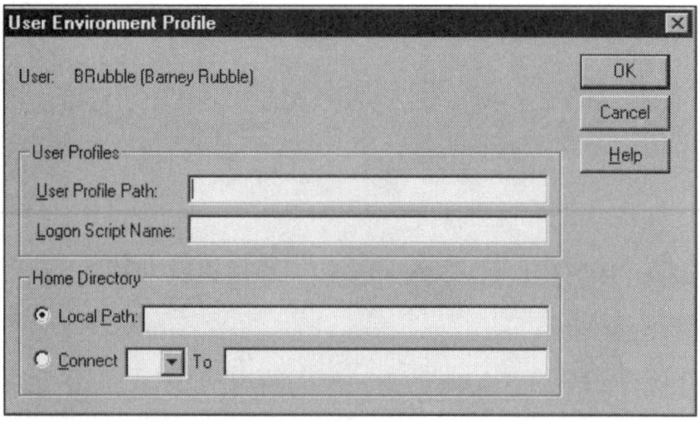

This screen allows you to point to where you have stored the user profile and the name of the logon script that the user should execute. You can give a user a path to their home directory, where they can store all that really private user stuff. This directory can be on any server or share.

User profiles contain those settings and configuration options specific to the user—installed applications, desktop icons, color options, and so forth. This profile is built from system policy information (for example, those things that a user has access to and those things that a user can and cannot change), the default user profile, and permitted, saved changes that a user makes to customize their desktop.

Remember that mandatory profiles can be created by changing the profile suffix from .DAT to .MAN. This resets profile settings to the mandatory values each time a user logs on. While it saves time and prevents users from mangling their desktop settings on a permanent basis, the downside to this implementation is that if the domain controllers are unavailable, users cannot log on, even with cached profile information.

NOTE   User profiles deal with a specific user. User policies deal with all users of a domain.

How do you tell which groups a user is a part of? The Group Memberships screen (see Figure 3.3) shows you which groups a user is a member of and to which groups a user can be added.

F I G U R E 3.3: Group Memberships

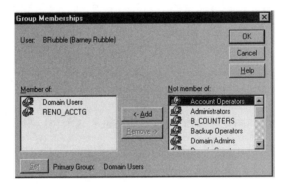

Although the Group Memberships screen shows you where you add a user to a group, you still don't know how and why groups interact.

Managing Windows NT Groups

Windows NT uses a very sophisticated group model that consists of local groups and global groups. At its simplest, in a multiple-domain environment, you create users and global groups in the domain. Users get placed in global groups. Local groups are created on individual NT computers to give access to resources of that server or workstation. Global groups are made a part of local groups, and the users can access the resources.

Global Groups

Global groups are simply users from the same domain grouped together. Global groups can contain only user accounts from their domain—they cannot contain other groups.

While a global group can contain only users in its domain, it is not limited to receiving permissions from only that domain. Global groups can be granted permissions to access resources in other domains. Global groups are created only on NT servers functioning as domain controllers using User Manager for Domains.

Local Groups

Unlike global groups, which can receive authentications from outside their domain boundaries, local groups can receive permissions only on the computer in which they were created. Local groups are created to grant permission to resources or allow users to perform specific tasks. Local groups can be made up of local user accounts, users from within their domain, users from trusted domains, and global group accounts both from their domain and from any trusted domains.

Default Groups

The types of groups described above are those that you can create. NT has taken some of the work out of planning for groups by creating some default groups to do various management tasks:

- Domain Users—global group containing all domain users except the user Guest

- Domain Guests—global group giving limited access and containing the user Guest

- Domain Admins—global group that allows administrator permissions to the entire domain

- Guests—local group for server guests containing the global group Domain Guests

- Print Operators—local group for the members that are assigned to administer domain printers

- Replicator—local group for the accounts that support directory and file replication in the domain

- Server Operators—local group for the members that can administer domain servers

- Users—local group for ordinary users. Contains the global group Domain Users by logging on locally and conducts sharing, hard drive, and backup operations

- Backup Operators—local group for backing up and restoring the server regardless of directory and file permissions

- Administrators—local group that has full control over the server. Includes the Administrator local user account and the Domain Admins global group

- Account Operators—local group that can access both the server's local SAM and domain SAM (if the server is a domain controller)

NOTE   Always remember that in the Microsoft-selected model of group management, users are always put in global groups. Global groups are added to local groups. Local groups are always assigned access permissions. Users are never put in local groups.

Administering Account Policies

There are other ways of improving the security settings of a user account. One way is to alter the default account policies. This is another section under-emphasized by the exam writers, but is very important for the network administrator.

- *Account policies* are the defaults that the administrator sets to handle various security issues.

Account policies are handled through User Manager for Domains. System policies are administered through the System Policy Editor.

Account Policies

Account policies set broad policies for all the users of your domain. To access the Account Policies page, start User Manager for Domains and choose Policies ➤ Account (see Figure 3.4).

F I G U R E 3.4: Account Policy options

Setting default user security is key to this utility. However, setting user security is a two-edged sword. The network and data are more secure, but your end users will probably whine about the changes. The Account Policy page offers the following selections:

- Maximum Password Age—for password restrictions, the administrator can set the Maximum Password Age. If you work in an environment where security is not an issue, you may choose Password Never Expires. If security is an issue, there is a setting that forces passwords to be changed every so many days. Keep in mind as you view this figure that the default is set to 42 days. While decreasing the amount of time a password is active may make great sense from a security point of view, the chances that your users will understand why they have to change their passwords so often are slim to none.

- Minimum Password Age—this forces a user to keep a password for at least a certain period of time. By default, users can change their passwords immediately.

- Minimum Password Length—how long must a password be? If no changes are made, blank passwords are permitted. If you increase the minimum password length, your users will have to start thinking before typing. Most experts say that six to eight characters is about the right length, but Microsoft doesn't have a particular policy.

- Password Uniqueness—you have heard the stories of the user who kept the same password for years and years. By the time the user left the company, everyone knew his or her password. This is almost as bad as having no password at all. Password Uniqueness, which is turned off by default, will remember a number of passwords, forcing the user to come up with something new every time the password must be changed, even if changing only capitalization (recall that passwords are case sensitive). You get to choose the length of the history list.

- Account Lockout—this is an attempt to prevent hackers from attempting to access your network over and over again. If Account Lockout is enabled and someone tries to log onto a valid user account unsuccessfully so many times, the account will be locked and the user will not be able to log onto the system. You can set the number of bad logon attempts, reset the count after so many minutes, and set the lockout duration. Once the account is locked, the hacker doesn't know if it is locked for 10 minutes or an hour and 10 minutes. At that point, there are probably easier networks to attack.

- Forcibly Disconnect Remote Users from Server When Logon Hours Expire—if you select this checkbox, it will cause users who are working when the allowed time expires to be kicked off the system. If this option is not selected, the remote server user can continue to use the system, but cannot open any new sessions.

- Users Must Log On in Order to Change Password—this selection makes your users change their passwords before they expire. If the password expires, the end user will have to contact the administrator, and the administrator will have to reset the password.

At this point, you know the types of users and groups. You know how each user and group interacts with the others. You know the Microsoft-approved method of putting users in global groups and putting global groups in local groups. You know all about the default types of users and groups and how to standardize some of the user settings. There is also a way to check on the changes that are made to the user database. It is called auditing.

Auditing Changes to the User Account Database

NT allows you to audit what is happening to user accounts and who is making changes or performing certain tasks. Don't get bogged down with auditing, but if you know how to use it, it can come in handy. It can certainly help answer an exam question or two.

Setting an audit policy can help spot security breaches. By default, auditing is turned off. You can change the audit policy through User Manager for Domains by choosing Policies ➤ Auditing. Take a good, close look at Figure 3.5.

F I G U R E 3.5: Audit Policy screen

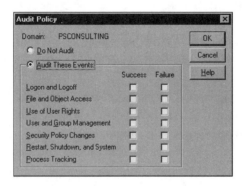

You have a limited amount of options for auditing. Remember that if you turn on auditing, it may help you track down a security breach. However, it will also put a serious load on your server, perhaps slowing response time.

As you can see from the options on the Audit Policy screen, you can audit the success or failure of seven common network events. The information is stored in a security log. You can view the log by using the Event Viewer.

Necessary Procedures

This objective encompasses several routine management procedures that need to be addressed.

Creating a Global User Account

To create a global user account, fire up User Manager for Domains and open the New User dialog box:

1. Click Start.

2. Select Programs.

3. Select Administrative Tools.

4. Click User Manager for Domains. The New User dialog box appears. (See Figure 3.1 earlier in the chapter.)

NOTE You can also create a new user by using the Administrative Wizard, or by starting User Manager for Domains and choosing User ➤ New User.

Using the New User dialog box, you can enter the basics to create a new user. Start with a unique user name. In many cases, Username will differ from the next field—Full Name. Depending on corporate standards, the user name might be GGovanus and the full name might be Gary Govanus.

- Description—an optional field for location, title, or any indentifying information.

- Password—can be up to 14 characters and is case sensitive. You can force the new user to change the password at the next logon.

TIP Some applications or services require a special account to start the service. If this is the case, enable the checkboxes for User Cannot Change Password and Password Never Expires.

- Account Disabled—disables the user account. If you want an account to be available when a user returns from a short leave, you can disable the account. The account will be inactive until the user returns from leave. This is also a good way to store user accounts that may be set up as templates, without them being illegally used.

- Groups button—gives the administrator the ability to add users to global and/or local groups.

- Profile button—activates the User Environment Profile screen, specifying where the user profile is stored, the name of the login script, and where the user's home directory is located. (See Figure 3.2 earlier in the chapter.)

NOTE See the next objective for an in-depth discussion of user profiles.

- Hours button—you can force your users off your network by setting the hours during which they can access the network.

TIP Using the Hours button is an especially handy trick when you are trying to get a clean backup with as few open files as possible.

- Logon To button—specifies which workstations a user may log onto. The default is All. If this is selected, a maximum of eight workstations can be assigned.

- Account button—allows you to expire an account and specify the account type. The account types are Global Account for a regular user in the domain and Local Account for a user from an untrusted domain. (See Figure 3.1 earlier in the chapter.)

- Dialin button—allows the user to access the server using remote access service (RAS).

NOTE   Remote access service will be discussed further in Chapter 4.

Creating a User Template

One of the ways to create a large number of users with the same requirements is to create a user template or model user. The user template is configured exactly the way you want your new users configured, except this account has the Account Disabled field enabled. When it is time to create the new account, you simply copy the model and provide the information necessary to make the account unique. The following fields can be copied:

- Description
- Groups
- Profiles
- Hours
- Logon To
- Account
- Dialin

The mandatory fields include:

- Username
- Full Name
- The Account Disabled checkbox is always cleared when an account is created by copying a template. The User Must Change Password at Next Logon checkbox is set.

To create and use a template:

1. If you are logged on as an administrator, go into User Manager for Domains and create a model user with all the properties that will be the defaults for the new group of users. Be sure to select the Account Disabled checkbox. Consider using an account name that represents the fact that this account is a template, such as Finance Template. Add the user.

2. Highlight the user you have just created and press F8 to copy the user. Notice that the Username and Full Name fields are blank, and that the Account Disabled checkbox has been cleared.

Deleting User Accounts

To delete a user account:

1. Log on as an administrator.

2. Start User Manager for Domains.

3. Select the user account to be deleted.

4. Either choose User and Delete or simply press the delete key.

5. Agree to the screen asking if you really want to delete the user.

6. Choose Yes to actually delete the user.

7. Close User Manager for Domains.

Renaming Users

When you change the name of the account, nothing else about the account changes. To change the user name of an account:

1. Log on as an administrator or a similar superior being.

2. Start User Manager for Domains.

3. Select the user to be renamed from the User account list.

4. Choose User ➤ Rename.

5. Change the Username and click OK.

Exam Essentials

The information in this section is so important that you will see questions on it in exam after exam. If you get it right the first time, the rest is easy. Know placement!

Know the relationship between global groups, local groups, and users.   Global groups exist at the domain level and can be added to local groups if the local group exists on a server that is a member of a domain that trusts the global group's domain. Local groups can be created on any Windows NT workstation or server within the domain. Global groups are limited to containing user accounts from the domain. Local groups can consist of users from the domain, global groups from the domain, or global groups from a trusted domain. Global groups are used to organize users; local groups are used to grant rights and permissions to resources.

Know what can be done to a user account.   User accounts can be renamed. If you have a user who is leaving the company and their replacement needs access to the same information, simply rename the account and change the password. This process is completed using the User Manager for Domains utility. The default Administrator and Guest accounts can be renamed, but not deleted.

Know what happens when you delete a user account.   Once a user account has been deleted, the only way to re-create the account is to start over. Accounts are not re-created using the exact same user name again.

Know which groups have the right to log onto an NT server locally by default.   The system-created accounts are Server Operators, Account Operators, Backup Operators, and Print Operators. By default, they have the right to log onto an NT server locally.

Know the privileges granted by default to the various groups. Backup Operators can back up files to tape and restore files from tape only when logged on locally.

Know how logon hour restrictions affect users. If a user is allowed to log on from 7:00 A.M. to 6:00 P.M., what happens to the user when 6:00 P.M. arrives? If there are no system policies set, the user will be allowed to continue the session, but will *not* be allowed to establish new connections.

Know what happens when a user's logon time has expired with the Forcibly Disconnect selection enabled and with the Forcibly Disconnect selection cleared. With the Forcibly Disconnect selection enabled, the user will be disconnected from all connections and then logged off. With the Forcibly Disconnect selection cleared, the user will be allowed to continue with the current connection, but cannot establish any new connections.

Know how to expire an account and how to reactivate it. To instantly expire the account, start User Manager for Domains, double-click the user, choose Account, select the End Of button, and fill in the date for the account to expire. This is similar to disabling it. To reactivate the account, start User Manager for Domains, double-click the user, choose Account, and either select the Never button or advance the date in the End Of field to a date in the future.

Know how to create user accounts using a template. Start User Managers for Domains, highlight the template account, and press F8 to copy the account and provide a new user name, full name, and password.

Know how to set an audit policy. Setting an audit policy can be a useful tool for troubleshooting security problems. If you audit the failure of logon and logoff attempts, it may show that hackers are attempting to gain entry to the network. The audit log is viewed using the Event Viewer.

Key Terms and Concepts

Account policy: Settings governing password restrictions, ages, and account lockouts.

Auditing: Keeping track of certain successful or failed key events on the network computers.

Disabling an account: Temporarily suspending access. The account can be reactivated at a later time. This is done manually and cannot be automated.

Expiring an account: Used for temporary or seasonal workers. You provide a date for when the account expires. After that date, the account cannot be accessed without administrator intervention.

Global account: A normal user account in an NT domain. Most network user accounts are global accounts.

Global group: A group that can be used in its own domain's member servers and workstations, and those of trusting domains. In all those places, it can be granted rights and permissions, and can become a member of local groups. However, it can contain only user accounts from its own domain.

Local account: A user account provided on a computer for a user who does not have or does not wish to log into a global account.

Local group: A group that can be granted permissions and rights only for its own resources. However, it can contain user accounts and global groups both from its own domain and from trusted domains.

Permissions: Windows NT security settings you place on a shared resource that determine which users can use the resource and how they can use it.

Policy: Default settings for a variety of NT objects.

Rights: Define a user's access to a computer or domain and the actions that a user can perform on the computer or domain. User rights permit actions such as logging onto a computer or network, adding or deleting users in a workstation or domain, and so forth.

Trusted relationship between domains: A link between domains that enables pass-through authentication, in which a trusting domain honors the logon authentication of a trusted domain. With trust relationships, a user who has a user account in one domain can potentially access the entire network.

Sample Questions

1. The basic Microsoft understanding of groups is as follows:

   A. Local groups can be placed in global groups.

   B. Global groups should be placed in local groups.

   C. Never use local groups; always use global groups.

   D. Never use global groups; always use local groups.

   Answer: B—Microsoft recommends that you place all users in global groups and make global groups members of local groups.

2. Which of the following statements is true?

   A. Global groups can contain members from multiple domains.

   B. Global groups must contain members from multiple domains.

   C. Local groups can contain members from multiple domains.

   D. Local groups must contain members from multiple domains.

   Answer: C—Global groups can contain only members from their own domains. Local groups can contain global groups from different domains; therefore, local groups can contain members from different domains.

Create and manage policies and profiles for various situations. Policies and profiles include:

- Local user profiles
- Roaming user profiles
- System policies

Control is a wonderful thing, especially when you are a network administrator. People on your network can do so many things to make your life more challenging. Just the thought of it can keep a person up nights.

Fortunately, there are ways around the problem. NT provides you with tools called policies and profiles that allow you to maintain some semblance of order and control over the workstations on your network. As you can see from the objective, there are local user profiles, roaming user profiles, and system policies—which entail control over the local user, control over the user who roams from system to system, and control over hardware profiles.

Critical Information

What kinds of things do you need to control? Often, the mundane, routine things. The Chief Executive Officer was roaming through the office and saw someone with wallpaper that was customized in a manner not appropriate to corporate life. The CEO reflected on this and decided that all users in the company will hereby use a custom-designed wallpaper showing the corporate logo. You control wallpaper choices through profiles and policies.

Local User Profiles

Local user profiles store information on how a user has configured their computing environment. This isn't really flashy stuff; it is more everyday information such as:

- Have you ever wondered where the information is stored that lets 32-bit applications know the last few documents you accessed? It's in the profile.

- How does the computer know to reattach all those connections to all those shares and printers? It's in the profile.

- How does the computer remember where you put all the bookmarks in Help? It's in the profile.

The subdirectory on every Windows NT machine that contains the user profile information is \WINNT\Profiles. Under that folder, there is a subfolder named for each user. Those subfolders contain a file called NTUSER.DAT. This file contains all the registry entries. There are also folders for Application Data, the Desktop, Favorites, Personal, Start Menu, and other information that pertains to a specific user.

When a user logs onto a system for the first time, the system knows there is no local user profile, so it goes out to the network to look for a roaming user profile. If there is no roaming user profile, NT creates a local user profile subdirectory for the user in the \WINNT\Profiles directory. NT then needs to provide the user with some of the basics, so it gets the information from the \WINNT\Profiles\Default user directory.

At this point, the user has the default profile settings. Any changes that the user makes will be stored in the local user profile for the new user. The next time the user logs onto the local machine, the user is presented with the system just the way it was left.

There are occasions when you do not want a user to be able to change the desktop. How do you keep that from happening? Easy, just configure the system the way you want it for the tech-weenie-wannabe and save the settings by logging out. Go back into the system as another user and change the name of the NTUSER.DAT file to NTUSER.MAN. When you add that little extension—.MAN—it changes the file to a mandatory profile. The user can change the desktop in a variety of fashions, but none of the changes will be retained.

Roaming User Profiles

With a roaming user profile, a profile is created and centrally stored. When a user logs onto a workstation on the network, the workstation checks for a roaming user profile, finds it, and *voila*—the desktop looks just the same, no matter where the user logs on from.

What happens if there are a local user profile and a roaming user profile, and the local user profile is more recent? NT is nothing if not polite; it will ask which profile you want to use. Otherwise, it will just go with the roaming user profile.

When the user logs off, the new profile is saved (if it is not mandatory or the user has not logged on as guest), and any changes that have been made are saved for posterity.

Now that you know how to standardize your desktop, be sure to share the wealth. Other people on the network roam, too, so you may want to give them the flexibility of a roaming profile.

TIP   The path to the roaming user profile is specified using User Manager for Domains.

System Policies

System policies are created with the System Policy Editor. Using system policies, you will be able to maintain machine configurations and user policies from one machine.

The System Policy Editor operates in either Registry mode or System Policy mode. Since the objective mentions system policies rather than Registry mode, apparently the exam writers think system policies are more significant.

Registry mode allows you to edit all sorts of interesting things. Take a look at Figure 3.6.

FIGURE 3.6: Local Computer Properties

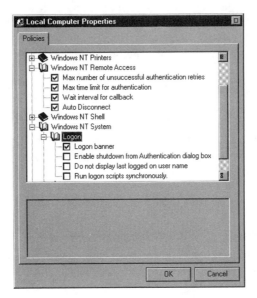

Several things jump out at you while looking at this screen:

- You can specify which applications to run at startup.

- You can create hidden drive shares for workstations or servers.

- From the Windows NT Remote Access section, you can set the maximum number of unsuccessful authentication attempts and for the system to automatically disconnect.

- From the Windows NT System\Logon section, you can specify a specific logon banner or make sure the name of the last user who logged on is not displayed.

System Policy vs. Registry Mode

How does System Policy mode differ from Registry mode? System Policy mode is like Registry mode, but with an *attitude*. If there is a setting in the registry and a system policy conflicts with the registry, the system policy takes precedence.

You can find the system policy file. For NT systems, the file is named NTCONFIG.POL. Suppose you want to impose a set of restrictions on machines that the user cannot change. How is that accomplished?

Use the System Policy Editor to make the changes you want replicated across the network. Save the file as NTCONFIG.POL in the \WINNT\System32\Repl\Import\Scripts folder on the boot partition of the domain controllers.

NOTE If system policy information is being stored for Windows 95 machines, the filename should be CONFIG.POL instead of NTCONFIG.POL.

When a computer attempts to log onto the network, it will check for the system policy. When the computer finds the NTCONFIG.POL file that affects the user or the computer, it brings this information into the registry and configures the workstation accordingly.

NOTE   If the changes are made in System Policy mode rather than Registry mode, the changes will overwrite the local registry. What a great topic for an exam question!

Necessary Procedures

The previous section examined the different types of profiles, but did not address how to create or change the settings. For a local user profile, there is not much to do, because it is automatically created and administered by NT. The configuration and dissemination of the roaming user profile are more challenging.

Creating a Local User Profile and a Mandatory User Profile

Local user profiles are created when the user logs on and makes changes to the computer. When the user logs off, these changes are saved in the file \WINNT\Profiles\UserName\NTUSER.DAT. To change this profile to a mandatory profile, change the extension from .DAT to .MAN. This changes the file to read only. Remember that with a mandatory user profile, if the NT domain controllers fail, the user will not be able to log onto the domain.

Creating a Roaming User Profile

Roaming user profiles are created from User Manager for Domains, which is accessed as follows:

1. Choose Programs ➤ Administrative Tools ➤ User Manager for Domains.

2. Double-click Administrator.

3. Select Profile. (See Figure 3.2 earlier in the chapter.)

4. In the User Profile Path, enter a universal naming convention (UNC) path to the \WINNT\Profiles directory. The syntax for a UNC path is *Servername**Foldername**Subfoldername*\WINNT\Profiles.

5. Close the User Enivironment Profile box by clicking OK.

6. Close the User window by clicking OK.

7. Close User Manager for Domains.

You may think nothing has changed. However, go to a different machine and log on as administrator. Your new profile will follow you.

Copying a User Profile to Make It a Remote User Profile

Create a central repository for user profiles on a server attached to the network, such as *Servername\Profile\Username*, and share the directory. Then, do as follows:

1. Start Control Panel.

2. Double-click System.

3. Choose the User Profiles tab.

4. Select the profile for the user you want to copy and click Copy To. You will be prompted to enter a path to the location of the share: *Server Name\Profile\Username*.

5. Under Permitted to Use, make sure the appropriate user name is selected.

Creating and Implementing a System Policy

There are many ways and reasons to set system policies. In this example, a system policy will be created to ensure that the name of the last user to log onto a system is not displayed. This policy will be replicated throughout the network to all NT systems.

Log on as administrator and do as follows:

1. Choose Programs ➤ Administrative Tools ➤ System Policy Editor.

2. Choose File ➤ New Policy.

3. Click Default Computer.

4. Click Windows NT System.

5. Click Logon.

6. Check the box next to Do Not Display Last Logged On User Name.

7. Select OK.

8. Choose Save As and save the file as NTCONFIG.POL on the domain controller in the \WINNT\System32\REPL\Import\Scripts folder.

Exam Essentials

There was lots of useful information in this section. The exam writers love to concentrate on questions of filenames and locations, so as you read this section, pay close attention to those topics.

Know where user profiles are stored. User profiles are stored in the \WINNT\Profiles*Username* folder of any Windows NT computer.

Know the name of the user profile file. The user profile file is called NTUSER.DAT.

Know how to make a local user profile a mandatory profile. Change the name of NTUSER.DAT to NTUSER.MAN.

Know what happens when the domain controller that contains the mandatory user profile is down and the user logs onto the network. The user's locally cached profile will be used. If a mandatory profile is set, the user will not be able to log on.

Know where shortcuts are stored on a local machine. Shortcuts are stored as part of the local user profile. The information will be stored in the \WINNT\Profiles*Username*\Desktop directory.

Know how profiles are accessed. During logon, NT looks for a local user profile. If it does not find a local user profile, it will look for a roaming user profile. If it cannot find a roaming user profile, it will create a local user profile using the default user settings.

Know how to create a roaming user profile. Copy the user's workstation local profile to a shared network path. Enter the UNC network path in the User Environment Profile dialog box.

Know what happens when a local user profile and a roaming user profile both exist.   If a local user profile is older than a roaming user profile, the roaming user profile is used. If the local user profile is newer than the roaming user profile, NT will ask which profile the user wants to use.

Know the two modes available in the System Policy Editor. The two modes are Registry mode and System Policy mode.

Know the difference between Registry mode and System Policy mode.   Registry mode changes the registry. System Policy mode allows you to control system policies for all NT computers in the domain. If a system policy exists that conflicts with the registry entry, the system policy entry will be used.

Know the name of the system policy file for NT and where it is stored for replication.   The system policy file is called NTCONFIG .POL. It is saved to the \WINNT\System32\Repl\Import\Scripts directory on the primary domain controller.

Know the name of the system policy file for Windows 95.   The name of the policy file for Windows 95 workstations is CONFIG.POL.

Key Terms and Concepts

CONFIG.POL: The name of the file that stores system policies for Windows 95 client workstations.

Local profile: Information stored on a local computer that reflects how the end user has configured the system.

Mandatory profile: A local profile that the end user cannot change.

NTCONFIG.POL: The name of the file that stores system policies for Windows NT workstations and servers.

NTUSER.DAT: The name of the file stored in the \WINNT\ Profile*Username* directory that contains all the settings in the local profile.

NTUSER.MAN: The name of the file stored in the \WINNT\ Profile*Username* directory that contains all the settings in the mandatory user profile. When you change the extension of .DAT to .MAN, it turns the profile file into a read-only file.

Registry mode: A way the System Policy Editor can be used to edit the registry of either local computers or other computers in the domain.

Roaming profile: Profile created for a user who accesses more than one computer. The user's look and feel will remain the same, no matter what computer is being accessed.

System Policy Editor: The utility used to create system policies. Available through Programs ➤ Administrative Tools ➤ System Policy Editor.

System Policy mode: A way the System Policy Editor can be used to mandate registry settings throughout the domain. Settings changed in the system policy files will override local registry settings.

Sample Questions

1. Suppose that your boss is a control freak. He wants to make sure that each NT workstation has exactly the same system policies. Each workstation is attached to the network, and the users must always log onto the domain before starting work. How can you keep your boss happy?

   A. Create a system policy file and export it to each workstation the first time it logs on.

   B. Create a system policy file for each end user and copy it to the user profiles directory on the domain controller.

   C. Create a system policy file and copy it to each workstation's WINNT folder.

   D. Create a system policy file that will affect all end users and copy it to the NETLOGON folder of the PDC.

Answer: D—Create a system policy file that will affect all end users and copy it to the NETLOGON folder of the primary domain controller.

2. After you created a system policy and stored it in the NETLOGON directory so that people can access it, you find that the policy is virtually ignored by several systems on your network. What is a possible cause?

   A. The computers may have a local policy that conflicts with the system policy.

   B. The user on the computer is logging onto the domain as administrator, nullifying any policy changes.

   C. The user on the computer is logging onto the domain as guest, nullifying any policy changes.

   D. You screwed up.

   Answer: A—If there is a conflict between a local policy and the system policy, the local policy takes precedence. Answer D is never an option, is it?

3. How do you change a user profile to a mandatory user profile?

   A. Change the extension in the NTUSER.MAN file to NTUSER.DAT.

   B. Change the extension in the NTUSER.DAT file to NTUSER.MAN.

   C. That is covered in the rights and permissions section of this book, and you haven't gotten that far yet.

   D. Store the profile in the \NETLOGON directory of the PDC with the filename NETUSER.DAT.

   Answer: B—If you change the extension in the NETUSER.DAT file to .MAN, it makes the user profile a mandatory user profile.

Administer remote servers from various types of client computers. Client computer types include:

- Windows 95
- Window NT Workstation

It is not always possible to go directly to the server to perform administration tasks. After all, servers are usually stored in locked rooms on the other side of the building. It is much more convenient to be able to perform routine tasks, such as checking the event log or starting User Manager for Domains, directly from your desktop workstation.

If your desktop workstation is running Windows 95 or Windows NT Workstation, you are in luck. Within five minutes, your system can access the tools necessary to administer a network remotely.

Critical Information

When Microsoft designed the remote administration tools, it considered the usual administration mind-set. Let's face it, you want the fastest, biggest, baddest computer your company can afford for your workstation. If you can run Windows NT Workstation, you will have more flexibility than if you have "just" a Windows 95 computer. Actually, the tools are somewhat different for each operating system, but, hey, any excuse to get a new computer.

Windows 95

If your workstation is running Windows 95, has an extra 3MB of disk space, and runs the Client for Microsoft networks, you can configure the system to access the following items:

- Event Viewer—viewer used to view the system log.

- Server Manager—powerful utility that allows you to monitor and manage all aspects of your network, including active users, shares, replications, alerts, and services.

- User Manager for Domains—utility that allows you to create and manage users and groups. This utility allows the administrator to set account policies, user rights, and audit accounts as well as manage trust relationships with other domains.

- File Security—the ability to set rights and permissions for files.

- Print Security—the ability to set rights and permissions for various print objects.

- Some utilities to help you manage NetWare services.

NOTE   The system must be at least a 486DX/33.

Windows NT Workstation

If, on the other hand, your workstation is running Windows NT Workstation and is a 486DX/33 with at least 2.5MB of disk space, you can access the following items:

- DHCP Manager—gives you the ability to configure a dynamic host control protocol (DHCP) manager on a network segment. A DHCP host will pass out IP addresses to workstations on the network segment.

- Remote Access Administrator—utility that allows you to administer RAS connections to the system.

- Remote Boot Manager—utility for the administration of images for diskless workstations.

- Services for Macintosh—administration tools for the Macintosh environment.

- Server Manager—powerful utility that allows you to manage all aspects of your network, including users, shares, replications, alerts, and services.

- System Policy Editor—utility that allows you to edit system policies. In Registry mode, you can edit any computer on the network.

- User Manager for Domains—utility that allows you to create and manage user and group accounts.

- WINS Manager—utility that allows you to manage Windows Internet name service (WINS). WINS is the Microsoft method of resolving Internet protocol (IP) addresses to Microsoft networking names.

As you can see, the list is different for each OS, but definitely skewed toward the NT Workstation side.

Necessary Procedures

Before you can configure your workstation to be able to remotely administer an NT server, you have to teach NT Server to work and play well with others. The NT Server installation does not prepare the system to pass out administrative tools to every Tom, Dick, and Windows 95 machine. Once the preliminary work of preparing the server is done, it is easy to install the workstation configuration tools.

Copying Client-Based Administration Tools

Installing client-based administration tools is a two-step process. First, you prepare the server. Second, you install the tools on the workstation.

1. Start Network Client Administrator by selecting Start ≻ Programs ≻ Administrative Tools ≻ Network Client Administration.

2. Select the Copy Client-Based Network Administration Tools radio button and click OK.

3. You can share files by providing a path name to the files, you can copy files to a new directory and then share, or you can use an existing shared directory. At the top of the dialog box, enter the path to the NT installation CD. Then, select the second option. You are given a destination path of C:\Clients\Srvtools by default and a share name of SetupAdm. At this point, the files will be copied and the share will be created automatically.

Now that the share has been created, you can go back to your workstation and use NT Explorer to attach to the share you have just created. Once you have attached to the share, go into the \WINNT folder and execute SETUP.BAT by highlighting the filename and double-clicking it. When the installation is finished, the remote tools will be available.

Exam Essentials

The exam writers did not spend much time covering the objectives in this section. However, there may be a few questions, revolving around operating systems and setup procedures.

Know the two operating systems that can be used to administer a Windows NT server remotely.   The two desktop operating systems that can be used to remotely administer a Windows NT server are Windows NT Workstation and Windows 95.

Key Terms and Concepts

Remote administration: Administering an NT network from a Windows 95 workstation or Windows NT Workstation, rather than directly from the server.

Sample Questions

1. Remote administration is accomplished by:

   A. Dialing in and using a RAS connection

   B. Using RCONSOLE and an SPX connection

   C. Using a workstation running Windows for Workgroups

   D. Using a workstation running Windows NT Workstation

   Answer: D—Remote administration can be accomplished from either a properly configured workstation running Windows 95 or a Windows NT workstation.

2. Which operating system provides the best remote management ability?

   A. DOS

   B. Windows 3.1

   C. Windows 95

   D. Windows NT Workstation

   Answer: D—Windows NT provides the greatest flexibility.

Manage disk resources. Tasks include:

- Copying and moving files between file systems
- Creating and sharing resources
- Implementing permissions and security
- Establishing file auditing

It's about time! We work in the Information Technology business, and so far, all we have talked about is technology. We finally get to start talking about what to do with information. Information needs to be managed and protected, which is what this objective is all about.

Let's explore how NTFS and FAT work together. What happens to the attributes given to a file stored on an NTFS system when it is moved to a FAT system? When NTFS was mentioned earlier, there were references to permissions and file rights. What are those things and how are they implemented?

Users access files through network share points. How are these share points created and what characteristics do they have? When should a share point be created? Can you hide a share point? How do you control access to information on the share point? Can you make sure that unauthorized users do not get into the payroll section? Worse yet, how will you know if someone does get into a private area and accesses a file they are not supposed to access?

Even though a lot of information is presented, don't panic. This is more real-world material than exam material. The exam writers seem to have skipped much of it. Go figure.

Critical Information

Before beginning this objective, let's take a look at the logistics behind the layout. The objective starts out with a discussion of the effects on a file when that file is moved or copied from one file system to another.

You know from the discussion of file systems in Chapter 1 that the NT file system (NTFS) has some capabilities that plain, old FAT doesn't have, such as local directory- and file-level security and compression. The first part of this objective traces what happens to the compression attribute when the file is moved from a compressed area to an uncompressed area and what happens if the file is copied.

If you can copy or move a file from one drive to another, you must be able to access that file. Access to a file is provided through a combination of things, but foremost is the ability to find the location of that file. Users access remote files, directories, or entire drives through share points. Share points, unfortunately, don't just magically appear—the administrator has to create them. Fortunately, this can be done in a variety of ways.

Once the user has access to an area using a share point, some restrictions may need to be placed on what a user can do in a particular share. For example, if you have created a share to reference a Human Resources policy manual, you may not want everyone to be able to rewrite the vacation policy to suit their own needs. This is where folder- and file-level security come into play. NT has several levels of share access security. In addition, if the share is located on an NTFS partition, additional local security can be applied to the folder or file. Each of these levels of security is applied in a specific order with predictable results.

To summarize, the file exists on a disk. That disk may be compressed. If the file is moved or copied, you know what happens to it. The file is accessed through a share point. The procedure for creating share points will be covered. The file is protected by share-point security and (if the file is on an NTFS partition) NTFS security. Is there a way to monitor and ensure that the file is accessed only by those users who are supposed to be allowed to access it? Yes, it's called auditing. The last section of this objective examines how you can audit a file to make sure only the right people are gaining access to it.

NOTE For a complete discussion of the differences between NTFS and FAT, see the section in Chapter 1 on file systems. The current section will assume that you understand the differences between the two file systems.

Copying and Moving Files between File Systems

NTFS offers several advantages over the FAT file system. Security, obviously, is one of the biggest advantages. Another advantage that NT offers is the ability to maximize your investment in disk subsystems by implementing file compression. The level of compression may not be as extreme as in programs such as Stacker or even DOS 6.22, but compression is still available—every little bit helps.

Compression and local-level security are only available on NTFS partitions. You made the call on whether to use NTFS or FAT back in Chapter 2 when you installed the operating system. If you chose the FAT file system and now want to change to NTFS, you can do that. Conversion is a relatively painless process using the CONVERT.EXE command-line utility.

NOTE Conversion works only from FAT to NTFS. There is no utility that converts from NTFS to FAT. For information on how to convert from FAT to NTFS, see the "Necessary Procedures" section of this objective.

Copying a file, by definition, is creating a mirror image of that file. Moving a file, by definition, is picking that little sucker up and putting it somewhere else, and then deleting the original. This issue arises when you cross compression boundaries.

Instance one: A file called C:\Data\Docs\RESUME.DOC is copied from an uncompressed partition to D:\Data\Docs\RESUME.DOC, which is on a compressed partition.

Result one: The original RESUME.DOC maintains its attributes. It stays the same (uncompressed). The copy of RESUME.DOC takes on the attributes of the partition it is placed in, so in this case it becomes compressed.

This is common sense. The original stays the same, the new file takes on attributes of its new home. What about when a file is *moved* from one location to another? The same thing occurs. The file takes on the attributes of the new home.

Instance two: RESUME.DOC is moved from a folder on an uncompressed partition to a folder on a compressed partition.

Result two: The only copy of the document becomes compressed.

NTFS compression can be handled at the drive level, the directory level, and the file level. Once compression has been implemented, compression of new files happens automatically. It is a completely transparent process that the application or user will not see.

In general, if files are copied, they will inherit the attributes of their new homes. If files are moved, the attributes of the files will stay the same, unless the files are moved across partitions. In this case, the file takes the attributes of its new home.

As is the case with most compression utilities, there may be a performance hit when you are working with compressed files. NT is much better than other utilities for minimizing the performance degradation. NT compression is also an intelligent process. When a file is marked for compression, NT takes a close look at that file. If NT determines that the performance hit does not justify the disk space saved, the file will not be compressed.

NOTE See the "Necessary Procedures" section for information on how to compress a file, folder, or drive.

Now that you understand compression and what will happen to a file if you choose to move it, the procedure for creating the shares that give people access to the network can be explored.

Creating and Sharing Resources

In this case, sharing resources means sharing folders. Folders are shared so that other people on the network can use the information or applications in the folder. You create a share so users can put their stuff on your network, in the *Servername*\Users*Username* sub-folder. You also put shares on the network so users can access the network version of Excel, from *Servername*\Apps\Excel. Another share might point to the *Servername*\Shared\Data\Budgets area.

Just because you have created a folder called Data with a subfolder called Budgets, it does not mean that anyone else can see the folders. On the contrary, nothing is visible by default. For users to see a directory, the administrator must make the concerted effort to share the directory. Do your users want to remember all those UNC paths? These are the same people who have a difficult time remembering their password—you don't want them to have to remember *Servername*\Shared\Data\Budgets. To make sure users can remember where things are, administrators create shares and make them available under a readable share name.

The administrator can share any directory on the network if the administrator has been given the LIST permission. If a user on a remote computer has blocked the administrator from having the LIST permission, chances are the user does not want the information spread across the network, so the administrator cannot create a share.

NOTE   If you are not sure what the LIST permission is or what it is good for, don't worry. A discussion of all permissions comes up next.

So, how are shares created? For a deeper look at creating and implementing sharing, skip ahead to the "Necessary Procedures" section. The current section will offer just a broad overview. Shares can be created using NT Explorer, My Computer, the command prompt, or Server Manager.

Look closely at Figure 3.7. To access this dialog box, open My Computer, browse to the folder and highlight it, right-click, and choose Sharing. Once the Sharing tab is displayed, choose Shared As and enter the share name—in this case, Applications. You can also add a comment so users will know what the share is for. You will notice that you can set a limit of users who can hack away on this share. You can allow the Maximum Allowed for the server or set a number of users with which you feel comfortable.

F I G U R E 3.7: Sharing a drive using My Computer

Using NT Explorer or My Computer to create a share is not the only way of doing it—it is just one of the most convenient. You can also create a share using File Manager (if you still use File Manager). If you happen to work in Server Manager, you can also create a share while doing normal management tasks. For the GUI-challenged or those of us who still feel most comfortable at a command prompt, you can use the Net Share utility. Each of these methods will be discussed in the "Necessary Procedures" section.

In addition to the shares that the administrator creates, if you are using an NT-based system that has a hard-coded access control list (ACL), you will find that there are at least two hidden shares. These hidden shares are the C$ share, which shares the root computer's C: drive, and the ADMIN$ share, which shares the root of the NT installation. These shares give administrators a path to the \WINNT directory or the operating system directory. Remember that a share name ending in $ results in a hidden or nonvisible share.

Implementing Permissions and Security

Shares have been created. It is time to start thinking about what kinds of permissions you want to grant users or groups of users for each one of the shares. The best way to start this process is to ask yourself some simple questions. Using the answers to the questions, you can make some decisions on share permissions.

To start, realize that by default all shares are granted Full Control to the Everyone group. Look at each share and ask, Who needs to do what to this share? If the share you are looking at is a data directory, your users will need to be able to see the filenames, open the files, write to the files, and even delete the files. If the directory you are looking at is a folder that houses an application, your users may just need to read the filenames and execute the files. Why do the permissions for the folders differ? You don't want your users to be able to go in and delete an executable file on which the rest of the network depends.

TIP   For exact information on permissions to run a specific application, be sure to read the documentation that came with the application.

Permissions are applied at various levels by various processes. For example, there is a share-level permission. If the share points to a folder on an NTFS partition, local computer permissions can point to the folder or directory.

Share-Level Permissions

Taking this one step at a time, let's start with share-level permissions. When you create a share using NT Explorer, you open NT Explorer, track to the folder you want to share, highlight the folder, and right-click. Click Share to open the Properties page for the folder.

NOTE For more information on creating shares using NT Explorer, please review the "Necessary Procedures" section of this objective.

Looking closely at the Share tab of the Properties page, you will notice a button marked Permissions. Click the Permissions button to bring up the Access Through Share Permissions (or ATS permissions) screen (see Figure 3.8).

FIGURE 3.8: Access Through Share Permissions

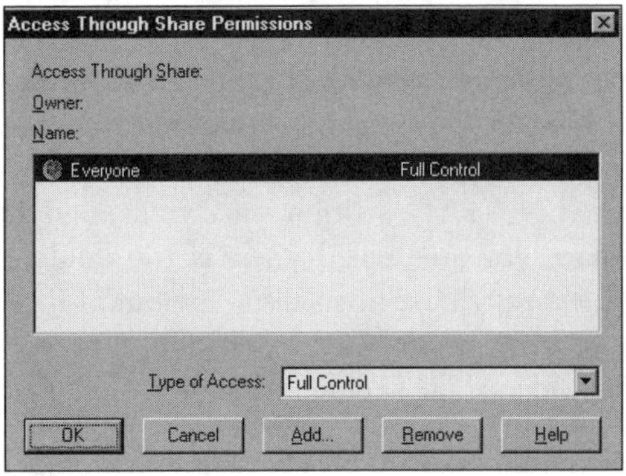

By default, the ATS share allows the group Everyone to have Full Control access to the share. If you use the Type of Access drop-down menu, you will see four types of share permissions you can control: Full Control, Change, Read, and No Access. See Table 3.1 for more information on these ATS share-level permissions.

TABLE 3.1: Share-Level Permissions

Access Through Share Permission	Permissions Granted
Full Control	The user can read or see a folder, subfolder, or file; execute an application; write to a closed file; and delete a folder or file. If the share resides on an NTFS partition, the user can also take ownership of the resource and change permissions.
Change	The user can read or see a folder, subfolder, or file; execute an application; write to a closed file; and delete a folder or file.
Read	The user can read and execute permissions to the share, folders, subfolders, and files.
No Access	The user can connect to the share, but will not be able to access any resources.

Share permissions deal with shares, and shares can point to folders regardless of the file system on which the folder resides. So, you can have a share that points to a folder on a FAT file system partition. If the share is on a FAT partition, once you assign the ATS permissions to the share, you are done. If there is a subfolder or file that needs more or less restrictive access, you are out of luck. Folder level is as deep as security gets on a FAT partition. If deeper security is necessary, the folder or file should reside on a drive that is based in NTFS.

If the share resides on an NTFS partition, another set of permissions can be granted to the local file or folder. This can get a little tricky. For example, suppose you are going to the bank to get some documents out of your safe-deposit box. When you arrive at the bank, you have to sign in to get the permission to go down to the vault; this is your logon security. Once you are down in the vault, you have to show identification to prove that you are whom you say you are. This second level of security could be considered share security. Once you prove whom you really are, you give your key to the person in charge of the vault so that they can open your box and give you access. When the teller finally takes the key to determine your access, that is NTFS security.

When determining what a user can really do, you must consider the share permissions granted to the share and the NTFS permissions granted to the folder or file. This is called the user's effective permissions to a folder. A user may get conflicting permissions from a variety of sources. One group may grant Full Access, another group may grant Limited Access, and the end user may have been given No Access as an individual permission. Is it possible to sort it all out? Yes, if share and NTFS permissions are applied, the most restrictive permissions take precedence. This is especially true of the No Access permission. If you have been given the No Access permission, either as an individual user or as a member of a group, you have no access, regardless of any other permissions you may have been assigned by other group memberships. You can attach to the share, but you cannot see anything.

WARNING   It is common for a question about permissions to have the sample user be a member of a group that is granted No Access. The question will usually be long and involved, and then asks what the user can actually do. If the words No Access show up in relation to a user, the answer is *nothing.*

Do all these share permissions appear to be Greek to you? Let's examine permissions and what all those funky letters mean.

To do anything, each permission is made up of one or more actions. There are six basic actions, four of which apply to both share and NTFS permissions (see Table 3.2).

TABLE 3.2:   System Actions

Permission	Actions
Read (R)	Users can read or see a file. Usually used in conjunction with Execute.
Write (W)	Users can add data to a file.

T A B L E 3.2: System Actions *(cont.)*

Permission	Actions
Execute (X)	Users can execute a file. Usually used in conjunction with Read.
Delete (D)	Users can delete a file.
Change Permissions (P)	NTFS permission—users can change the access level of other users on this file or folder. Granted as part of Full Control if the share is on an NTFS partition.
Take Ownership (O)	NTFS partition—users can claim ownership of a file. Granted as part of Full Control if the share is on an NTFS partition.

NOTE These actions also play a role in the auditing of files.

Given this information, let's reexamine the ATS share permissions. Full Control is self-explanatory. By default, when you create a share, the group Everyone has Full Control over the share and its folders, subfolders, and files. The newest user on your network can delete anything on the share. If security is an issue on your network, this could pose a problem.

Change gives the user or group the ability to perform the following actions: Read (R), Execute (X), Write (W), and Delete (D). So, the user or member of the group can read, execute, write, and delete information in the share.

The share Read permission grants the user or group the ability to read and execute files on the share. It is usually granted to application executable files—files with the extension .EXE or .COM.

No Access lets the user or member of the group attach to the share, but they cannot access any information from the share.

Directory-Level Permissions

What about the NTFS permissions? NTFS permissions are permissions granted to *local* files and directories on a host computer. These permissions can be granted by the owner of the directory. Separate permissions can be granted at the directory and file levels. The directory-level permissions are listed in Table 3.3.

T A B L E 3.3: NTFS Directory-Level Permissions

Directory-Level Permission	Permissions Granted
No Access	Users cannot access the directory at all.
List	Users cannot access the directory, but can see the contents of the directory.
Read	Users can read data files and execute application files.
Add	Users cannot read any information from the directory or even see the files that are stored in the directory, but can add data to the directory.
Add and Read	Users can see information in the directory and add information (new files) to the directory. Users cannot modify existing files in the directory.
Change	Users can see files in the directory, add files to the directory, modify files in the directory, and delete files from the directory (or even delete the whole directory). Users can also change the attributes of the directory.
Full Control	Users can do everything they can do with Change, but can also make changes to resources they do not own.

Permissions given to a directory flow down into the directory. If you have given the group EXCEL_Users the Read permission to the folder D:\Applications\Excel, a member of that group can execute the file EXCEL.EXE.

File-Level Permissions

There are times when security needs to be taken one step further, down to the individual file level. Suppose you have a folder that contains files with the payroll information for the next fiscal year. During the budget process, the payroll file is open so certain users can make changes. When the payroll process for the year has been finalized, you want users to be able to read the file, but not make changes to it. Meanwhile, in the same folder, there are files that the management team needs to change. In this case, you would simply change the permissions on the payroll file to allow people to only read the file. When you make the change to just one file, all the other files are not affected. See Table 3.4 for an explanation of file-level permissions.

TABLE 3.4: NTFS File-Level Permissions

File-Level Permission	Permissions Granted
No Access	Users cannot access the file at all.
Read	Users can read a data file or execute it if it is an application file.
Change	Users can read, execute, modify, or delete the file.
Full Control	Users can read, execute, write to, or delete the file, and change permissions or take ownership away from the owner of the file.

To set NTFS permissions for a folder or file, highlight the folder or file, right-click, and select Properties. From the Properties page, select the Security tab and then choose Permissions.

NOTE Step-by-step directions for setting ATS and NTFS permissions are found in the "Necessary Procedures" section, following the discussion of auditing.

Establishing File Auditing

How security-conscious is your place of business? Some businesses consist of only family members and security is nonexistent. Everyone has full access to everything. Other businesses are *very* security-conscious and make every effort to ensure against the inappropriate use of corporate information.

One way to check the security of those ultra-sensitive documents or folders is to enable auditing. Auditing will not allow you to choose which folders, subfolders, and files you want to audit, but it will provide you with a way of determining who is accessing the files.

You can audit the success or failure of the following actions by any user or group of users:

- Read
- Write
- Execute
- Delete
- Change Permissions
- Take Ownership

After you enable auditing, the results of the audit are written to the event log.

NOTE   For more information on enabling auditing, see the "Necessary Procedures" section.

Necessary Procedures

For some system administrators who have been around for a while, the FAT file system may offer some solace, because it is understood. If, however, you want features such as security or data compression, NTFS is a must. There is a one-way conversion method.

Converting a Drive from FAT to NTFS

There is a one-time-only conversion of drive partitions from FAT to NTFS. This is done using a command line, CONVERT.EXE. To convert a partition:

1. Log on as administrator.

2. Select Start ➤ Programs ➤ Command Prompt.

3. The convert syntax is shown below. To convert the D: drive from FAT to NTFS, the command-line syntax would be as follows:

CONVERT D: /FS:NTFS

NOTE   You can access the following information by going to the command prompt and typing **Convert /?**.

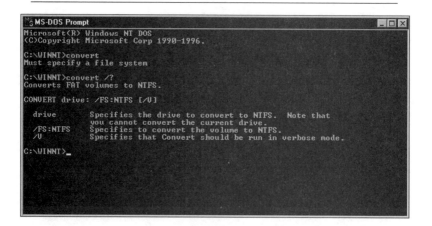

```
MS-DOS Prompt                                              _ □ ✕
Microsoft(R) Windows NT DOS
(C)Copyright Microsoft Corp 1990-1996.

C:\WINNT>convert
Must specify a file system

C:\WINNT>convert /?
Converts FAT volumes to NTFS.

CONVERT drive: /FS:NTFS [/V]

  drive       Specifies the drive to convert to NTFS.  Note that
              you cannot convert the current drive.
  /FS:NTFS    Specifies to convert the volume to NTFS.
  /V          Specifies that Convert should be run in verbose mode.

C:\WINNT>_
```

4. The /V parameter can be used if you want to use Verbose mode. Verbose mode can be outputted to a file so that you can keep a record of what the utility accomplished. The syntax for that would be as follows:

CONVERT D: /FS:NTFS /V > *FILENAME.TXT*

WARNING   Sometimes, there are so many ways of doing something that it almost clouds the issue. It is nice to have a choice, though. Choose the method you feel the most comfortable with and go for it.

Compressing a File, Folder, or Drive

You can set compression at the file level, the folder level, or the drive level. There are several ways to accomplish compression. This section will demonstrate the use of NT Explorer and the command-line utility COMPACT.EXE.

To compress a file or multiple files using NT Explorer:

1. Open NT Explorer and locate the files to be compressed.

2. Highlight the files to be compressed. You can select multiple files by using the Shift+click or Ctrl+click method. Shift+click allows you to select multiple individual files; Ctrl+click allows you to select a block of files.

3. Right-click to bring up the Properties page.

4. Enable the Compressed checkbox.

5. Click OK.

To compress a folder or multiple folders using NT Explorer:

1. Open NT Explorer and locate the folders to be compressed.

2. Highlight the folders to be compressed. You can select multiple folders by using the Shift+click or Ctrl+click method. Shift+click allows you to select multiple individual folders; Ctrl+click allows you to select a block of folders.

3. Right-click to bring up the Properties page.

4. Enable the Compressed checkbox.

5. Click OK.

When you compress a folder, all the files in that folder take the compressed attribute. Subfolders will *not* be compressed unless you enable the Also Compress Subfolders checkbox on the NT Explorer warning screen. You will receive the warning screen for each folder you select.

To compress a drive or multiple drives using NT Explorer:

1. Open NT Explorer and locate the drive to be compressed.

2. Highlight the drive to be compressed. You can select multiple drives by using the Shift+click or Ctrl+click method. Shift+click allows you to select multiple individual drives; Ctrl+click allows you to select blocks of drives.

3. Right-click to bring up the Properties page.

4. Enable the Compress *Drive Letter*:\ checkbox.

5. Click OK.

When you compress a drive, all the files in the root folder take the compressed attribute. Subfolders will *not* be compressed unless you enable the Also Compress Subfolders checkbox on the NT Explorer warning screen. In this case, you are not prompted for each subfolder.

NOTE   If a folder, subfolder, or drive is compressed, files that are created in these areas in the future will be compressed.

TIP   You can uncompress drives, folders, subfolders, and files by using NT Explorer to highlight the appropriate selections, right-clicking, and clearing the Compressed checkbox.

To use COMPACT.EXE:

1. Open a command prompt by selecting Start ➤ Programs ➤ Command Prompt.

2. The syntax for COMPACT.EXE is as follows:

```
COMPACT [/C :  /U] [/S[:DIR]] [/A] [/I][/F]
[/Q][FILENAME]
```

See Table 3.5 for an explanation of COMPACT.EXE command-line switches.

T A B L E 3.5: COMPACT.EXE Command-Line Switches

Switch	What It Does
/C	Compresses
/U	Uncompresses
/S	Compresses an entire subfolder tree. [:DIR] allows you to specify the subfolders to compress (if it is not the current folder).
/A	Compresses hidden and system files. The only file that cannot be compressed is the NTLDR hidden system file.
/I	Ignores error messages and keeps compressing
/F	Forces compression
/Q	Quiet mode
filelist	Lists individual files to be compressed, separated by a space

NOTE If you decide to compress a disk using either the COMPACT.EXE command-line utility or NT Explorer, be sure to allow plenty of time for the process to continue. While timing will certainly vary with the size and makeup of your files, compressing a 2GB drive takes approximately 45 minutes. The compression finished with an 18 percent compression ratio.

Creating a Share

There are several ways to create a share—by using NT Explorer, My Computer, Server Manager, or the Net Share utility.

To create a share using NT Explorer:

1. Open NT Explorer.

2. Open directories until you locate the folder that you want to share.

3. Highlight the directory name and right-click.

4. Select Sharing from the drop-down menu. This will open the Sharing tab of the Properties dialog box.

NOTE You can also reach the Properties dialog box by highlighting the directory name, right-clicking, and choosing Properties. From the Properties menu, select Sharing.

---

5. When you reach the Sharing tab, you will notice that the default share name is the name of the directory. Some users are not excited about having a share name such as APPS_EXCEL. So, you can enter a new name for the share—one that is more user friendly. When you change the name of the share, it does not change the name of the directory—it just presents users with a name that makes sense to real people rather than computer people.

There is an opportunity to change the path, but if you have to do that, why did you choose this folder in the first place?

You will notice there is also a spot for comments. Comments are optional, and be careful, because what you enter will show up next to the share in NT Explorer.

To create a share using My Computer:

1. Open My Computer.

2. Click the drive letter on which the target folder resides.

3. Open directories until you locate the folder that you want to share.

4. Highlight the directory name and right-click.

5. Select Sharing from the drop-down menu. This will open the Sharing tab of the Properties dialog box.

6. When you reach the Sharing tab, you will notice that the default for the directory is Not Shared. Click the Shared As radio button. The usual share name is the name of the directory. Some users are not excited about having a share name such as APPS_EXCEL. So, you can enter a new name for the share—one that is more user friendly. When you change the name of the share, it does not change the name of the directory—it just presents users with a more user-friendly name.

To create a share using Server Manager:

1. Log on to the computer as administrator.

2. Start Server Manager by choosing Start ➤ Programs ➤ Administration Tools ➤ Server Manager.

3. Highlight the server name.

4. Choose Computer from the top menu, then select Shared Directories.

5. In the Shared Directory menu, click New Share.

6. Fill in the information on the New Share page, including Share Name, Path, and a comment.

7. Finally, you can add the maximum number of users allowed or choose to allow a specific number of users.

Net Share is a command-line utility. As such, you start the process by opening a command prompt. To create a share using Net Share, choose Start ➤ Programs ➤ Command Prompt. The syntax for the Net Share utility is shown below.

```
MS-DOS Prompt
Microsoft(R) Windows NT(TM)
(C) Copyright 1985-1996 Microsoft Corp.

C:\>net share /?
The syntax of this command is:

NET SHARE sharename
          sharename=drive:path [/USERS:number | /UNLIMITED]
                               [/REMARK:"text"]
          sharename [/USERS:number | /UNLIMITED]
                    [/REMARK:"text"]
          (sharename | devicename | drive:path) /DELETE

C:\>
```

As an example, suppose you need a temporary share to point to D:\Applications\Excel. You want to call the share Excel and allow 10 users to access the share.

From the command prompt, the syntax would be as follows:

```
Net Share Excel=d:\applications\excel /users:10
```

To delete the share, the syntax would be as follows:

```
Net Share Excel /delete
```

Setting Share Permissions

You can set share permissions only on network shares. ATS permissions are usually assigned to a group, rather than an individual.

NOTE As you have already seen from the discussion of creating shares, there are several ways of accessing the Properties page for a share, folder, or file. In the examples that follow, NT Explorer is the utility of choice.

To set ATS permissions:

1. Log onto the network as administrator or a user with Full Control over the share.

2. Start NT Explorer by selecting Start ➤ Programs ➤ Windows NT Explorer.

3. Browse to the share where the permissions will be applied. Highlight the share and right-click.

4. Click Sharing.

5. Click Permissions.

6. With the Access Through Share Permissions screen showing, click Add, which brings up the Add Users and Groups window.

7. Select the group that will receive the permissions, highlight the group, and click Add.

8. In the lower half of the Add Users and Groups window, use the Type of Access drop-down menu to choose No Access, Read, Change, or Full Access.

9. Click the appropriate choice. This will bring you back to the Add Users and Groups window.

10. Click OK to return to the ATS Permissions screen.

11. Click OK to return to the share's Properties window.

12. Click OK to return to NT Explorer.

Setting NTFS Folder- and File-Level Permissions

To set lower-level (folder or file) permissions, you must use NTFS permissions. NTFS permissions are not available for FAT partitions.

NOTE   NTFS permissions are usually assigned to a group, rather than an individual.

To set NTFS permissions:

1. Log onto the network as someone who has ownership over the folder or file.

2. Start NT Explorer by selecting Start ➤ Programs ➤ Windows NT Explorer.

3. Browse to the folder or file where the permissions will be applied. Highlight the folder or file and right-click.

4. Click Sharing.

5. Click Security.

6. Click Permissions. This brings up the Directory Permissions window.

7. With the Directory Permissions window showing, click Add, which brings up the Add Users and Groups window.

8. Select the group or user that will receive the permissions, highlight the group or user, and click Add.

9. In the lower half of the Add Users and Groups window, use the Type of Access drop-down menu to choose No Access, List, Read, Add, Add and Read, Change, or Full Access.

10. Click the appropriate choice. This will bring you back to the Add Users and Groups window.

11. Click OK to return to the Directory Permissions window.

12. At the top of the Directory Permissions window, there are two radio buttons.

   - If you select Replace Permissions on Subdirectories, it will push the changes down to any subdirectories.

   - If you select Replace Permissions on Existing Files, it will push the changes down to any files.

13. Click OK to return to the folder's Security tab.

14. Click OK to return to NT Explorer.

Establishing File Auditing

Before you can configure auditing, you must turn it on. Auditing is turned off by default. To enable auditing:

1. Start User Manager for Domains by selecting Start ➤ Programs ➤ Administrative Tools ➤ User Manager for Domains.

2. Click Policies.

3. Click Audit.

4. Select the Audit These Events button.

5. Enable the checkboxes for the events you want to audit. Your choices involve the success or failure of the following items:

   - Logon and logoff

   - File and object access

   - Use of user rights

- User and group management

- Security policy changes

- Restart, shutdown, and system

- Process tracking

6. Click OK. Auditing is now enabled for the domain.

To start auditing activities of a specific folder or file, access the Auditing tab by choosing Properties ➤ Security ➤ Auditing. To select auditing:

1. Log on as an administrator or equivalent user.

2. Start NT Explorer by selecting Start ➤ Programs ➤ Windows NT Explorer.

3. Browse to the folder or file you want to audit. Highlight the folder or file and right-click.

4. Select Properties.

5. Click the Security tab.

6. Click Auditing.

7. At the top of the Directory Auditing window, you can select Replace Auditing on Subdirectories or Replace Auditing on Existing Files.

  - Replace Auditing on Subdirectories will start the audit process for all current and new subfolders.

  - Replace Auditing on Existing Files will start the audit process for all current and new files.

8. Click Add.

9. Select the users or groups you want to audit. Click Add after each selection.

10. When the selection of users and groups is complete, click OK.

11. Enable the appropriate checkboxes for the actions you want to audit.

12. After you have selected the actions to audit, click OK to begin auditing.

Auditing writes the information to the event log. This is a processor-intensive task and should be undertaken with great care.

Exam Essentials

Exam questions for the objectives in this section will show up on exam after exam. Know the different file systems and understand what each can do.

Know how to convert a drive from FAT to NTFS. Use CONVERT *drive letter:* /FS:NTFS.

Know the ramifications of converting a drive from FAT to NTFS. You can convert drives from the FAT file system to NTFS. You cannot convert drives from NTFS to FAT.

Know how to compress files, folders, or drives. If the files are stored on an NTFS partition, you can highlight the files, folders, or drives you want to compress using NT Explorer, right-click, select Properties, click Compress, and click OK. There is also a command-line utility, COMPACT.EXE.

Know the various methods of creating a share. You can create a share by using NT Explorer, My Computer, Server Manager, or the Net Share command-line utility.

Know how to create a hidden share. You can create a hidden share by adding $ to the end of the share name—for example, C$ or ADMIN$.

Know how to set ATS permissions. You can assign ATS permissions through the Properties page of the share. From the Properties page, select Permissions.

Know how to set NTFS folder- and file-level permissions. You can assign NTFS permissions through the Properties page of the share. Select the Security tab to begin the process.

Know the effect when a user or group has the No Access permission to a share. If a user has been given the No Access permission to a share or folder, either by an individual assignment or through a group assignment, the user will not be able to access that share. Assignments granted through other means cannot override the No Access assignment.

Know the effects of file auditing. When you enable file auditing, it lets the administrator see what has been done with a file. The audited information is displayed in the event log.

Key Terms and Concepts

Access control list (ACL): Hard-coded list of users and groups with permissions to various hidden shares. Also, a list of users and groups that have been provided permissions or rights to a resource.

Access Through Shares permissions (ATS permissions): Permissions granted at the share point, at the folder level.

Add: Directory-level permission that allows the user to add information to the directory. With just the Add permission, the user cannot read any information from the directory or even see other files stored in the directory.

Add and Read: Directory-level permission that allows the user to add information to a directory and see information already stored in the directory.

CDFS: CD file system.

Change: Permission that allows the user to read, execute, write, and delete folders, subfolders, and files at the share level and below.

Change permissions: An action that allows the user to change permissions to the file for others.

Delete: An action of deleting a file.

Execute: An action of running or executing a file.

FAT (file allocation table): DOS-based file system.

File auditing: Configuring the server to keep track of various actions or events that occur to a given resource.

Full Control: Permission that gives the user full rights to the share, including the permission to determine ownership.

List permission: Directory-level permission that allows the user to see the contents of the directory, even if the user cannot gain access to the directory.

Macintosh-accessible volume: Server-based share that is available to users of Apple's Macintosh.

No Access: Users can connect to a share, but will not be able to access any resources.

NTFS (new technology file system): NT file system designed for drives or partitions greater than 400MB.

Permission: Windows NT settings you set on a shared resource that determine which users can use the resource and how they can use it.

Read: Assigns Read and Execute permissions to the share, folders, subfolders, and files. Also an action of reading a file.

Share: To make resources, such as directories and printers, available to others.

Share name: A name that refers to a shared resource on a server. Each shared directory on a server has a share name, used by PC users to refer to the directory. Users of Macintoshes use the name of the Macintosh-accessible volume that corresponds to a directory, which may be the same as the share name. *See also* Macintosh-accessible volume.

Share permissions: Used to restrict the availability over the network of a shared resource to only certain users.

Shared directory: A directory to which network users can connect.

Shared network directory: *See* shared directory.

Shared resource: Any device, data, or program that is used by more than one other device or program. For Windows NT, shared resources refer to any resource that is made available to network users, such as directories, files, printers, and named pipes. Also refers to a resource on a server that is available to network users.

Take Ownership: An action that allows the user to take ownership of a file.

User rights: Define a user's access to a computer or domain and the actions that a user can perform on the computer or domain. User rights permit actions such as logging onto a computer or network, adding or deleting users in a workstation or domain, and so forth.

Write: An action of writing information to a file.

Sample Questions

1. Given the default permissions assigned to groups, which groups would you need to belong in to create a share?

   A. Administrators

   B. Backup users

   C. Guests

   D. Users

   Answer: A—Administrators can create shares.

2. Suppose that a user is a member of three groups—Administrators, MIS, and Apps_Acctg. There is a share created called Accounting. The Administrators group has Full Control permissions to the Accounting share. The MIS group has been assigned No Access

permissions, and the Apps_Acctg group has been given the Change permission. What can the user do with the share?

A. The user has full rights to the share, granted to them through their membership in the Administrators group.

B. The user can read or see a folder, subfolder, or file; execute an application; write to a closed file; and delete a folder or file. These are inherent in the Change permission the user received through their membership in Apps_Acctg.

C. The user can attach to the share, but cannot see or do anything. This is a result of the No Access permission given to the MIS group.

Answer: C—In the Microsoft security model, all bets are off when the No Access permission is granted. If you are given No Access permission because of your membership in any group or by an explicit assignment to your user account, you have no access to the share.

3. A user has been given Change permission to the H_R share. The share points to a folder that resides on a FAT partition. The Human Resources Director comes to you and asks that the user retains Change permissions to the share, but the Director would like more restrictive permissions placed on the Salary_99 file. Can you help the Human Resources Director?

A. Yes—NT will allow you to add file-level permissions to the Salary_99 file. Because the file is on a FAT partition, file-level security is allowed.

B. No—NT will not allow you to add file-level permissions to the Salary_99 file. Because the file is on a FAT partition, file-level security is not allowed.

C. Yes—The user is accessing the file through a share, which implies that they are a remote user. Because the user is a remote user, the format of the drive the share resides on has no impact.

Answer: B—Because the share points to a folder on a FAT partition, only share-level permissions will apply.

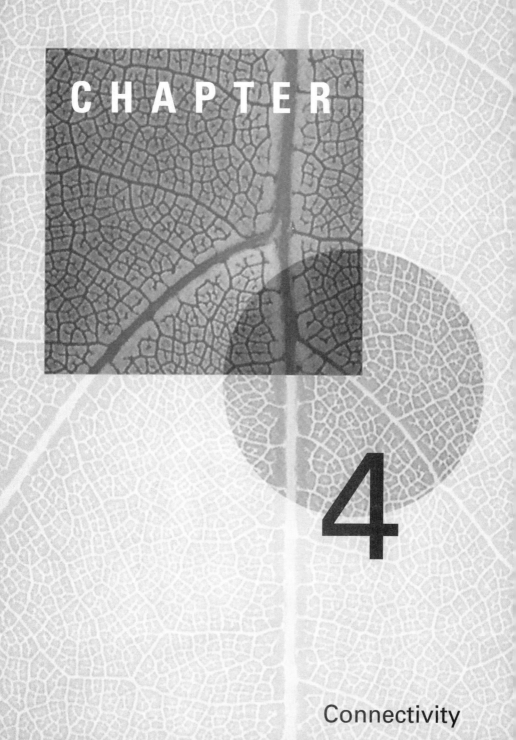

CHAPTER

4

Connectivity

Microsoft Exam Objectives Covered in This Chapter:

▶ **Configure Windows NT Server for interoperability with NetWare servers by using various tools. Tools include:** *(pages 229 – 238)*
- Gateway Service for NetWare
- Migration Tool for NetWare

▶ **Install and configure remote access service (RAS). Configuration options include:** *(pages 239 – 260)*
- Configuring RAS communications
- Configuring RAS protocols
- Configuring RAS security
- Configuring dial-up networking clients

There are very few "pure" networks in the world. Most networks are a combination of a legacy system purchased over the years, a couple of servers with operating systems mandated by some piece of software, a few odds and ends purchased by the "last guy," and a few new pieces of technology (mostly new toys bought for image not function).

Into this mess, you wish to bring a little order and stability—good luck! Given the state of many networks, one of the most important criteria for new systems is interoperability. When you add to this the ability to grow with technology, you have only a handful of potential operating systems worthy of consideration.

Microsoft Windows NT has a few design features that make it the perfect choice for today's networks. One of these features is NT's modular design. Every function that an NT server can perform is designed as a separate subsystem of the operating system. This modular design means that NT can be updated to meet the needs of future technologies. It also means that third-party developers can add functionality to the base operating system. These are important features in a business world that can't decide what the power tie of the week should be, let alone standardize a set of services for the network.

By the end of this chapter, you should be comfortable discussing the various tools available to connect an NT network to the world.

Configure Windows NT Server for interoperability with NetWare servers by using various tools. Tools include:

- Gateway Service for NetWare
- Migration Tool for NetWare

No discussion of networking is complete without discussing Novell's NetWare. In the not-too-distant past, Novell owned over 90 percent of the worldwide networking market. Even today, that percentage is probably still over 50. Given this, you will probably have to connect to a NetWare server at some point in your career.

Even if you believe the experts who claim that NetWare is a *legacy* operating system and that Novell is on a downward spiral to oblivion, common sense tells you that NetWare servers will be around for a long time. With Novell's current market share, it will take years for NT to replace the NetWare servers currently installed.

One of the features of Windows NT is its ability to coexist with a NetWare environment. This means companies can ease into an NT network, while maintaining the NetWare services that they currently use.

Critical Information

Because of the number of Novell networks in existence, Microsoft tests heavily on the skills necessary to add an NT server to a Novell NetWare environment. You will find NetWare-related questions on many of the MCSE examinations. Make sure that you are comfortable with the topics covered for this objective before you take the MCSE exam.

Gateway Service for NetWare

There are two ways to configure your network so that your clients can access NetWare servers:

- Install Client Service for NetWare (CSNW) on each NT workstation that might need to access a NetWare server.

- Install Gateway Service for NetWare (GSNW) on an NT server and use it as a gateway to the NetWare environment.

CSNW is not listed in the exam objectives, but you should know what it is and when to use it. CNSW is software loaded on the *client* computers. This software allows them to directly connect to and communicate with NetWare servers. (The clients will also have to have the NWLink IPX/SPX-compatible network protocol installed and configured as one of their protocols.) CSNW should be used if your clients extensively use the NetWare servers or if you have a lot of users who will use the NetWare servers simultaneously.

It might not be convenient or necessary to configure CSNW on your clients. Another option is to install GSNW on an NT server. GSNW acts as a gateway to the NetWare environment. When clients need to access services on a NetWare server, they send the request to the GSNW service on the NT server. It, in turn, passes the request to the NetWare server.

GSNW offers two benefits to the network administrator. First, only one computer (the NT server) has to have special software installed (GSNW). Second, the gateway server is the only computer that has to have NWLink installed and configured. Anytime you can bring management of a service to your server, rather than your workstations, you save time and effort. In addition, the GSNW connection uses only one NetWare connection regardless of the number of clients connected through it, while each CSNW connection uses an individual, which can be limited by the number of access licenses held.

The downside to this configuration is that all of your clients that need to access NetWare services must share this one connection. If you have a large number of users or your users access the NetWare server continuously, you will get better performance by using CSNW on your clients.

When configuring GSNW, you need to configure the NT side and the NetWare side. On the NetWare side, you must:

1. Create a user account with the same name and password configuration as on the gateway account on the NT server.

2. Assign to the NetWare user account created in step 1 all necessary trustee rights to NetWare network resources.

3. Create a group account named NTGATEWAY.

4. Make the user (from step 1) a member of this group.

WARNING   Since all users share this one account to access the NetWare server, the account must include all permissions that any GSNW user might need. In other words, you cannot set up different permissions for each NT client that might access the NetWare server. This might be a security issue in your environment.

Once the NetWare accounts are created, you configure the GSNW on the NT server. This process will be explained in the "Necessary Procedures" section. Once you have configured, you create shares on your NT server that point to a resource on the NetWare server. From the user's perspective, these shares look like any other share points on the NT server.

Remember that GSNW is designed for an environment in which NetWare access is light and intermittent. If your clients need continuous access to the Novell servers or you expect a high level of traffic, you should configure CSNW on your clients.

Migration Tool for NetWare

There are many reasons to migrate from a NetWare to an NT environment—you might purchase software that requires NT (an issue that is becoming more and more common), you might want to limit your network to a single operating system for ease of administration, or you might just be pushed into it by upper management. Whatever the reason, Microsoft has provided a tool to make the migration process smooth and painless.

The Migration Tool for NetWare (MTFN) can be found on your NT server in the *Windows root*\System32 directory. The executable file is named NWCONV.EXE. MTFN allows you to easily transfer information from a NetWare server to an NT server. MTFN performs the following tasks:

- Preserves user account information, including logon and station restrictions.

- Preserves uscr login scripts. Microsoft Windows NT supports network login script commands.

- Offers control over how user and group names are transferred.

- Offers control over passwords on the transferred accounts. NT cannot read network passwords, so all passwords must change.

- Offers control over how account restrictions are transferred.

- Offers control over how administrative privileges are transferred.

- Creates a volume for network users.

- Selects which files and directories to transfer.

- Selects the directories to which transferred files will be copied.

- Preserves effective rights on files and directories (only if copied to an NTFS volume).

This tool transfers user information and data from one server (NetWare) to another (NT), but it does not upgrade an existing NetWare server to Windows NT. This is actually the best form of migration. If, at any time, you are not happy with the results, you can reformat the new NT server to get back to where you started.

TIP If you are migrating multiple NetWare servers, you do not have to replace each computer. Migrate each one in turn, testing the results before moving on. After you have confirmed that the migration was successful, you can take down the NetWare server. At this point, if the hardware supports NT, you have the computer for your next NT server.

Necessary Procedures

Microsoft has spent a lot of marketing dollars trying to convince users of Novell's NetWare to move to Windows NT Server. One of the biggest selling points is that the network does not have to be moved completely to NT—the two operating systems can coexist on the same network. You will see questions about this topic on many of the MCSE exams, and most of those questions will be of a "how to" nature. So, spend some time getting familiar with the procedures involved in connecting to a NetWare environment.

Configuring Gateway Service for NetWare

GSNW is installed like any other NT service. In the Services tab of NT Server's Network applet, click Add. There are no configuration options during the installation, but as in all network service changes, you will be asked to restart your server. After this restart, you will be presented with a window that asks for your preferred NetWare server or Tree and Context. The former is used in bindery-based NetWare 3.*x* environments, the latter in NetWare 4.*x* NDS (Novell directory service) environments.

1. In Control Panel, you will find a new applet, GSNW, which is used to manage your NetWare gateway. The opening screen of GSNW allows you to change the default server, set some default print parameters, and determine whether clients should run a login script when they connect to the NetWare server.

2. Click the Gateway button. Enable the gateway and enter the NetWare gateway account and password defined earlier.

3. You are ready to allow your clients access to resources on the NetWare server. Create shares that point to those resources. In the Configure Gateway dialog box, click Add to get the New Share dialog box.

4. Give the share a name and define the UNC path to the resource. Define the mapped drive letter if desired. You can also limit the number of users that can simultaneously access the resource, although the default is Unlimited.

5. Once the share is configured, you can set permissions like on any NT share. Click the Permissions button in the Configure Gateway dialog box.

Remember that the Novell permissions set on the gateway account, which are more restrictive in nature, will overrule any permissions you set here.

From the client, the new share appears as if it is located on the NT server, which is acting as the Novell gateway.

Using Migration Tool for NetWare

Migration Tool for NetWare is found in the *Windows root*\System32 directory. The executable is NWCONV.EXE. When you run it, it will ask you for the source and destination servers.

You can then configure the migration itself. Click the User Options button in the next dialog box and configure the migration parameters for user and group accounts. You can configure:

- How passwords should be handled. Remember that NT cannot read the NetWare password. You have three options: Users will have no password, password will be the same as the user name, or users will have a default password. You can also force users to change their new password the first time they log onto the NT domain.

- How Migration Tool should deal with duplicate user names. You have four options: Log an error but do nothing, ignore the problem and skip the user, overwrite the existing NT account, or define a prefix to be added to the user name.

- How to deal with duplicate group accounts. You have three options: Log an error and skip the group, ignore the duplicate group completely, or define a prefix to be added to the group name.

- How to handle accounts with supervisor privileges on the Net-Ware server. You can add those accounts to the domain admins group. (By default, they do not inherit any administrative privileges in the NT domain.)

The next step is to configure the file transfer between the two servers. On the MTFN main screen, click the File Options button. Here, you can decide which files and directories should be transferred and where they should be copied. By default, everything is copied to the NT server—remember to change the default settings so that the Novell management directories are not copied (you won't need NetWare management tools on an NT server).

This utility has a great function that can save you hours of time and prevent a catastrophic failure—the ability to run a trial migration. The trial migration attempts the migration without actually transferring any information. This allows you to determine any problems you will run into and correct them before they occur. The trial migration creates a series of three log files:

- LOGFILE.LOG—Describes the setting you configured for the migration.

- SUMMARY.LOG—Summarizes the activity, reporting which servers were involved, how much disk space was required, how many user accounts were migrated, and how many files and directories were migrated.

- ERROR.LOG—This is probably the most useful log file during a trial migration. It lists areas where the utility encountered a problem. It lists duplicate user names, duplicate group names, etc. This provides you with a list of problems that you can correct before performing the actual migration.

Once you're ready to go, click the Migrate button. Remember that this process will take quite a bit longer than the trial migration and places a huge system load on the servers. Schedule this to be done during low usage times. This time, the files actually have to be copied from server to server.

Exam Essentials

Interoperability with NetWare is very important to the success of Windows NT Server. Be sure you're comfortable with the following topics.

Understand Gateway Service for NetWare (GSNW). GSNW is a service that creates a connection between an NT server and a NetWare server. This connection can then be used as a point of access to NetWare resources. The point is to allow the clients of your NT domain access to NetWare resources without having to configure any special software on each client.

Understand the network setup for GSNW. On the NetWare server, you must create a user account that the GSNW service can use to log onto the network. You must also create a group named NTGATEWAY and make the user account a member. Assign any necessary trustee rights to this network group account.

Know when it is appropriate to use GSNW and when it is not. GSNW is best when your users need occasional access to NetWare resources. Remember that all users share one channel to the NetWare server. If too many users access it, performance will decrease. On the plus side, however, only one licensed connection will be established to the NetWare server, which reduces the number of client licenses you will have to purchase for your NetWare environment.

Understand the migration process from NetWare to NT. Use Migration Tool for NetWare to migrate users, groups, files, and directories from a NetWare server to an NT server. This tool allows you to configure which users and groups will be migrated and what should happen in the event of duplicate names. It provides a method for controlling NT passwords for migrated NetWare user accounts since the passwords cannot be transferred. It also allows you to control the data that are migrated, both the content and the destination.

Key Terms and Concepts

Client Service for NetWare (CSNW): Software loaded at the client that allows a direct connection to a NetWare server.

Gateway Service for NetWare (GSNW): An NT server service that provides a point of access to NetWare servers.

Migration Tool for NetWare (MTFN): A utility that migrates users, groups, files, and directories from a NetWare server to an NT server.

Sample Questions

1. Which of the following items is loaded on client computers to allow direct access to Novell NetWare servers?

   A. CSNW (Client Service for NetWare)

   B. GSNW (Gateway Service for NetWare)

   C. NCS (Novell connection software)

   D. Novell TCP/IP services

   E. NWLink IPX/SPX Compatible Transport

   Answer: A, E—To allow a client to access a NetWare server directly, you must load both the appropriate protocol (NWLink) and a NetWare redirector (CSNW).

2. Which of the following features are benefits of GSNW?

   A. Only the server needs to load NWLink.

   B. NetWare resources look like NT shares to your clients.

   C. Each user can have their own set of permissions on the NetWare server.

   D. Since only one session is created to the NetWare server, performance is enhanced.

   Answer: A, B—The server providing the GSNW service is the only NT computer that must communicate directly with the Novell environment. Thus, it is the only computer that must load NWLink. Since all NetWare resources look like a shared resource on that NT server, no retraining is necessary for your users.

Install and configure remote access service (RAS). Configuration options include:

- Configuring RAS communications
- Configuring RAS protocols
- Configuring RAS security
- Configuring dial-up networking clients

RAS (remote access service) allows a workstation computer running NT to connect to remote systems using just the POTS (plain old telephone system). When the client connects, the workstation is treated just like any other client. The user can access the network, check e-mail, get documents, and do just about anything they would do from their desk, except that now they are using a laptop.

NOTE There is a lot of testable material in this objective. Although the exam designers have not given it the attention of printing or disk configuration, there are some questions out there. Be aware and study hard!

Critical Information

The purpose of RAS is to allow for communications between a local host and hosts that operate from remote locations, utilizing just telephone lines. RAS can, however, be configured to work with ISDN and X.25 connections, as well as some WAN implementations such as asynchronous transfer mode (ATM). The purpose of this book is not to describe the multiple ways that RAS can interface with the telephone company. This book is designed to give you a broad overview of the product and get you through the exam, so it will stick to client-to-network communication using a dial-up connection.

For RAS to work, you need to create a mini-network. A network is nothing more than two systems with some information to share, a physical communication medium to share the information over, and rules to govern the transmittal of information. The first part of the objective involves the server piece of RAS—how to configure the server so it can "answer" the call when it comes. When the server answers the call, it must "talk" with the client using a specific set of rules. So, the available protocols and how to configure them to work with a dial-up client will be discussed. To hold any kind of discussion, you must have two parties. So, configuration of dial-up networking clients will be discussed. Finally, there have to be some rules for this discussion. The server needs to prove that the workstation is who it says it is, so RAS security will also be covered.

Configuring RAS Communications

The best place to start is always the beginning. If you are going to con-figure a system to which your workstations can call in and get informa-tion, something should be there to answer the phone. In this case, it will be your NT server. In an earlier chapter, communication products that allow you up to 256 dial-up connections from a single multiport expan-sion modem card were mentioned. RAS will take advantage of systems like that, as well as just a plain old modem hooked up to a COM port.

The first question to ask yourself is, What is the main goal of this communication channel? In some cases, your main goal may be to provide dial-up service to all those sales people and executives out there traveling around the country. If your company is small, you may not have a lot of sales people or high-powered executives traveling all over the country selling your company's wares. You may, however, have a remote site that needs to communicate with the home office and doesn't need all the power of a T-1 line. In that case, an ISDN line may be just the ticket. ISDN stands for integrated services digital net-work. ISDN is a faster, better version of what you normally think of as a modem connection. However, an ISDN does not use a modem. In fact, it is a purely digital data path from start to finish. It does require an adapter, which most people casually call a modem, but no modu-lation or demodulation actually occurs. A modem, on the other hand, requires an analog connection provided by the public switched tele-phone network (PSTN), generally referred to as the phone company.

NOTE Anytime you want faster and better, that usually translates into *more expensive*. Costs vary on ISDN service around the world, but it is safe to say that it is more expensive than a standard dial-up line.

Modems modulate and demodulate the signals between two computers, sending the signal over the phone line. Your computer speaks digital. The phone company speaks analog. A modem turns a digital signal into an analog signal on the sending end, and turns the same signal from analog to digital at the receiving end.

The key word in the definition of ISDN is digital. With ISDN, you are now using a phone line that speaks digital, so there is no translation necessary. The ISDN modem or router just sends digital signals over a line that understands how to deal with ones and zeros. You have a cleaner, faster communication link. If you are planning on connecting two sites, you may look at installing ISDN service. However, in some places, it may not even be available. In others, the cost may be prohibitive. In some areas, it may be just the solution for which you are looking. When judging cost, keep in mind that ISDN service is like having two phone lines. Therefore, you would expect it to cost twice as much as a single phone line. Because there are two channels, you get twice the speed. Because it is digital, and analog modems rarely give you their rated speed, it is usually more than twice as fast.

You are now over the first hump—should you use ISDN or a regular phone line? If you are going to use the dial-up capabilities of the phone company, the phone line has to be dedicated to RAS communications. RAS is *very* selfish—it doesn't want to share. So, if your system is configured to dial out and notify you when the power goes out, or if you are running a fax-server solution using a modem and phone line, you need to add more hardware. RAS requires its own line with its own modem.

If you are installing an ISDN device, follow the manufacturer's directions. The ISDN device is slightly more challenging to install than a modem. Make sure you have somewhere to connect to (another ISDN connection) and make sure you have all the paperwork the phone company left for you when they installed the ISDN line. There are some interesting parameters that you will need to configure, such as SPIDs (service profile IDs). SPIDs identify which services the ISDN line is providing. The SPID looks like a normal 10-digit phone number, except that there are two of them.

NOTE   Installing modems was covered in Chapter 2. This section will assume that the modem is installed and dedicated to RAS communications.

After all these decisions have been made and all the hardware has been installed, the installation of RAS is really anticlimactic. Since RAS is a networking service, it is installed through the Network applet in Control Panel. It is just a matter of NT copying some files off the installation CD and linking the RAS with the modem or communication device you already have configured. Part way through the installation process, the system will begin asking you questions about protocols, which is a great segue into the next section of this objective.

TIP   For a step-by-step discussion of the installation of RAS, see the "Necessary Procedures" section of this objective.

Configuring RAS Protocols

RAS supports the big three protocols—TCP/IP, NWLink, and NetBEUI. How it supports all those protocols does require some explanation. The explanation even requires some explanation, because you are about to be buried in a flow of acronyms.

TDI

The first acronym is TDI (transport driver interface). The TDI is an interface specification to which all Windows NT transport protocols must be written so that they can be used by higher-level services such as RAS. In other words, you will read that all of the dial-up protocols must be TDI-compliant.

PPP and SLIP

The next two acronyms deal with communication-framing protocols—the set of rules that allows communication devices to negotiate how information will be framed or blocked as it is sent over the network. The two framing protocols that RAS can use are point-to-point protocol (PPP) and serial line Internet protocol (SLIP).

Since SLIP is the granddaddy of framing protocols, it is just an implementation of Internet protocol (IP) over a serial line. Developed for use by UNIX computers, SLIP has been improved on and replaced, by and large, by PPP.

PPP is a data-link-layer transport that performs over point-to-point network connections such as serial or modem lines. PPP can negotiate with any TDI-compliant protocol used by both systems involved in the link and can automatically assign IP, domain name service (DNS), and gateway addresses when used with transmission control protocol/Internet protocol (TCP/IP).

Now that the terms are defined, an overview of protocols can be provided. When a dial-up client accesses a RAS server, it will use PPP as its network-layer protocol. Think of PPP as the Ethernet or token ring of the dial-up world.

NOTE   SLIP is an older version of PPP. Although you *can* configure an NT RAS server to dial out using SLIP, in most environments, SLIP has gone the way of CP/M.

Once a modem is connected to a RAS server, it can support TCP/IP, NWLink, and/or NetBEUI. Each protocol can be bound to a modem, and a modem may have more than one protocol bound to it. Each of the three protocols have advantages and disadvantages, depending on the job you are configuring the system to do.

TCP/IP

TCP/IP is the standard protocol suite of the Internet. TCP/IP is a mature, stable, robust protocol suite that brings a lot to the table, including routing capabilities and the ability to handle less-than-perfect phone connections. However, while it is robust, it is not necessarily the fastest protocol out of the gate.

RAS using TCP/IP will allow the administrator to configure whether the client computer can access just the RAS server or the entire NT network. In addition, the RAS server controls how the client receives its TCP/IP address.

NWLink

NWLink is an Internet packet exchange/sequenced packet exchange (IPX/SPX) wanna-be. It is fast and efficient, and works well with interconnecting NetWare clients and servers. If you have a mixed environment with NetWare servers and NT servers, you are probably already aware of the advantages of NWLink. If you configure your RAS to use the NWLink protocol, you will not have to add a second protocol to those dial-up clients.

Like TCP/IP, NWLink can be configured to allow a RAS connection access only to the server or the entire network. You can also specify network-addressing and node-addressing selections through RAS protocol configurations.

NetBEUI

Of all the transport protocols, NetBEUI is the lightweight. NetBEUI is an efficient, simple protocol that protects against overuse of the network bandwidth. If you don't need to use TCP/IP or NWLink, Net-BEUI is the protocol of choice.

NetBEUI configuration allows the administrator to determine only whether a user can access just the server or the entire network from the RAS connection.

NOTE   See the "Necessary Procedures" section for a step-by-step discussion of the configuration of each of the protocols.

Configuring RAS Security

Once the client computer has called the RAS server and has connected, how do you protect your network against intruders? RAS has some built-in security features. You can configure the RAS connection security using permissions, encrypted passwords, point-to-point tunneling protocol (PPTP), and call back. If you look at the Administrative Tools menu, you will see a new utility listed, Remote Access Admin.

Permissions

When a user dials in and authenticates to a RAS, permissions are the first line of defense for the network. If a user has been granted Remote Access Permission, the user can log onto the RAS server. Using the Remote Access Admin utility, RAS permissions can be granted to all users of the server, revoked for all users of the server, or granted to individual users. Notice that permissions cannot be granted to global groups or local groups. Basic RAS permissions can also be granted through the User Manager utility. The Random Access Permissions screen is shown in Figure 4.1.

F I G U R E 4.1: Random Access Permissions

Call Back

One of the ways RAS enforces security is to call back the initiating client system to reestablish communication. This way, RAS is sure that the system calling is really what it says it is and can record the number it called to validate the user and minimize long-distance charges borne by the client. Call-back features can be set for each user with dial-up access. Notice in Figure 4.1 that you can configure three choices per user:

- No Call Back—Disables the call-back feature.

- Set by Caller—Prompts the caller for a number.

- Preset to—Calls back a user at a predefined phone number. The server will call back this number only for the user.

You cannot set call-back authentication for groups of users or a particular modem.

Passwords and Data Encryption

By now, just about everyone in the free world has heard the trials and travails of passing passwords and other information over phone lines and (gasp) the Internet. There are several ways of protecting information sent over phone lines—the most common is encryption.

When the client and the server begin to communicate, they use point-to-point protocol (PPP). To authenticate over PPP, RAS supports three authentication protocols:

- Password authentication protocol (PAP)

- Challenge handshake authentication protocol (CHAP)

- Microsoft extensions of CHAP (MS-CHAP)

You might anticipate that protocol selection is done through the Remote Access Admin tool, but your anticipation would be misguided. The protocol selection is done from the Network Configuration window of Remote Access Setup (see Figure 4.2).

FIGURE 4.2: Network Configuration of RAS

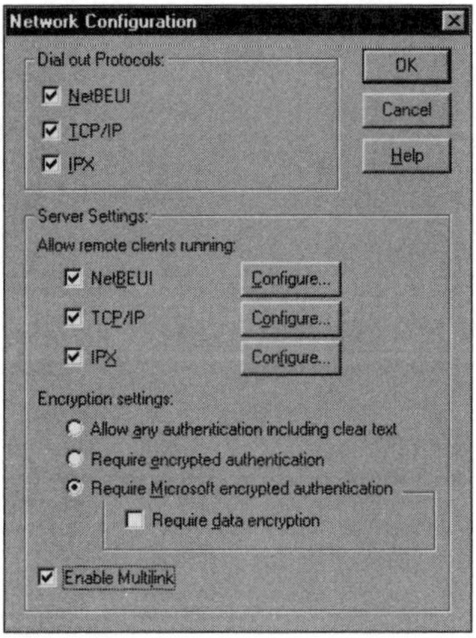

As you can see from Figure 4.2, the three settings show up under the heading Encryption Settings. The default selection is MS-CHAP, although that does not appear to be an option. It is just camouflaged by calling it Require Microsoft Encrypted Authentication. When you configure a client to call the RAS, it will encrypt its password via MS-CHAP. Using MS-CHAP ensures that the system on the other end of the phone is at least using Windows 95 or above for an operating system.

If the Require Data Encryption button is selected, not only is MS-CHAP used, but the data that are sent over the phone lines are also encrypted.

Suppose that you have a diverse environment that is not Microsoft-centric. That is the politically correct way of saying that you have some bit-head who wants to dial in from a UNIX box. Since that system cannot use MS-CHAP, something else needs to be provided. You can require encrypted authentication. This option sets up the system to run CHAP as well as MS-CHAP.

The final selection you can make involves those systems that do not support encrypted password authentication. In that case, you can check Allow Any Authentication Including Clear Text. This is the free-for-all method of system access.

Another security feature mentioned above is point-to-point tunneling protocol (PPTP). PPTP is a new NT 4 feature. It is Internet centered and uses a two-step approach to connecting the client to the server:

1. Connect the client to the Internet.

2. Use the Internet to create an encrypted link to the RAS server. In some areas, this is called creating a virtual private network (VPN).

NOTE   If you use this approach, the RAS server must be attached to the Internet.

Multilink
By filling the Enable Multilink checkbox in Figure 4.2, you are allowing RAS to combine multiple serial signals into one. This is especially helpful when dealing with the two channels of ISDN, because now you can take full advantage of both channels. Multilink will also allow you to link regular modems together.

There is a catch—to use multilink, both computers have to be running NT and both must have multilink enabled. Furthermore, it is important to remember that multilinking is not possible with the call-back option enabled.

Configuring Dial-Up Networking Clients

At this point, you have configured the server, but now the server needs something to talk to. So, you need to configure the client workstation to call into the RAS server.

From a Windows NT workstation client, you may need to install RAS services to provide for dial-up networking capabilities. For a Windows 95 client, dial-up networking needs to be installed.

NOTE For more information about how to install and configure RAS services on a Windows NT workstation machine, see the excellent publication from Sybex, *Windows NT Workstation Study Guide,* by Gary Govanus and Bob King.

When the fundamental services, such as RAS services, are in place, it is time to get specific—configuring the client to dial into a particular RAS server. Before beginning, you need to know the ground rules for that server, such as what is the phone number, what protocols does it use, and what kind of security does it offer.

Once that information is in place, you create a new dial-up connection in the RAS phone book. Create one entry for each server the system needs to access. If the network's dial-up requirements are complicated, you can even create login scripts to automate much of the process, such as what would be needed for a SLIP-based UNIX server.

The final step in the process is to test the new service. Dial into the RAS server, connect, and make sure you have access to the resources on the remote server. Once you have disconnected, your remote access system is in place.

NOTE Scripting is simple programming. It is also outside of the scope of this book and this exam. The documentation is available at WINNT\System32\RAS\Script.DOC.

Necessary Procedures

There is a lot to do in this section. This objective is all about configuring. While the first section of the objective gave an overview of the decisions to be made and the items to be ordered, this section is where the meat of the process lies—actually doing the work.

The exam developers approached this section in a logical fashion. The first three areas examine how to install RAS on the server, how to configure the protocols that the systems will use, and how to lock down security.

The last section takes you away from the server and toward the workstation. The client-side configuration is a dial-up configuration, similar to configuring the system to dial into AOL or CompuServe.

Configuring RAS Communications

RAS is a network service and is installed like most of the other network services—from the Network applet in Control Panel. Before beginning to install RAS or any network service, be sure to have the NT installation CD handy, or at least have access to the files it contains. To install and configure RAS:

1. Log onto the computer as administrator.

2. Choose Start ➤ Settings ➤ Control Panel.

3. Double-click the Network icon.

4. Open the Services tab by clicking it. Since RAS is not installed, click Add. This will open the Select Network Service window, which is a selection of all the services available but not currently installed on your server.

5. Scroll down to Remote Access Service, highlight it with a single click, and then click OK. This will open the Windows NT setup screen. This window asks for the location of the NT setup files. Provide the appropriate location and click the Continue button. At this point, the Installation Wizard copies the files it needs to the places it needs to put them.

6. The next window you are presented lists all the RAS-capable devices attached to the server. If you have more than one modem attached to the server, the drop-down menu will allow you to select the device for RAS communications. If you haven't installed a modem, you can choose Install Modem or Install X.25 from this screen. Once you have chosen your RAS-capable device, click OK.

NOTE RAS is selfish. The communication channel must be dedicated to RAS. If you want to use the channel for something else, you will have to stop RAS and restart it when you are finished.

7. At this juncture, you should see the Remote Access Setup screen. Instead of continuing at this time, click Configure.

8. When you click Configure, it opens the Configure Port Usage screen, which allows you to specify how you want the port used. Make your selection from the choices below and click OK to return to the Remote Access Setup screen.

- Dial Out Only—If you are configuring this server to dial into another RAS connection and you want this machine only to dial out, this is the appropriate selection.

- Receive Calls Only—If your RAS connection will not be going out looking for work and dialing into other servers, this is the appropriate selection. It is also the default selection.

- Dial Out and Receive Calls—This selection provides two-way communication.

9. You should now be back at the Remote Access Setup screen. Click Continue to open the RAS Server NetBEUI Configuration window.

Configuring RAS Protocols

The first protocol that is configured is the simplest, most basic network protocol—NetBEUI. You will also be prompted to provide information about TCP/IP and NWLink.

1. The RAS Server NetBEUI Configuration window allows you to choose how far your NetBEUI clients can go. Do you want them to access the entire network or just this particular computer? Make your choice by selecting the appropriate radio button and then click OK.

2. The next screen is the RAS Server TCP/IP Configuration screen. This screen is a little more complicated than the NetBEUI screen. There are several decisions to make before continuing.

- The first set of radio buttons will allow you to decide how far the TCP/IP client will be allowed to go. Again, as with Net-BEUI, the choices are Entire Network or This Computer Only.

- Now, things begin to get interesting. You will have to make some decisions about TCP/IP addressing.

- The first radio button is a "cop out" button. By selecting Use DHCP to Assign Remote TCP/IP Client Addresses, the server will pass the buck to a DHCP server to provide the IP address.

- If you choose Use Static Address Pool, it will let this service decide which of the IP addresses to assign to each connecting device.

- You can also check the box at the bottom of the screen that allows the remote client to request a predetermined IP address from either the DHCP server or the static pool. After making the appropriate selections, click OK.

NOTE Notice that there are Begin and End selections as well as Excluded Ranges under Use Static Address Pool. For a more complete discussion of TCP/IP addressing, read Sybex's *MCSE: TCP/IP Study Guide.*

---

3. When you click OK, it brings up the next (and last) protocol to configure—IPX. There are several decisions to make here also.

- The top selection of radio buttons allows you to choose whether the IPX client uses the entire network or just this computer.

- The next selection of radio buttons allows you to choose whether network numbers are allocated automatically or within the range you provide.

- In the bottom of the screen, there are two checkboxes. If you check the first, it will give the same network segment number to all IPX clients. If you check the second, it allows the client computer to select its own node address.

4. Click OK and close the RAS installation wizard.

5. Agree to allow NetBIOS broadcasts for IPX clients.

6. Click OK to close the Network Configuration window.

7. Finally, select Yes to restart the computer.

Configuring RAS Security

RAS security is configured using both the Remote Access Admin utility and the Network Configuration window from the Remote Access Setup screen. The security settings involved with the Admin tool revolve around granting dial-up access rights to the server and call-back selections.

Encryption information and selections are made through the Network Configuration tool.

To provide dial-up access:

1. Start the Remote Access Admin utility by selecting Start ➤ Programs ➤ Administrative Tools (Common) ➤ Remote Access Admin.

2. From the Remote Access Admin screen, click Users to show users with access to this server. To provide access to users from another domain or another server, even if it is across a slow link, choose Server ➤ Select Domain or Server, and then choose the domain you would like to administer. To actually select the domain, double-click the domain name in the Select Domain window. Once this has been accomplished, the users in the other domain will show up in the Remote Access Admin screen.

3. Click Permissions to show the Remote Access Permissions screen.

4. The Remote Access Permissions screen will show you the users associated with this system. By using the selection buttons to the right, you can Grant All access to dial-up networking or Revoke All access from dial-up networking. To grant individual users the right to dial up, highlight the user account and select the Grant Dialin Permission to User checkbox at the bottom of the screen. (Remember that RAS permission can also be granted in the User Manager utility.)

5. You can also use this screen to provide three levels of Call Back support:

   - No Call Back—Disables the call-back feature.

   - Set by Caller—Prompts the caller for a number.

   - Preset to—Calls back a user at a predefined phone number. The server will call back this number only for the user.

To change the default encryption scheme for passwords and data:

1. From the NT Server desktop, highlight Network Neighborhood and right-click.

2. Click Properties.

3. Click the Services tab and highlight Remote Access Services.

4. Click the Properties button to bring up the Remote Access Setup screen.

5. Click the Network button. This brings up the Network Configuration window.

NOTE The selection and configuration of protocols has already been discussed, so the items in the top half of the Network Configuration window will be skipped in the current discussion.

---

6. The default encryption setting is Require Microsoft Encrypted Authentication. This provides for MS-CHAP. If you fill the Require Data Encryption checkbox, it will encrypt not only the password, but any data flowing between the RAS server and the client.

   ▪ Select Require Encrypted Authentication if you are providing access to non-Microsoft-based operating systems, such as UNIX. This provides for CHAP-based encryption in addition to MS-CHAP.

   ▪ Select Allow Any Authentication Including Clear Text, which allows all three methods, including no encryption.

Configuring Dial-Up Networking Clients

On a Windows NT computer, before you can connect to the RAS server, you must have RAS services installed. If you are using NT Server, refer to the first section of "Necessary Procedures" to install RAS.

Once RAS has been installed, you must configure a dial-up connection in the RAS phone book. To configure the dial-up connection:

1. Double-click the My Computer icon on the desktop.

2. Double-click the Dial-Up Networking icon.

3. If this is the first entry in your phone book, you will get a nagging screen that tells you the phone book is empty. Click OK. After you pass the annoying screen, click New to start the New Phonebook Entry wizard.

4. Type in the name of the phone-book entry and then click the Finish button.

5. You need to enter a name for the dial-up entry you are creating. The receiving server name seems appropriate, don't you think?

6. Did you notice the Dial Using box? Select the modem to use.

7. Click the Use Telephony Dialing Properties option.

8. Enter the area code and phone number of your RAS server in the Phone Number input lines.

9. Does your RAS server have more than one phone number? If so, you can check the Alternate button and add any other phone numbers to call.

10. Click the Server tab. Select the protocol that your RAS server uses. The protocols must match between the client and the server for communication to take place.

11. The security must also be the same on the server and the host, so click the Security tab. Since this is a nonsecure network, check Allow Any Encryption Including Clear Text.

12. Click OK to save the settings and then click Close. You may be prompted to restart your computer, but in this case, it is not necessary.

Exam Essentials

The exam writers really like the objectives in this section, so study carefully.

Know the three call-back modes and when they should be used.   The three call-back modes are No Call Back, Set by User, and Preset. No Call Back bypasses call-back security. Set by User prompts the user for a number where they can be reached. Preset makes the system always call a specific number.

Use No Call Back if security is not an issue. Use Set by User if your users are travelling or at a client site. Use Preset when dealing with remote sites that will not move around.

Call-back options cannot be set if multilink is enabled.

Know the differences between SLIP, PPP, and PTPP. SLIP (serial line Internet protocol) is IP over a modem. This is an outdated protocol. PPP (point-to-point protocol) is used with serial or modem communications to provide IP communications, and it can provide additional features such as data compression and DNS and gateway addressing. PPP has largely replaced SLIP. Windows NT servers can establish SLIP connections only when dialing out or originating a SLIP session. PPTP (point-to-point tunneling protocol) is PPP with security and is used with the Internet to create an encrypted link to the RAS server. In some areas, this is called creating a virtual private network (VPN).

Key Terms and Concepts

ATM (asynchronous transfer mode): WAN communication implementation.

Call back: A part of RAS security. You can configure the RAS server to return the call of the system needing access.

CHAP (challenge handshake authentication protocol): Password security protocol used by RAS systems to communicate with non-Windows systems.

IPX: Internet packet exchange protocol.

ISDN (integrated services digital network): Provides communications over special phone lines using digital communications.

Modem: From modulate/demodulate. Computer hardware that will turn a computer's digital signal into an analog signal that can be sent over a phone line. The modem at the receiving end will then turn the analog signal into a digital signal that the computer can understand.

MS-CHAP: Microsoft's implementation of CHAP. Default RAS selection. Used to provide secure password authentication between a RAS server and Microsoft Windows 95 or Windows NT clients.

Multilink: RAS can combine several serial signals into one, using either ISDN or modems.

NetBEUI: Microsoft networking protocol. Efficient, simple protocol that will not provide routing, but can be used in RAS sessions.

NWLink: Microsoft's implementation of the IPX/SPX protocol. Installed to be compatible with Novell networks. Can be used by RAS servers as a networking protocol.

PAP: Password authentication protocol.

POTS: Plain old telephone system.

PPP (point-to-point protocol):   A data-link-layer transport that performs over point-to-point network connections such as serial or modem lines. PPP can negotiate with any transport protocol used by both systems involved in the link and can realize data-transfer efficiencies, such as software compression, and automatically assign IP, domain name service (DNS), and gateway addresses when used with transmission control protocol/Internet protocol (TCP/IP).

PSTN (public switched telephone network):   The phone company.

RAS: Remote access service.

RAS permissions: Front-line security to determine whether the user has the right to log onto the RAS server.

SLIP (serial line Internet protocol):   An implementation of Internet protocol (IP) over a serial line. SLIP has been replaced, by and large, by PPP.

SPID (service profile ID):   ISDN-required configuration information. The ISDN phone number.

SPX: Sequenced packet exchange protocol.

TCP/IP (transmission control protocol/Internet protocol):   The standard protocol suite of the Internet.

TDI (transport driver interface):   A specification to which all Windows NT transport protocols must be written to be used by higher-level services such as RAS.

Sample Questions

1. What are the three RAS call-back options?

    A. No Call Back

    B. Preset

    C. Set by User

    D. Only if asked

    Answer: A, B, C—The call-back options for RAS are No Call Back, Preset, and Set by User.

2. Which dial-up line protocols does RAS support?

    A. PPP

    B. TCP

    C. SLIP

    D. IPX/SPX

    E. UDP

    Answer: A, C—PPP and SLIP are the only two dial-up line protocols listed.

3. What is multilink?

    A. The ability to have two or more modems handling different calls at the same time

    B. The ability to have two or more modems call out at the same time

    C. The ability to use more than one communication channel for the same connection

    D. The ability to have two network interface cards in the same system at the same time

Answer: C

CHAPTER

5

Monitoring and Optimization

Microsoft Exam Objectives Covered in This Chapter:

▶ **Monitor performance of various functions by using Performance Monitor. Functions include:** *(pages 263 – 279)*
- Processor
- Memory
- Disk
- Network

▶ **Identify performance bottlenecks.** *(pages 279 – 284)*

While studying for the various MCSE exams, you have probably learned about numerous tools, services, and applications that can be added to an NT server. Each change you make to a server will influence its ability to perform other functions. In this chapter, a few tools that measure the effects of change on both your servers and the network will be discussed. The objectives for this portion of the exam cover your ability to use tools to gather information about your network and analyze the data gathered.

Managing your server is much like managing your family budget. Your family budget has a limited amount of resources. Those resources have to be used to accomplish certain things—you must pay for housing, transportation, and food. These things are mandatory and must be budgeted before anything else. At the same time, you'd like to be able to provide a few luxuries for yourself and your family—a vacation, a second car, or maybe a pool for those hot summer days. Managing a family budget is often more about juggling expenses than managing money.

Your server is the same type of environment. You have limited resources—a certain amount of memory, hard disk, and CPU with which to play. With those resources, you have to provide certain services to your users—e-mail, shared data, print services, and backups. Once again, the act of managing the environment involves balancing needs against resources.

To truly manage your network, rather than react to it, you need a set of tools that allow you to measure the impact of each service on both an individual server and the network as a whole. Once you have that information, you can manage your resources to optimize performance and efficiency.

By the end of this chapter, you will be able to gather information, analyze it, and make changes to optimize your network.

Monitor performance of various functions by using Performance Monitor. Functions include:

- Processor
- Memory
- Disk
- Network

When you troubleshoot any kind of complex system, one of the most important skills is knowing what to look for—the questions you ask and how you interpret the answers are critical to both problem solving and optimization on your network. In this section, the Performance Monitor counters to track on each of the major subsystems of an NT server will be discussed.

Critical Information

While any given environment might stress other particular components, there are four main physical components to any NT server: processor, memory, disk, and network. These four areas are good indicators of the health of your system. When monitoring any NT server, always start with these four components and then add any of the other additional NT objects that might be appropriate in your environment.

Performance Monitor

Performance Monitor is the tool provided by NT to gather statistics at the server. Performance Monitor uses objects and counters to describe the statistics that can be gathered. An object is a subsystem, while a counter is a specific statistic of an object.

Performance Monitor has a list of 12 objects that can be monitored. Some software creates its own counters when you install it. Specific objects and counters will be examined later in this chapter. Each of the four main subsystems has an associated object with counters that you should track.

When creating your baseline, you will often want to gather statistics while a specific process happens. Backups, for instance, often strain both the servers involved and the network. Unfortunately, most companies do their backups during nonpeak hours or, in other words, during your personal time. You can use the AT command to start Performance Monitor automatically. The AT command allows you to schedule a start time for any process or application. Using the AT command, you can make Performance Monitor load and begin collecting data automatically. This can come in handy when you want to gather information on a regular basis or you are not available to start the process manually.

Once you've collected your data, you'll want to analyze it. Performance Monitor can save data in a format that many commercial applications can read. When you dump the statistics into a database or spreadsheet, it is called *creating a measurement database*. If you use a database or spreadsheet, it allows you to track information over time. Performance Monitor does not have this innate ability—it shows either current information or statistics since the server was booted. You can easily export Performance Monitor data in a format that a program such as Microsoft Excel can import. This allows you to take advantage of the various tools that the application might have—such as Excel's excellent graphing abilities. When you present your data to management, it is much more effective to use a graph than columns of numbers.

When gathering information, you will often track a lot of counters and check those counters frequently. How often Performance Monitor checks the values of counters you are tracking is called the *interval*. If your interval is set low, NT will gather the values often, which can result in huge data files. Microsoft suggests that after you have analyzed the data, you relog the information with a larger interval. This will reduce the size of the log file, but still leave you information for trend analysis and comparison.

Performance Monitor offers many ways to view the statistics that it gathers. You will need to be familiar with each of them for the exam.

Chart View

Chart view provides a real-time chart showing the values of the counters you have chosen. The first step is to add the counters to your view, as shown in Figure 5.1. Highlight the appropriate object and then pick a counter from the list.

F I G U R E 5.1: Add to Chart

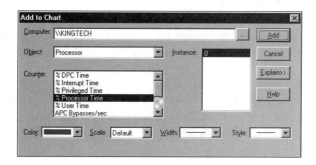

When you have added all of the counters you want to chart, click Cancel. The chart will show the value of those counters in real time, as shown in Figure 5.2.

F I G U R E 5.2: A real-time Performance Monitor chart

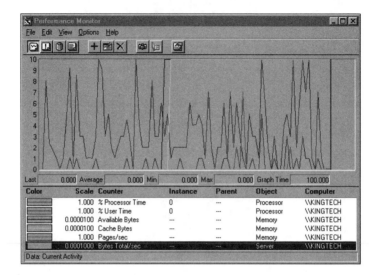

Report View

Report view shows the same information as Chart view. However, with Report view, the values are shown in the form of a text-based report. As in Chart view, the report data are updated in real time.

Log View

Log view allows you to save the data to a file. In Log view, you do not pick counters—all counters for the objects you chose will be tracked. Rather than the data being shown as they are collected, the data are saved to a file for later analysis.

Alert View

Alert view is different from the other three views. With Alert view, you set a threshold for a counter. When this threshold is reached, you can make Performance Monitor run an application that pages you, for instance.

Processor

To determine whether the processor is the bottleneck, monitor the counters listed in Table 5.1.

T A B L E 5.1: Processor-Related Counters in Performance Monitor

Counter	Acceptable Value	Description
% Processor Time	Under 80 percent	If the processor is busy more than 80 percent of the time, it is likely that the processor is the bottleneck.
% Privileged Time	Under 80 percent	This is the amount of time that the processor is busy performing operating-system tasks.
% User Time	Under 80 percent	This is the amount of time that the processor is busy performing user tasks, such as running a program.
Interrupts/ sec	Varies	This is the number of hardware interrupts generated each second. Each type of processor can handle a different number. On a 486/66, this number should be under 1,000; on a Pentium 90 system, this number could run as high as 3,500. If this number is consistently high, the system probably has an IRQ conflict or a piece of hardware that is going bad.
System: Processor Queue Length	Less than 2	This represents the number of threads that are ready to execute, but are waiting for the processor.
Server Work Queues: Queue Length	Less than 2	This represents the number of threads in the queue for a given processor.

If the bottleneck is your processor, you can:

- Add a faster processor
- Add another processor
- Move processing to another server

NOTE These are Microsoft's proposed solutions. In reality, you very seldom have the option of adding another or faster processor. Upgrading the processor in today's quagmire of choices (Pentium, Pentium Pro, Pentium II, etc.) is never as easy as it sounds. As for adding a processor, few administrators would buy a multiprocessor motherboard and leave a slot open.

Memory

Before the counters that determine whether memory is your system bottleneck are discussed, how NT uses memory needs to be reviewed.

Memory in an NT system can be divided into two classifications: paged and nonpaged. Paged memory is used by most applications. It can be made up of either physical RAM or virtual memory (hard disk space). Nonpaged memory is used by programs that cannot be "paged" to the hard disk. The operating system and its components use nonpaged memory.

NT uses a virtual memory model. In this model, applications that can use paged RAM are given a full set of memory addresses with which to work. The operating system keeps track of actual physical memory. When memory is full, the OS will move "pages" of memory to a file on the hard drive (PAGEFILE.SYS). If that code is needed later, it will be moved back to physical memory. By using a virtual memory model, your applications can use more memory than is physically available (up to the limits of your hard drive).

Whenever the data that a program needs are not in RAM, they must be acquired from the hard drive. This process is called a *hard page fault*. If you have a consistently high number of hard page faults (over five per second), it could indicate that performance is being significantly degraded since there is not enough memory available on the server. The goal on an NT server is to have enough memory in the server so that most data requested are found in memory. (Obviously, the first time the data are used, they will have to come from the disk. But after that, if you have enough memory for file caching, it can greatly increase performance.)

TIP To appreciate the importance of file caching, compare the access speeds of your memory and your hard disk. Hard-disk access times are measured in milliseconds or thousandths of a second. Memory is measured in nanoseconds or millionths of a second.

Monitor the counters listed in Table 5.2 to determine whether memory is your bottleneck.

TABLE 5.2: Memory-Related Counters in Performance Monitor

Counter	Acceptable Value	Description
Pages/sec	0–20	The number of pages that were either not in RAM when requested or needed to be moved to virtual memory to free up space in RAM. This is really a measurement of disk activity related to memory management.
Available Bytes	Minimum of 4MB	The amount of available physical RAM at any point in time. This number will usually be fairly low, because NT will utilize memory that is available and free it up as needed.
Committed Bytes	Should be less than the physical amount of RAM in the computer	This indicates the amount of memory in use. If the number is greater than the amount of physical RAM in the machine, you need more memory.
Pool Non-Paged Bytes	Should remain steady	This is the memory used by nonpaged processes (i.e., the operating system). If this number fluctuates, it could indicate that a process is not using memory correctly.

If memory is the bottleneck on your server, the fix is simple—add more RAM. With today's prices, you are shorting the true performance of your server by allowing a RAM bottleneck to occur.

Disk

The disk is usually the slowest component on your computer. NT compensates for this by using file caching and memory management to reduce the number of disk accesses. Often, what appears to be a disk problem is really just a lack of memory, so be sure to watch both subsystems—disk and memory.

Before you can track disk counters in Performance Monitor, you must turn on those counters. The disk counters are not activated by default, because tracking physical-disk access used to add measurable overhead to the workstations and servers that ran older Intel processors. Today's CPUs aren't affected to nearly the same degree, but the counters still must be turned on and off.

To activate the disk counters, type **diskperf –y** at a command prompt. If your disks are configured as a RAID set, type **diskperf –ye**.

NOTE   The added overhead of tracking disk counters is constant once they are activated—not just when you are monitoring them. You should turn them off when you are not actively watching them. To turn them off, type **diskperf –n** at a command prompt.

Once you have activated them, you can monitor the counters listed in Table 5.3.

TABLE 5.3:   Disk-Related Counters in Performance Monitor

Counter	Acceptable Value	Description
%Disk Time	Under 90 percent	This is the amount of time that the disk drive is busy. If this number is consistently high, you should monitor specific processes to find out exactly what is using the disk. If you can, move some of the disk-intensive processes to another server.
Disk Queue Length	0–2	This value represents the number of waiting disk I/O requests. A high number indicates that I/O requests are waiting for access.

TABLE 5.3: Disk-Related Counters in Performance Monitor *(cont.)*

Counter	Acceptable Value	Description
Avg. Disk Bytes/ Transfer	Depends on use and type of subsystem	The larger this number is, the more efficiently your disk subsystem is working. This value depends on the type of access—are your users saving many small files or a few large ones? It also depends on the types of disks and controllers.
Disk Bytes/ sec	Depends on use and type of subsystem	The larger this number is, the more efficiently your disk subsystem is working. This value depends on the types of disks and controllers.

If you find that the disk subsystem is the bottleneck, you can do the following things:

- Add a faster controller and disk drive. (See Chapter 1 for a comparison of the various disk technologies.)

- If using RAID, add more disks to the set. This spreads the work across more physical devices.

- Move disk-intensive processes to another server to spread the workload.

WARNING   None of these solutions is really a simple fix. If you add a faster controller, it will help only if your disks are compliant with the controller type. If they are not, you will have to replace the disks as well to gain any benefit. As for the RAID solution, to add a disk, you need to have a slot open and the funding for more hardware. As for moving the process to another server, you need to have a server that is not too busy to accept the extra workload. The proper solution to this problem is to have prevented the problem in the first place. Proper capacity planning (projecting throughput needs, comparing technologies, and implementing the best solution) is the best fix.

Network

Due to the complexity of today's networks, monitoring the network portion of your environment can be a difficult task. The network doesn't end at your NIC card—the network includes the entire infrastructure that makes up your enterprise. Everything attached to your network could be a potential problem. To monitor a network, you have to be familiar with all of the components on that network—the routers, the wiring, the protocols, the operating systems, etc.

Don't try to fix the entire network, try to find out which component is causing the problem and fix that.

Performance Monitor has a few counters, listed in Table 5.4, that can help you determine where the problem lies. A few of the counters analyze the overhead on the server itself, while others give an overview of what is happening on the wire.

TABLE 5.4: Network-Related Counters in Performance Monitor

Counter	Acceptable Value	Description
Server: Bytes Total/ sec	Varies	This counter shows the number of bytes sent and received through this server. It is a good indicator of how busy the server is.
Server: Login/sec	Varies	Use this value to determine the authentication overhead being placed on the server. If this number is high and other services are slow, it might indicate the need for another domain controller.
Server: Login Total	Varies	This is the number of login attempts this server has serviced since the last time the server was started. Can be used to justify another domain controller.

T A B L E 5.4:   Network-Related Counters in Performance Monitor *(cont.)*

Counter	Acceptable Value	Description
Network Interface: Bytes sent/ sec	Varies	Used to determine whether a particular network interface card is being overused.
Network Interface: Bytes total/ sec	Varies	This is the total number of bytes sent and received through a particular NIC.
Network Segment: %Network Utilization	Usually lower than 30 percent	This shows the percentage of network bandwidth in use. This number should be lower than 30 percent for most networks. Some network technologies can sustain a higher rate.

The Network Segment object is not available until you install the Network Monitor Agent as a service on the server. Once this service is installed, Performance Monitor will put the NICs in promiscuous mode when you are monitoring Network Segment counters. When in promiscuous mode, a NIC processes *all* network traffic, not just those packets destined for the server. This can add a tremendous amount of overhead to the server.

Each protocol that you add to your server also has its own counters. These counters allow you to determine the overhead being placed on your server by each protocol. Most of these counters have no acceptable range of values. The values will depend upon the hardware, topology, and other protocols used on your network.

NetBEUI and NWLink
These two protocols have similar counters, listed in Table 5.5.

TABLE 5.5: NetBEUI- and NWLink-Related Counters in Performance Monitor

Counter	Acceptable Value	Description
Bytes Total/sec	Varies	This is the total number of bytes sent and received using this protocol. This counter is an excellent way to compare network overhead created by various protocols.
Datagrams/sec	Varies	This is the total number of nonguaranteed datagrams (usually broadcasts) sent and received.
Frames sent/ sec	Varies	This is the number of data packets sent and received.

TCP/IP

The counters listed in Table 5.6 will not be available unless both the TCP/IP protocol and the SNMP service are installed on the server.

TABLE 5.6: TCP/IP-Related Counters in Performance Monitor

Counter	Acceptable Value	Description
TCP Segments/ sec	Varies	This is the total number of TCP frames sent and received.
TCP Segments re-translated/sec	Varies	This is the total number of segments retranslated on the network.
UDP datagrams/sec	Varies	This is the number of UDP-based datagrams (usually broadcasts) sent and received.
Network Interface: Output Queue Length	Less than 2	This is the number of packets waiting to be transmitted through a particular NIC. A high number can indicate a card that is too busy.

The following strategies are potential fixes if the network is your bottleneck:

- Upgrade the hardware at the server. Add a faster NIC, add RAM, or upgrade the processor.

- Upgrade the physical components of your network, such as routers and bridges. Shift to higher-speed network protocols such as 100BaseT Ethernet.

- Decrease the number of protocols used on your network.

- Segment your network to split the traffic between segments.

- Add servers to split the workload.

Necessary Procedures

This objective primarily concerns your ability to use Performance Monitor. You must understand the available options before taking the exam.

Creating a Baseline Using Performance Monitor

To build a baseline, you use the Log view in Performance Monitor. First, pick the objects that you want to track. Remember to start with the four main subsystems. At a minimum, you will want to track processor, memory, disk, and whatever objects are available for protocols in use on your network. Save this log to a file. You will use this file—the baseline—as a basis for comparison. Performance Monitor can use this file later as the input material for graphs or reports.

Relogging Your Data at a Longer Interval

Use the Log view in Performance Monitor.

1. Choose Options ➤ Data from.

2. Choose Log File and browse to your baseline log file.

3. Build the log again, using the same steps as before—only this time, change the interval.

4. When you start the log, it will save information at the new interval, reducing the size of the log file.

WARNING Although this method is great for archiving trends, the resulting log file contains less-accurate data. Since you have reduced the sampling rate, the resulting information will be less detailed in terms of time.

Exporting Information to Another Program

Build a chart using your log file. Choose File ➤ Export Chart. Save the chart in a format your application can import.

Exam Essentials

Trying to outsmart the exam writers at Microsoft is often an exercise in futility. There is one common thread throughout—they want to ensure that you have the skills necessary to provide your environment with an efficient NT network. The following items are critical to that goal.

Understand NT's virtual memory model. NT extends physical RAM by using disk space. When a program needs memory, NT will allocate physical RAM. IF there is not enough RAM available, NT will move a "page" of memory to the PAGEFILE.SYS file on the hard drive. To the application that originally placed that information in memory, it appears as if the data are still in RAM. When that application needs the data again, NT will page something else to disk and place it in physical RAM for use.

Know the difference between paged and nonpaged memory. Paged memory can be "paged" to the PAGEFILE.SYS file. Nonpaged memory contains data that cannot be moved to virtual memory (usually, this code will be part of the operating system).

Know how to activate the disk counters in Performance Monitor. From a command prompt, type **diskperf –y**. In a RAID implementation, type **diskperf –ye**.

Know the suggested fixes for bottlenecks in each of the four major subsystems. These fixes are as follows:

- Processor:
  - Add a faster processor.
  - Add another processor.
  - Move processing to another server.

- Memory:
  - Add RAM.

- Disk:
  - Add a faster controller and disk drive. (See Chapter 1 for a comparison of the various disk technologies.)
  - If using RAID, add more disks to the set. This spreads the work across more physical devices.
  - Move disk-intensive processes to another server to spread the workload.

- Network:
  - Upgrade the hardware at the server. Add a faster NIC, add RAM, or upgrade the processor.
  - Upgrade the physical components of your network, such as routers and bridges.
  - Decrease the number of protocols used on your network.
  - Segment your network to split the traffic between segments.
  - Add servers to split the workload.

Be familiar with the counters discussed in this section. Reread this section, paying close attention to the counters listed. They are the counters that are most likely to be mentioned on the exam.

Key Terms and Concepts

Counter: A specific statistic that can be tracked.

Datagram: A term usually used to describe a nondirected packet on the network (broadcasts, acknowledgments, etc.).

Frame: A term usually used to describe a directed packet of data.

Interval: In Performance Monitor, a setting that determines how often data are updated.

Nonpaged memory: An area of memory that cannot use virtual RAM. Usually used by the operating system.

Object: An NT subsystem that can be monitored.

Paged memory: An area of memory that can be extended using virtual memory space.

Virtual memory model: A memory system that uses hard-drive space as if it were RAM.

Sample Questions

1. Which of the Performance Monitor views displays a real-time graph?

   A. Chart

   B. Report

   C. Log

   D. Alert

   Answer: A

2. Which of the Performance Monitor views allows you to save data for later analysis?

   A. Chart

   B. Report

C. Log

D. Alert

Answer: C

Identify performance bottlenecks.

NT servers are used for a lot of different tasks. Microsoft defines three main server environments—File and Print, Application, and Domain. Each of these environments will stress different components of a server. In this section, each of these environments will be defined, and which components they will utilize most heavily and the specific objects and counters that you will track to analyze each environment will be discussed.

WARNING Microsoft has made a big assumption when discussing each type of server environment—the assumption is that the server is used to provide only one service. In most networks, servers perform multiple services. In a real-world network, you will have to analyze how each function affects all other functions that the server performs.

Critical Information

For each server environment, you will need to know its main function and the importance of each of the four main subsystems for each environment.

File and Print Server

A file and print server is used by users to acquire and save data, to load server-based software, and as a print server. A breakdown of this type of server is given in Table 5.7.

NOTE The values in the following tables represent relative importance. Some components may have equal values.

T A B L E 5.7: File and Print Server

Subsystem	Importance to Environment*	Critical Information
Memory	1	Servers use memory to cache the files that users request. Caching a frequently used file can increase process performance by over 100 percent.
Processor	2	Each network connection uses processor time at the server.
Disk	3	Since most connections are used to save or retrieve data, the disks can have an impact on performance. However, since servers use file caching, memory will have a bigger impact.
Network	3	Every transaction will add to the traffic on the network, but this is usually not the bottleneck on a file and print server.

*1= highest; 4=lowest

Application Server

An application server is a client/server environment. In a client/server environment, the actual processing happens at the server, not the client computer. A good example is a database server. The client runs a small piece of software called a front-end, which is used to formulate a query of the database. The server runs the actual database software. When the front-end sends a query, the server looks through the database and returns only the results. Notice that most of the processing happens at the server. The details of this environment are listed in Table 5.8.

T A B L E 5.8: Application Server

Subsystem	Importance to Environment*	Critical Information
Memory	2	Each application or service you add to a server will use memory. Most client/server-based applications use a lot of memory. Make sure the server has sufficient memory for both the operating system and the application.
Processor	1	As discussed above, most of the actual processing occurs at the server.
Disk	3	This is a tough one to categorize. If the application is disk intensive (a database, for instance), the disk could be a potential bottleneck. In most cases, though, its impact will be negligible compared to the processor and memory.
Network	4	Client/server-based applications put very little traffic on the network. Instead of transferring a large amount of data to be processed by the client, only the pertinent information is transferred.

*1= highest; 4=lowest

Domain Server

A domain server is a server that is involved in providing network management services. This server will be a domain controller, a DHCP server, a WINS server, etc. Most communication will be server to server, rather than client to server. The components of a domain server are listed in Table 5.9.

TABLE 5.9: Domain Server

Subsystem	Importance to Environment*	Critical Information
Memory	1	Each service the server provides will use memory.
Processor	2	Each network connection will use processing time. Domain controllers need to synchronize the SAM and act as login servers for users.
Disk	3	Domain servers are usually not disk intensive.
Network	1	All transactions will involve the network. Limited connection speed will slow down the overall operation of the workstations while waiting for server processes such as security authentication.

*1= highest; 4=lowest

Now that you know the different kinds of servers that might be found in your environment and which subsystem(s) is most important to each, you can use this information to choose what to include in your baseline. For each of the "big four" subsystems, you will need to know which counters to watch and what ranges of values are acceptable for each environment.

Exam Essentials

Most of the optimization techniques covered in the remaining chapter will assume that you understand the different types of environments in which an NT server might be used. Know these before continuing.

Know the three types of server environments and the importance of the four main subsystems for each. The three types of environments are File and Print, Application, and Domain. Review Tables 5.7, 5.8, and 5.9 to understand the relative importance of the four main subsystems to each environment.

Key Terms and Concepts

Application server: A server that acts as the back-end for a client/server-based application.

Client/server: An application process that is divided into two parts—the server code that does the actual request processing and client code that communicates requests to the server.

Domain server: A server that performs network management tasks.

File and print server: A server that provides data storage and print services to the network.

Sample Questions

1. On a file and print server, which of the four main components is most likely to be the bottleneck?

   A. Memory

   B. Processor

   C. Disk

   D. Network

   Answer: A—Memory is used to cache users' data requests. If not enough memory is available, the system will spend too much time accessing its hard drives.

2. On an application server, which of the four main components is most likely to be the bottleneck?

   A. Memory

   B. Processor

   C. Disk

   D. Network

   Answer: B—Since most of the actual processing of data occurs at the server, the processor becomes a critical component.

3. On a domain server, which of the four main components is most likely to be the bottleneck?

   A. Memory

   B. Processor

   C. Disk

   D. Network

   Answer: A, D—The function of a domain server is to handle network management tasks. Also, keep in mind that every connection to a server uses memory.

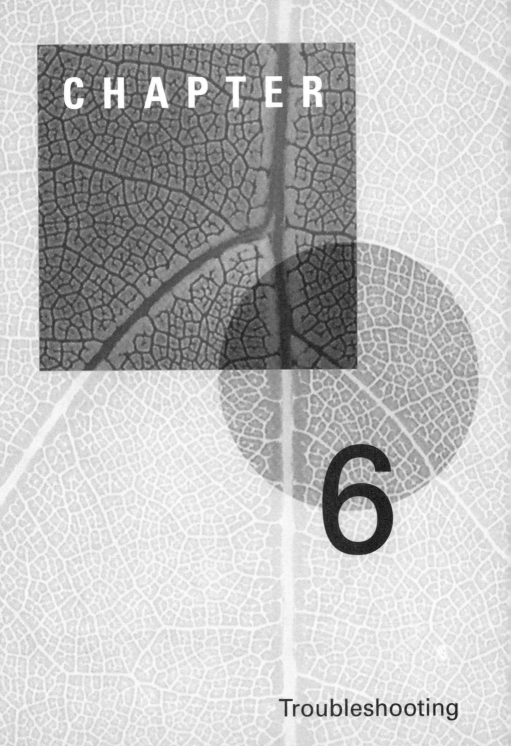

CHAPTER

6

Troubleshooting

Microsoft Exam Objectives Covered in This Chapter:

▶ Choose the appropriate course of action to take to resolve installation failures. *(pages 287 – 290)*

▶ Choose the appropriate course of action to take to resolve boot failures. *(pages 290 – 301)*

▶ Choose the appropriate course of action to take to resolve configuration errors. *(pages 301 – 308)*

▶ Choose the appropriate course of action to take to resolve printer problems. *(pages 309 – 317)*

▶ Choose the appropriate course of action to take to resolve RAS problems. *(pages 317 – 320)*

▶ Choose the appropriate course of action to take to resolve connectivity problems. *(pages 320 – 328)*

▶ Choose the appropriate course of action to take to resolve resource access and permission problems. *(pages 328 – 331)*

▶ Choose the appropriate course of action to take to resolve fault-tolerance failures. Fault-tolerance methods include: *(pages 332 – 340)*
- Tape backup
- Mirroring
- Stripe set with parity
- Disk duplexing

The objectives for this chapter cover the actions you should take to correct a specific set of problems. Some of these problems occur often in the workplace, while others occur rarely. Whether the problems are common or rare, knowing how to correct them is a very big part of being a network administrator.

Learning to troubleshoot technical problems is a lifelong process. You can pick up some useful tips by reading books or taking classes, but you can never know everything—experience plays a big role in developing troubleshooting skills. However, this book can act as a starting place to help you build a "troubleshooting database" in your head.

Each section features a specific set of steps to take when troubleshooting a particular problem. For the exam, it is important to know these steps.

Choose the appropriate course of action to take to resolve installation failures.

In the real world, installation failures can be fairly common. They are also the most fortunate type of problem, because they manifest before the server has been placed in production. While you are usually under a deadline during installation, there is usually less pressure to fix the problem immediately.

Critical Information

An NT installation might fail for many reasons. The easiest way to avoid installation problems is to purchase equipment that has been tested to be compatible with Microsoft Windows NT. Microsoft provides a tool—the NT hardware qualifier (NTHQ) utility—that will help you determine whether your equipment is on the tested list. This tool is found on your NT Server CD-ROM or can be downloaded from the Microsoft Web site. NTHQ tests your hardware to determine whether any components are not on the list.

WARNING   Always download the latest version of NTHQ from the Microsoft Web site. The version found on your CD-ROM will not contain information about hardware that has been certified since the CD-ROM was created. Before you purchase equipment, you can access the compatibility list on the Web site. Make it a policy to specify *NT 4.0 certified* when you talk to vendors.

Some specific problems that you might encounter will now be examined.

Media Errors

If you get an error message that indicates that a particular file cannot be copied or is corrupt during an installation of NT, it could indicate a media error. Try using another CD-ROM if you have one. If not, try using another method of installation. For example, copy the I386 directory to the C: drive (assuming it is a FAT partition) and try the installation from there. Another option is to copy the I386 directory to another server, sharing the directory, and then install from that share point.

Nonsupported SCSI Adapter

If your CD-ROM is attached to a SCSI adapter that is not supported by NT, you can lose the ability to read from it halfway through the installation process, after the server has been restarted under NT. Unfortunately, even if the CD-ROM manufacturer provides an NT SCSI driver, you cannot use it until after NT is fully installed. If you run into this problem, you will have to use the techniques listed in the "Media Errors" section. Try installing from a share point on another server. Or, boot to DOS, copy the I386 directory to the C: drive, and install from there.

Insufficient Disk Space

Insufficient disk space is really just poor planning. Know the minimum requirements before you start the installation, and make sure your hardware meets or exceeds them. The only fix for insufficient disk space is to provide NT with enough disk space either by deleting an existing partition or by adding another drive.

Failure of Dependency Service to Start

When the dependency service fails to start, it is usually a configuration error. Most of these errors result from network interface card (NIC) problems, requiring you to go back to the network setup section of the installation and ensure that the protocols are configured correctly, that you have chosen a unique computer name, and that the NIC settings are correct.

Inability to Connect to the PDC

Ensure that you have entered the domain name correctly, that the NIC settings are correct, and that you have chosen the correct network protocols. This problem is quite common—it usually occurs when you try to install a BDC on a computer that has a nonsupported NIC. If NT doesn't provide a NIC driver, the card cannot initialize and you cannot communicate with the server.

Error in Assigning a Domain Name

When you install a PDC, ensure that the domain name is not already in use on your network. The domain name cannot be the same as any other domain or computer name.

Failure of NT to Install or Start

When NT fails to install or start, it usually indicates that a piece of hardware is not compatible with NT. Run NTHQ to determine which component is not on the hardware-compatibility list and replace the component.

Exam Essentials

If you know what problems you might encounter, it can help you avoid them.

Understand the various reasons that an NT installation might fail. The most common reasons for failure are either human error or incompatible hardware.

Key Terms and Concepts

HCL (hardware-compatibility list): A list of hardware that has been tested and approved for use with Microsoft Windows NT.

NTHQ (NT hardware qualifier): Software that checks your hardware to ensure that all components are on the hardware-compatibility list.

Sample Questions

1. Which of the following actions should you take if you encounter a media error when installing NT?

   A. Try another NT CD-ROM.

   B. Try another method of installation—across the network, copy the I386 to the local drive first, etc.

   C. Give up and try another operating system.

   Answer: A, B—Although answer C might seem like the easiest method in the short term, it is not a Microsoft-recommended solution.

▶ Choose the appropriate course of action to take to resolve boot failures.

Nothing is worse than a server that won't finish the boot process. You are left staring at an obscure error message or, worse, at a stop screen filled with what appears to be hieroglyphics. In this section, the most common error messages, their causes, and the appropriate actions to take to correct the problems will be discussed.

Critical Information

NT goes through four distinct phases during the boot process. For the MCSE examination, you will need to know what happens in each phase. After the stages have been examined, specific errors and possible solutions will be examined.

NT Boot Phases

The four boot phases are as follows:

- Initial

- Boot loader

- Kernel

- Logon

Initial Phase

During the initial phase, the computer performs a power on self test (POST), during which it determines how much memory is installed and whether the required hardware is available. During this process, the computer executes the BIOS and reads the information stored in CMOS to determine what storage devices are available, the date and time, and other parameters specific to the hardware.

In CMOS, the computer will read the type and configuration of possible boot devices. Based upon this information, it will determine which device it should examine to find operating system boot information. If your computer is configured to boot from the hard drive, your computer will read the first sector in an attempt to find the master boot record (MBR). The MBR contains critical information for the boot process—a list of partitions defined on the disk, their starting and ending sectors, and which partitions are active. (The active partition is the one that the computer will attempt to boot from.) If there is no MBR on the disk, the computer cannot boot to an operating system. This is why many computer viruses attack the MBR.

Once the computer has determined which partition it should look to for boot information, it will access that partition and read the partition boot sector (PBS). The PBS contains operating system–specific information. In the case of Windows NT, it directs the computer to load a file called NTLDR (NT loader), which is found in the partition root folder. If the PBS is missing or corrupted, you may see an error message that implies that no operating system was found, a nonsystem disk is being used, or a disk error has occurred. This is what happens when you restart your computer with a nonsystem floppy disk in the A: drive. There is no boot information on it, so the server doesn't know where to find the operating system.

Boot Loader Phase

Once NTLDR has been found and starts to load, the boot loader phase begins. During this phase, NT uses various programs to gather information about the hardware and drivers needed to boot. The following files will be utilized during this phase:

NTLDR—This is the operating system loader. It must be in the root directory of the active partition. NTLDR remains the overall conductor of the NT startup process.

BOOT.INI—This is an important text file that controls which operating system will be loaded. The user will see a menu offering various operating system choices. NTLDR expects to find this file in the root directory. The BOOT.INI file will be discussed in more detail later in this section.

BOOTSEC.DOS—If the computer is configured to dual boot between NT and another operating system, the NT installation program will gather all of the information needed to boot the other OS and place it in this file. When the user chooses to boot to another OS, NT will call this file.

NTBOOTDD.SYS—This is a device driver used to access a SCSI hard drive when the SCSI controller is not using its own BIOS.

NTDETECT.COM—This is a program that attempts to analyze the hardware on the computer; it passes this information to the operating system for inclusion in the registry later in the boot process. NTDETECT.COM can detect the following components: computer ID; bus/adapter type; video, keyboard, and communication ports; parallel ports; floppy disks; and mouse/pointing device. While

NTDETECT.COM performs its function, it displays the following message on the screen:

```
NTDETECT V1.0 Checking Hardware…
```

NTLDR controls the initial startup of NT on the hardware. It also changes the processor from real-time to 32-bit flat memory mode, starts the appropriate miniature file system (NTLDR has code that enables it to read FAT and NTFS partitions), and reads the BOOT.INI file to display the menu of operating system choices.

Once NT has been selected and NTDETECT.COM has run its course, NTLDR will display the following message:

```
OS Loader V4.0
Press SPACEBAR now to invoke Hardware Profile/Last
Known Good menu.
```

If the spacebar is not pressed and there is only one hardware profile, NTLDR will load the default control set. If the spacebar is pressed, NTLDR will display a screen offering hardware profile choices and the option to use the last known good configuration. This is an important method to restore driver and configuration settings from the registry following changes that caused an operating system failure. The old settings are called from the registry's saved control sets and used in place of the erroneous settings.

Once the hardware configuration has been chosen, NTLDR will load the NT kernel—NTOSKRNL.EXE. NTLDR loads this kernel into memory, but does not initialize it at this point. Next, the boot loader loads the registry key—HKEY_LOCAL_MACHINE\SYSTEM. NTLDR scans all of the subkeys in CurrentControlSet\Services for device drivers with a start value of zero. These drivers are usually low-level hardware drivers, such as hard disk drivers, needed to continue the boot.

Kernel Phase

The boot loader phase ends when NTLDR passes control to NTOSKRNL.EXE. At this point, the kernel-initialization phase begins. The screen will turn blue, and you will see a message similar to the following one:

```
Microsoft  Windows NT™ Version 4.0 (Build 1381)
1 System Processor (16MB Memory)
```

The kernel then creates the HKEY_LOCAL_MACHINE\HARD-WARE registry key using information passed to it by the boot loader (gathered by NTDETECT.COM).

The next step is to load the device drivers. NTOSKRNL.EXE looks in the registry for drivers that need to be loaded, checks through their DependOnService and DependOnGroup values for dependencies, and determines the order in which drivers should be loaded. It then loads the services, reads and implements the specified parameters, and initializes the various services and drivers that are needed.

Logon Phase

An NT boot is not considered successful until a user successfully logs on. The Windows subsystem automatically starts WINLOGON.EXE. The Begin Logon box now appears on the screen. The user can press Ctrl+Alt+Delete to log on even though other services might still be initializing in the background.

The service controller performs one last sweep through the registry to locate any remaining services that need to be loaded. At this point, NT has just about finished the boot process.

When a user logs on, NT considers the boot to have been successful. Only then will it take the CurrentControlSet and copy it to create the last known good configuration (for use in the next boot of this computer).

Now that the boot process has been examined, some of the specifics required for the examination can be discussed.

BOOT.INI File

The BOOT.INI file is a text file located in the root of the boot partition. Here is an example of a BOOT.INI file for an NT server that is set up to dual boot with the Windows 95 operating system:

```
[boot loader]
timeout=30
default=multi(0)disk(0)rdisk(0)parition(1)\WINNT
[operating systems]
multi(0)disk(0)rdisk(0)parition(1)\WINNT="Windows NT
Server Version 4.0"
```

```
multi(0)disk(0)rdisk(0)parition(1)\WINNT="Windows NT
Server Version 4.0 [VGA mode]" /basevideo /sos
C:\="Windows 95"
```

A BOOT.INI file has two sections. In the [boot loader] section, you will find settings that control the defaults—how long the menu should be on the screen before a default is selected and which operating system should load if the user makes no selection. In the [operating systems] section, you will find the various choices that are presented to the user, and the path and switches for each of the operating system files. The ARC path conventions were discussed earlier. Now you see where that information is put to use. If there is no BOOT.INI file, the system will attempt to boot from the location where the NT installation program places boot files by default—the \WINNT directory on the active partition. If you have placed the operating system files in another location, the BOOT.INI file is critical to the boot process.

BOOT.INI Switches

You can use numerous switches within the BOOT.INI file to help control the way that NT boots. These switches are placed at the end of the line that describes the location of the operating system.

/basevideo—This switch forces NT to boot using a standard VGA driver, which allows an administrator to recover from installing an incorrect or corrupted video driver that disables video output. The NT installation program creates an operating system choice, annotated [VGA mode], in the BOOT.INI file that implements this switch. This allows you to fix a video driver problem by rebooting, choosing the VGA option, and replacing the bad driver.

/maxmem:n—This switch allows the administrator to specify how much physical memory NT can use. You can use this switch to troubleshoot various memory problems such as parity errors, bad SIMMs, etc.

/noserialmice=[COM x or COM x,y,z]—NT will occasionally detect a device on a communication port and assume that it is a mouse—even if it is another type of device. When this happens, that device will be unusable in Windows NT because a mouse driver will be loaded that uses that port. This switch disables detection on the communication port(s) specified. This can be used to prevent NT from issuing shutdown signals to a UPS during the boot process.

/sos—This switch will cause NT to display the names of drivers as they are loaded rather than the default progress dots.

/crashdebug—This switch enables the automatic recovery and restart capability in the event of a stop screen. This parameter can also be set in the System applet in Control Panel.

A number of switches relate to advanced troubleshooting techniques that will be covered later in this chapter. These switches configure NT to "dump" its memory contents into a file for analysis. You can configure where this memory dump file will be placed. Often, a problem will be so severe that the computer is inaccessible. With this type of error, you will want to configure the system to dump its memory to another computer's hard drive. The following switches control this transfer:

/baudrate=nnnn—This switch is used to configure the communication port if you are going to dump memory to another computer.

/debugport=comx—This switch sets the communication port to be used.

BOOT.INI Error Messages

Various error messages are commonly seen when there is a problem with the BOOT.INI file. If the BOOT.INI file is missing or the operating system line does not point to the NT operating system files, you will see the following message:

```
Windows NT could not start because the following file
is missing or corrupt:
    <winnt root>\system32\NTOSKRNL.EXE
Please reinstall a copy of the above file.
```

If the ARC path points to a nonexistent or inaccessible disk or partition, you will see the following error message:

```
OS Loader V4.0
Windows NT could not start because of a computer disk
hardware configuration problem. Could not read from the
selected boot disk. Check boot path and disk hardware.
```

```
Please check the Windows NT documentation about
hardware disk configuration and your hardware reference
manuals for additional information.
```

In either event, you can either edit the BOOT.INI file to correct the problem or restore the BOOT.INI file off of your emergency repair disk.

Last Known Good Configuration

If your Windows NT server refuses to boot after you have added new hardware or software, you can attempt to boot using the last known good configuration. The *last known good configuration* is the hardware configuration used during the last successful boot. Remember, though, that when you successfully log onto the computer, you will overwrite the last known good configuration with the current control set.

If one of the files used during the boot process has become corrupted, you can attempt to replace it with a good copy. You can accomplish this task in a couple of ways. If you boot to a FAT partition, you can boot to a DOS disk and copy the new file over the suspect file. The only file that is unique to the server's hardware is the BOOT.INI file. All of the other files are generic, so you can grab a copy from any other NT server. You can also expand a copy from the NT Server CD-ROM using the Expand –r utility.

Another way to replace suspect boot files is to use your emergency repair disk (ERD). You create the ERD by running the RDISK.EXE utility. This utility creates a disk with the following files on it:

SETUP.LOG—An information file that is used for verifying the system files

SYSTEM._—A copy of the system registry hive

SAM._—A copy of the security accounts manager database

SECURITY._—A copy of the security hive

SOFTWARE._—A copy of the software hive

DEFAULT._—A copy of the default hive

CONFIG.NT—The Windows NT version of the CONFIG.SYS file used to configure an NT virtual DOS machine

AUTOEXEC.NT—The Windows NT version of the AUTOEXEC.BAT file used to configure an NT virtual DOS machine

NTUSER.DA_—A copy of the *System Root*\Profiles\Default-User\Ntuser.DAT file

Files with an underscore (_) in their extensions are in compressed form and can be decompressed using the expand utility. By default, the repair disk utility will *not* back up the entire SAM or security files. Use the /s switch when running this tool to get a complete backup. If you do not use this switch, your repair disk will have a default user accounts database. If you have a problem with the registry and need to restore from the ERD, you will lose all of your user account information.

To restore from the ERD, you must boot from the setup disks provided with Windows NT Server (or create a set by using the CD-ROM). On the screen that asks whether you want to install NT or repair files, type **R** to select the repair option. After that, just follow the instructions.

The repair process can do the following things:

- Inspect the registry files—Replaces existing registry files with those on the ERD. Remember that you will lose any changes that have occurred since the last time you updated the ERD.

- Inspect startup environment—Attempts to repair a BOOT.INI file that does not list NT as an option in the user boot menu.

- Verify Windows NT system files—Verifies each file in the installation against the file that was installed originally (this is what the SETUP. LOG file is used for). If it finds a file that does not match the original, it will identify the file and ask whether it should be replaced.

- Inspect boot sector—Copies a new boot sector to the disk.

Exam Essentials

Understanding the boot process is critical to troubleshooting. For the exam, you should be comfortable with the information covered for this objective.

Know the four phases of the NT boot process and what happens in each phase. The *initial phase* is mostly hardware related. The computer does a POST, reads the CMOS, finds the boot device, and reads the master boot record.

In the *boot loader phase*, NTLDR gathers information about the hardware that is needed to boot. It reads the BOOT.INI file and displays the operating system menu, runs NTDETECT.COM to discover the computer's hardware, and loads NTOSKRNL.EXE.

The NT operating system initializes in the *kernel phase*. NTOSKRNL.EXE creates the hardware registry key using the information gathered during the boot loader phase, reads the registry to find out which device drivers need to be loaded, and loads services that are marked with a start value of zero in the registry.

The *logon phase* is the last phase. The WINLOGON service starts and displays the logon box. An NT boot is not considered successful until a user logs onto the machine.

Understand the function of the BOOT.INI file. The BOOT.INI file has two sections—[boot loader] and [operating system]. The [boot loader] section contains information about defaults—how long the menu should stay on the screen before a default operating system should be chosen and where that default operating system is located. The [operating systems] section contains the choices that the user will be presented with and the location of the available operating system files.

Know the BOOT.INI command switches and what functions they perform. These switches include /basevideo, /maxmem:n, /noserial-mice, /sos, /crashdebug, /debugport, and /baudrate.

Understand the last known good configuration. The last known good configuration is a saved copy of the CurrentControlSet in use the last time NT was successfully booted. It is overwritten when a user successfully logs on during the end of the WinLogon phase. Since the configuration information within it was sufficient to log on a user, you can always use it to bypass any major errors. You can then log on and correct the problem.

Understand the process involved in creating and using the emergency repair disk (ERD).   Use the RDISK.EXE utility to create an ERD. Remember to use the /s switch to ensure that your security and account information are backed up. You use the ERD by booting to the NT setup floppies and typing **R** for repair when asked whether you want to install NT or repair files.

Key Terms and Concepts

CMOS: Configuration information stored in a nonvolatile form that is used by the computer at boot. In the current discussion, this is how the computer knows which device to boot from.

Emergency repair disk (ERD):   A floppy disk that contains replacement copies of critical system files. You can use this disk to recover from boot problems caused by the deletion or corruption of these files.

Master boot record (MBR):   A section of the boot device that contains a list of the partitions on the disk and which partition is the active partition.

Partition boot sector (PBS):   A sector of the disk that contains operating system–specific boot instructions.

Power on self test (POST):   A process run by the computer to determine the amount of memory installed and confirm the existence of required hardware.

Sample Questions

1. What are the four phases of an NT boot (in the correct order)?

   A. Initial, Boot loader, Kernel, Logon

   B. Boot loader, Initial, Kernel, Logon

   C. Boot loader, Kernel, Initial, Logon

   D. Logon, Initial, Boot loader, Kernel

   Answer: A

2. A user is given the chance to use the last known good configuration in which phase of the NT startup?

   A. Initial

   B. Boot loader

   C. Kernel

   D. Logon

   Answer: B

3. The current configuration becomes the last known good configuration at which point in the boot process?

   A. After all services have successfully loaded in the kernel phase

   B. After a user successfully logs on

   C. After the BOOT.INI file has executed

   Answer: B—An NT boot is considered successful when a user logs on at that computer. At that point, the current configuration is considered to be valid, so it is written to the last known good configuration.

Choose the appropriate course of action to take to resolve configuration errors.

Almost everything you do on an NT-based computer will access the registry. The registry contains information about your hardware settings, the drivers needed to access that hardware, your user profiles, the software you have installed, etc. Each time you boot, the registry is read from and written to in order to determine what should happen. When you run a program such as Microsoft Word, the registry is read to determine where the program is located. When you log onto the system, the registry is read to build your security context. In other words, the registry is critical to the health of your server's operating system. Both Windows NT and Windows 95 have registry files, but the keys are not identical. This is one of the principal reasons that you cannot upgrade from Window 95 to NT.

The objectives for this section involve the tools that you can use to back up the registry and edit its contents. Always remember to do these two things in *that* order—back up, then edit. Since the registry is so important, you want to always have a current backup before you make any changes to the registry.

Critical Information

Before the tasks listed in this exam objective can be discussed, what the registry is and how it is structured must be examined. The *registry* is a database that contains NT configuration information. This database is organized in a hierarchical structure that consists of subtrees and their keys, hives, and values.

NOTE   Don't be intimidated by the term *hierarchical.* You are already familiar with a hierarchical structure—the DOS file system. If you understand the directory, subdirectory, and file structure of DOS, you can understand the structure of the registry. Hierarchical structures use a series of containers and subcontainers to organize the data that they hold.

The NT registry is made up of five subtrees, each of which holds specific types of configuration information. Each subtree holds keys that contain the computer or user databases. Each key can have specific parameters and additional subkeys. The term *hive* refers to a distinct subset of a key. You can back up a hive as a single file.

It is important that you know the five main subtrees and understand the type of information that is found in each one.

HKEY_LOCAL_MACHINE—Contains hardware and operating system configuration parameters for the local computer, such as bus type, processor, device drivers, and startup information. This is the subtree that is most commonly used in the troubleshooting process for operating system errors or crashes.

HKEY_CLASSES_ROOT—Defines file associations and configuration data for COM and DCOM objects.

HKEY_CURRENT_USER—Contains the user profile for the user that is currently logged in. You will find parameters for the user's desktop, network connections, printers, and application preferences.

HKEY_USERS—Contains all actively loaded user profiles, including a copy of HKEY_CURRENT_USER.

HKEY_CURRENT_CONFIG—Contains the current hardware configuration.

Backing up and Restoring the Registry

You can back up the registry in four ways:

- Choose Save Registry in the NT Backup utility found in the Administrative Tools (Common) group. This is the preferred method if you have a tape backup unit. This method can back up and restore the registry while Windows NT is running.

- Use the two command-line tools that can also back up and restore the registry while NT is running—REGBACK.EXE and REGREST.EXE. These tools are included in the Windows NT Resource Kit.

- On the Registry menu within the registry editor, click Save Key. This process saves a single key, and everything below it, to a file. Online restorations using this method are not guaranteed, so use the backup utility whenever possible.

- Create or update your emergency repair disk. Remember to use the /s switch to ensure a complete backup.

Editing the Registry

Most of the time, you will avoid editing the registry directly—you will use various tools to adjust the configuration of your environment, and these tools will write to the registry for you. There are, however, many optimization and troubleshooting techniques that will require you to use the registry editor. You use two modes when working with the registry—backup and read-only mode.

Backing up is a simple form of protection against a moment of clumsiness. Everyone makes mistakes; the trick is to be prepared for them. The best protection against yourself is a good backup.

An option in the registry editor allows you to use read-only mode. In this mode, you can look at parameters, do your research, and know that, at the very least, you didn't inadvertently make the problem worse. After careful consideration of your options, you can then go back into the editor and make changes to the registry (after making a good backup).

Many of the troubleshooting and performance optimization techniques that have been discussed required you to make changes to the registry. By default, only members of the administrator group can change the registry; normal users are limited to read-only access. NT ships with two tools designed for manual editing of the registry database—the Windows NT registry editor (REGEDT32.EXE) and the Windows 95 registry editor (REGEDIT.EXE). While both tools allow you to edit the registry, certain keys can only be edited using the NT version.

When you edit the registry, certain changes may take effect immediately, while others might require some action on your part. In general, when you edit values in the CurrentControlSet subtree, the computer must be restarted before changes will take effect. When editing values in HKEY_CURRENT_USER, the user will often be required to log off before changes take effect.

Necessary Procedures

Almost every course in the MCSE program includes at least one example of a change that you might have to make to the registry. If you understand the process, it will make your studying easier.

Using the Registry Editor to Back Up a Key

Both the NT and Windows 95 versions of the registry editor allow you to back up the registry. They accomplish this goal in different ways—the NT version, shown below, will save each subkey as a separate file, so you have to save each of the five main hives individually.

The Windows 95 version, shown below, will allow you to save the entire registry as a single file.

Creating or Updating an Emergency Repair Disk

The emergency repair disk creation utility, RDISK, allows you to create and update a repair disk as registry changes on your NT server. Run RDISK.EXE from a command prompt. The program will ask you for a floppy disk to copy the information to. Remember to use the /s switch when running RDISK.EXE so that you get a complete backup of the registry.

Using the Registry Editor to Search the Database

Both the NT and Windows 95 version of the registry editor allow you to search the database—there is, however, a difference in functionality.

REGEDT32.EXE allows you to search for any key by name; for instance, you could search for the CurrentControlSet key. The only problem with this is that you must know the correct name of the key.

REGEDIT.EXE gives you a few more choices as to what you can search for. You can search for the actual value or data within a key. This will come in handy if you are looking for information, but don't know which subkey it is in. For example, suppose that you have a problem with a device set to interrupt 5. In the NT version, you would have to know the name of the key in which this value was stored; in the Windows 95 version, you could search for the number 5.

Using the Registry Editor to Add or Edit the Value of a Key

To add or edit the value of a key:

1. Open REGEDT32.EXE.

2. Choose Edit ➤ Add Value.

3. You will have to determine what type of data will be entered. There are five types of data:

   - REG_BINARY—Represents data as a string of binary numbers

   - REG_SZ—Represents data as a string

   - REG_EXPAND_SZ—Represents data as an expandable string

   - REG_DWORD—Represents data as a hexadecimal value with a maximum size of 4 bytes

   - REG_MULTI_SZ—Represents data as multiple strings

Unless you are a software developer, you probably will not have to determine the type of data—just the value. You will choose the type based upon information found in a manual or reference material.

Using the Registry Editor to Troubleshoot a Remote Computer

You can use the registry editor to access the registry of a remote computer. You are allowed to access the HKEY_LOCAL_MACHINE and HKEY_USERS subkeys of the remote machine. Choose Registry ➢ Select Computer.

Exam Essentials

For this exam, you are not expected to understand every detail of the registry, but you are expected to know what it is used for, how it is organized, and the processes involved in backing it up and editing its content.

Know the five main keys and understand what type of data is contained in each.   The five main keys are as follows:

- HKEY_LOCAL_MACHINE

- HKEY_CLASSES_ROOT

- HKEY_CURRENT_USER

- HKEY_USERS

- HKEY_CURRENT_CONFIG

Know the four methods of backing up the registry.   To back up the registry, use the backup tool located in the Administrative Tools (Common) group, the two command-line utilities REGBACK.EXE and REGREST.EXE from the Windows NT Resource Kit, the registry editor, or the emergency repair disk.

Know the various functions of the registry editor utility.   Reread the "Necessary Procedures" section above. Know what you can accomplish using the registry editor and how to perform those tasks.

Key Terms and Concepts

Hierarchy: A structure used to store information. The registry is a hierarchical database made up of keys and subkeys that hold values.

Hive: A subtree and its values, including any subtrees below it. Think of the hive as a branch of a tree.

Key: A subtree that contains per-computer or per-user configuration databases.

Registry: A database that contains the configuration parameters necessary for the NT operating system to function.

Value: Within the registry, a specific parameter's setting.

Sample Questions

1. Which of the five main registry subtrees holds system startup information?

   A. HKEY_LOCAL_MACHINE

   B. HKEY_CLASSES_ROOT

   C. HKEY_CURRENT_USER

   D. HKEY_USERS

   E. HKEY_CURRENT_CONFIG

   Answer: A

2. Which of the five main registry subtrees holds file association information?

   A. HKEY_LOCAL_MACHINE

   B. HKEY_CLASSES_ROOT

   C. HKEY_CURRENT_USER

   D. HKEY_USERS

   E. HKEY_CURRENT_CONFIG

   Answer: B

Choose the appropriate course of action to take to resolve printer problems.

How many times have you had to trek all the way across the building, up four flights of stairs, and through a crowded hallway, only to find a gaggle of people standing around a printer getting mad because the printer doesn't work? Once you have added paper to the printer, the users are happy, but now you are the one who is mad and frustrated.

Critical Information

Printing problems are easy to resolve if you understand the printing process. Experience has shown that printing problems fall into two basic categories—SEU (stupid end user) problems and system problems. The SEU problems are easy to solve:

- Plug in the printer.
- Turn the printer back on.
- Put paper in the printer.
- Clear the paper jam in the printer.
- Put the printer back online.
- Redirect the user to the proper printer.

Troubleshooting printing subsystem problems can be more difficult. One technique to use when troubleshooting printing problems is to generate a mental flowchart of where the print job goes. If you can figure out which step along the way is causing the problem, you can usually understand how to solve the problem.

Printing from the workstation starts when an application sends output to the software-based printer at the workstation.

NOTE Remember from Chapter 2 that an HP LaserJet 5P is not a *printer*, it is a *print device*. The printer is the software that runs at the workstation to prepare the print job.

At this point, NT checks whether the workstation has the most up-to-date version of the printer driver. If it does, all is well. If it doesn't, NT downloads a copy of the print driver from the print server to the client.

The printer sends the job to the print spooler. The client (workstation) spooler writes the data to a file and sends a remote procedure call (RPC) to the server spooler. Then, the data are transferred from the workstation to the server spooler on the print server machine.

The print server machine sends the print job to the local print provider, which translates the information into something the printer can understand, and if necessary, adds a separator page to the print job. Separator pages are used, in some cases, to signal to the printer that a change in printer languages is coming—it needs to switch from Hewlett Packard's printer control language (HP PCL) to PostScript or back again.

When the local print provider is done with the job, it sends the job to the print monitor, which sends it to the appropriate printer port and printing device.

If you remember the process, you can check each step along the way. When you find out where the print job stops, you can reset the application that should handle the next step. If the job comes out garbled, make sure the printer driver is up to date or determine whether there is a SEU problem.

Necessary Procedures

Print troubleshooting can be divided into the following key areas:

- SEU (stupid end user) problems
- Applications (non-Windows)

- Print drivers
- Spooling
- Printing speed

Troubleshooting with SEU Tricks

When a group of end users has a printing problem, you usually find out about it when your pager goes off. Here is a list of SEU tricks:

1. Is the print device plugged in? The cleaning staff chooses the most creative places to plug in vacuum cleaners.

2. Is the printer cable attached at both ends?

3. Is the print device turned on? The end user may have told you that it is turned on, but is it really?

4. Does the print device have paper in it?

5. Does the print device need toner, ink, or a ribbon?

6. Is there a paper jam?

7. Is the paper the right size for the job the user wants to print?

8. Has someone replaced the letter-size input tray with the legal-size input tray?

9. Is the print device trying to tell you something? Check the control panel for messages or flashing lights. Read the manual and find out how to solve the problem.

10. Is there really something wrong with the print device, or is the SEU just confused? If the SEU is confused, straighten them out, politely.

11. Is the print device online? Did someone try to troubleshoot it themselves by taking the print device off-line and then forget to reset it?

Troubleshooting Non-Windows-Based Applications

Non-Windows-based applications can be tricky to troubleshoot, because they change the normal print routine. Here are some things to check:

1. Each non-Windows-based application needs to have its own set of print drivers. Does this application have the right drivers?

2. Each non-Windows-based application needs to be told where to go to print. Is this application network aware, do you have to use the NET USE LPT1: command or some other method of setting up the printer port? Read the manual.

Troubleshooting Print Drivers

Print driver problems manifest in strange ways—print jobs suddenly take on odd appearances. Here are the common print driver problems:

1. A print job is submitted for a small document. Instead of receiving their document, the user receives page after page of smiley faces or other strange characters. Make sure that the user has a PCL print driver selected in the application. This is a classic case of a print job using a PostScript driver to print to a PCL printer.

2. A print job is submitted for a document. You can trace the print job all the way to the printer, but nothing comes out. Other than with this job, the printer works fine. Check the print driver. The user may be sending a job formatted with a PCL driver to a PostScript printer. PostScript will not act on a job that is not formatted with the appropriate driver.

3. A print job comes out with garbage embedded in the document, especially in graphics. Check to make sure that tabs and form feeds are turned off for the job. This is primarily applicable to jobs going to PostScript printers and is a workstation setting.

4. When you find a print driver update, the update needs to be made only at the print server. Drivers need to be updated only at the print server—the print server will distribute the job to the clients.

Troubleshooting Spooling

Spooling is the act of copying a file from one spot to another. Spoolers must be running at both the print server and the workstation.

1. If print jobs get stuck in a print spooler, stop and restart the spooler. Choose Start ➤ Settings ➤ Control Panel ➤ Services ➤ Spooler.

2. You can also stop and start the spooler using the NET START SPOOLER and NET STOP SPOOLER commands from the command line.

3. By default, print spoolers are stored in the \WINNT\System32\ Spool\Printers folder. Be sure the disk that contains this folder has plenty of free disk space. Bad things happen when you try to print a 100MB file to a print spooler that resides on a drive with only 50MB free. Change the location of the print spooler from the Advanced tab of the Server Properties dialog box.

4. You can assign a separate spooler for each printer. Enter a path for the new spooler directory in the registry. The path will act as the data for the value SpoolDirectory . The printer name is also needed. The registry entry is HKEY_LOCAL_MACHINE\System\ CurrentControlSet\Control\Print\Printers*Printer*. Be sure to stop and start the spooler so that this will take effect.

5. If the computer that houses the print spooler suffers an unexpected shutdown, the jobs that are in the spooler should print when the print spooler is restarted.

NOTE   Print jobs in the spooler are made up of two files, *.SPL and *.SHD. The file with the .SPL extension is the actual spool file—the .SHD file is a shadow file. Check the spooler directory occasionally to clean out the old, corrupted files. You can tell which ones they are by the date and time stamp.

Troubleshooting Printing Speed

A *very* common complaint of end users is the speed of the network. Here are some things you can do to remedy this situation:

1. Print spooling is a background process. NT Workstation assigns it a process priority of seven. NT Server, on the other hand, gives it a higher priority of nine, which means that it is as important as a foreground application. If your NT workstation is just a print server, increase the priority. To change the priority, add a value called PriorityClass of type REG_DWORD to HKEY_LOCAL_ MACHINE\System\CurrentControlSet\Control\Print and set it with the priority class you desire.

TIP Priority is a funny thing—what you give to one, you take away from another.

---

2. Many times, third-party print servers are faster than NT-based print servers. Printers that have a built-in network card are usually the fastest providers.

NOTE One common printer manufacturer (Hewlett Packard) requires that the dynamic link control (DLC) protocol is installed so that a network interface can communicate with the rest of the system.

Exam Essentials

Printing is a favorite topic of the exam writers. The questions they ask sometimes don't have obvious solutions, so make sure to understand the following material.

Know that HP (Hewlett Packard) is different. Depending on which HP print device you use, it may require that the dynamic link control (DLC) protocol is loaded when you have a printer with an integrated network interface card. If, during installation, you do not see an option to install a port for the printer, DLC is not installed. Check the manual to see whether DLC must be loaded. On the exam, if the question mentions HP and not DLC, be suspicious.

Know that HP is different (part two). Suppose that DLC is loaded at the workstation and at the printer, and you still cannot print. Using the HP utilities, check whether another computer is attached to the print device using continuous-connection mode. If that is the case, the other user is hogging all of your resources.

Know what happens when a printer jams. If a job has been submitted and the printer jams, you can restart the document by going into the Printers folder and choosing Documents ➤ Restart.

Know what happens when a printer jams in a printer pool. If one printer of a printer pool jams, the job that is printing at the time of the jam will be held at that printer until the jam has been cleared. Other jobs will be routed to different printers in the pool.

Key Terms and Concepts

DLC (dynamic link control):   A protocol that is necessary to manage HP printers that have onboard network interface cards.

Print device: The hardware that puts the ink on the paper.

Print driver: The software component that allows the print devices to interface with the operating system.

Print server: A computer to which printers are attached and that is connected to the network.

Print spooler: Temporary holding areas for print jobs. Print spooler files are stored in the \WINNT\System32\Spool\Printers folder.

Printer: A software applet that runs at the client workstation. The printer takes the print job from the applications, and prepares it to traverse the system and come out as ink on paper at the print device.

Printing pool: A number of print devices that are connected to the same printer. The printer directs the print job to an available print device in the pool.

Sample Questions

1. Suppose that a user is installing a new HP print device on the network. The print device has it own network interface card. When the user tries to configure the device, they find that there is no

option to install a port for the printer. What is the most common cause of this situation?

A. The printer is corrupted.

B. The print spooler has some corrupted file in it.

C. The print driver needs to replaced.

D. This device uses both PCL and PostScript printing. Therefore, it doesn't need a printer port.

E. The DLC protocol is not configured on the workstation the user is using for a print server.

Answer: E—The most common cause of not being able to "talk" with an HP print device is the lack of a data link control (DLC) protocol configured at the print server. HP uses the DLC protocol to communicate with its print devices.

2. Suppose that a user has a big report due in the morning. They are trying to print that report to an HP printer that has an onboard network interface card using the DLC protocol. DLC is currently installed and working on their computer. Even after the user resets the printer, they still cannot print to it. What is the most likely cause of the problem?

A. The user isn't sending their print job to the HP printer; they are using a printer on a different floor.

B. The printer is out of paper.

C. Somewhere on the network, there is another computer hooked to the printer using DLC in continuous-connection mode.

D. The print device is currently servicing an Apple computer and will come back online when it is finished with the Apple print job.

Answer: C—If DLC is being used by another computer on the network in continuous-connection mode, no other system can connect to the printer.

3. A print job appears to be stuck in the print spooler. What should you do?

A. Sounds like lunch time!

B. Stop and restart the print spooler.

C. Go into the \WINNT\System32\Spool\Printers folder and delete all the files that are in the spooler, and then resend the job.

D. Turn the printer off and back on to reboot it.

Answer: B—If the print job becomes stuck, a quick fix is to stop and restart the print spooler. Investigate the size of the spooler file capacity and compare it to the total size of the print jobs being sent to it.

Choose the appropriate course of action to take to resolve RAS problems.

What is more frustrating than bringing a laptop home, getting set to do some work, dialing in, and not getting connected? You can take some actions to minimize this frustration.

Critical Information

When you troubleshoot remote access service problems, there is always two sides to the issue. You may know that your side is correct, but if the other side isn't configured exactly the same as your side, you are simply not going to talk. As a network administrator, the task is even more frustrating, because you are working with end users who are working with configurable software, cables, IRQs, internal or external modems, etc.—the list of things they can screw up is practically endless. Some common troubleshooting tools for RAS connections will be examined in the next section.

Necessary Procedures

Every administrator has their own troubleshooting style. One approach is to start from the wall and work back.

Troubleshooting Dialing Problems

Before you can establish modem communications, you have to be able to dial the phone. Here are some simple things to look for:

1. Does the phone line actually work? Is there an analog telephone you can plug into the line to make sure that there is a dial tone?

NOTE This sounds like common sense, but it is often the really simple things that haunt you. You can spend a long time reinstalling the modem, checking the connections, verifying the ports—only to find out that there was no carrier to begin with.

---

2. Now that you know there is a real phone line on the other side of the jack, are you sure the cable is good? Often, you use a different cable for your modem than you do for the phone. Replace the phone cable with your cable, if possible, and retest for a dial tone.

3. So, there is a real phone line running through your phone cable— plug the cable into your modem and try again.

4. If you still don't have a connection, start checking modem connections. If it is an internal modem, is it firmly in the slot? Did you screw it down? If so, unscrew it and reseat the card. Is it an external modem? Are the cables tight to the modem and the PC? Does the modem have power? Is the modem turned on? Is the modem working properly? Is it installed properly?

5. Is RAS installed properly? Have you selected Receive Calls Only? Have you selected Dial Out Only? Can you dial out with another simple terminal program such as HyperDialer?

Troubleshooting Connection Problems

Troubleshooting connection problems can be frustrating. Many different settings can get changed and mess up the works.

1. Are you dialing the right phone number?

2. Are both computers using the same type of authentication?

3. Are both sides of the conversation using the same protocols from within RAS?

4. Does the user account have dial-in privileges and is the call-back feature properly set?

5. Did you verify the user name, password, and domain name when dialing in?

6. If your user can dial in, appears to connect, and then gets disconnected after authentication, did you try to enable RAS logging? When in doubt, check the log file, DEVICE.LOG.

Exam Essentials

As you study this section, concentrate on where things are and how to get to them.

Know where the DEVICE.LOG file is kept. DEVICE.LOG is kept in the \Winnt\System32\RAS directory.

Sample Questions

1. All else has failed—it is time to read the log. Where are entries made for RAS logging?

    A. WINNT\DEVICE.LOG

    B. WINNT\System32\RAS.LOG

    C. WINNT\System32\RAS\DEVICE.LOG

    D. WINNT\System32\RAS\Ras.LOG

    Answer: C—The RAS log is kept in the WINNT\System32\RAS\ DEVICE.LOG file.

2. How do you view the RAS log?

    A. Use Event Viewer

    B. Use a text editor

C. Only through Word

D. Only through WordPerfect

Answer: A—The RAS log is viewed through the Event Viewer.

3. Your RAS connection is using call back with multilink over a regular phone line. How many numbers can you configure RAS to call back per call?

A. Unlimited

B. 1

C. 3

D. 5

E. 7

Answer: B—RAS can be configured to call back only one number using call back. Multilink is disabled when call back is set.

Choose the appropriate course of action to take to resolve connectivity problems.

Troubleshooting connectivity problems can be a complex process. At least two computers could be the cause of the trouble, not to mention the network components between them. In this section, assume that the problem is a configuration issue on an NT-based server.

In reality, before you start troubleshooting your NT configuration, you should ensure that the network is functioning properly. Luckily, this is usually an easy task. If two computers are having problems communicating, the first step is to see if *any* computers can communicate. Pick a computer on the same physical network and try to connect from there. If you can successfully attach, the problem is probably a configuration issue. If you cannot connect, you should begin by troubleshooting your network components, such as the wiring, routers, and other physical aspects of your network. Determine whether your outage is system wide or just located on a network segment.

Once you have determined that the problem is confined to a particular computer, you can begin the process of troubleshooting its configuration. To do this, you must understand the networking architecture of Microsoft Windows NT.

Critical Information

Both user-mode and kernel-mode network components are in the NT architecture. Like the rest of the operating system, the network components are modular—distinct components perform each network function. If you understand the architecture, it makes troubleshooting easier. Once you have analyzed the symptoms of the problem, you can usually determine which components are involved.

The discussion will begin with the components at the network interface card and work up to the user-mode components. The overall structure of the NT networking architecture is shown in Figure 6.1.

F I G U R E 6.1: NT architecture

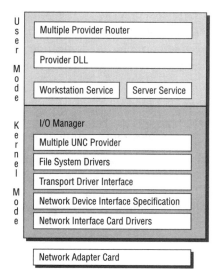

Network Interface Card (NIC) Drivers

Each type of NIC installed in your server will have a specific driver associated with it. The driver should be NDIS (network device interface specification) 4 compliant. (NDIS 3 compatible drivers will still work on an NT 4 server, but it is recommended that newer drivers be used.)

NDIS is a specification that defines how a NIC driver should communicate with the adapter, the protocols, and the operating system. Specifically, NDIS is a library of network functions that are predefined for NIC driver developers. NDIS acts as an interface layer between the driver and card, submits requests to the operating system, and allows the network drivers to receive and send packets independent of the operating system.

Typical problems at this layer of the architecture include corrupt, out-of-date, or missing drivers. Microsoft certifies all of the drivers found on the NT CD-ROM and those available for download from their Web sites. If you are using a card that is not on the hardware compatibility list, you should contact the manufacturer to determine whether they have an NT 4 driver.

Transport Protocols

The various protocols that can be used on an NT network were discussed earlier. Each of these protocols has its own tools and techniques for troubleshooting communication problems. Some of the more commonly used tools are described in Table 6.1.

T A B L E 6.1: Tools for Troubleshooting Protocols

Protocol	Troubleshooting Tool or Technique
TCP/IP	• PING the address of the remote computer. • Use IPCONFIG /ALL to check the IP configuration of the local computer. • Use IPROUTE to check the routing table.

T A B L E 6.1: Tools for Troubleshooting Protocols *(cont.)*

Protocol	Troubleshooting Tool or Technique
NWLink	• To check the IPX configuration of the local computer, type **IPXROUTE CONFIG** at a command prompt. • To view the SAP table, type **IPXROUTE SERVERS** at a command prompt. • To view the routing table, type **IPXROUTE TABLE** at a command prompt.
NetBIOS and AppleTalk	Neither of these protocols has a set of configuration tools. To troubleshoot these protocols, use Network Monitor to capture and analyze traffic.

Transport Driver Interface (TDI)

The TDI acts as the interpreter between the protocols and redirectors, and services above them. From a developer's perspective, the TDI acts as a common interface between these two layers. This makes writing NT networking modules easier, since the APIs (application programming interfaces) are well documented.

The server has a specific set of services that it can provide, but each protocol will ask for those services in a different way. The TDI is the interpreter because each transport protocol knows how to talk to it, and it knows how to talk to each of the services.

File System Drivers

The file system drivers are above the TDI. NT supports peer-to-peer networking, so NT Server and NT Workstation provide server services. All of the network server and redirector modules are written as file system drivers. From a developer's perspective, this makes writing networked applications easier—if the program needs to open a file, it can make the same sort of call whether the file is local or remote.

Redirectors

Redirectors provide the ability to access remote computer resources. The Windows NT system redirector allows access to Windows NT, Windows for Workgroups, LAN Manager, LAN Server, and a few other types of servers. When you design the redirector as file system drivers, it allows applications to make the same sort of call for local and remote files. The redirector runs in kernel mode, so it can take advantage of other kernel-mode modules (such as the cache manager) to increase performance; it can be dynamically loaded and unloaded; and it can coexist with other redirectors.

In addition to the NT redirector, some redirectors are used to connect to other operating systems, such as Novell NetWare and Banyan Vines. This is the true benefit of using a modular design—you can add functionality as needed.

Server Service

The server service also acts as a file system driver. It handles incoming requests for files from the network. It is composed of the following components: SRV.SYS and LanmanServer.

Multiple UNC (Universal Naming Convention) Provider (MUP)

The MUP handles requests for files that have names following the UNC standard. In the UNC standard, names begin with a double backslash (\\), which indicates that the resource exists on the network. The MUP receives these requests and recognizes that the requested resource is remote. It then passes the request to each registered redirector until one recognizes the requested name.

Multiple Provider Router (MPR)

One of the registered redirectors that the MUP will hand requests to is the MPR. The MPR is specifically designed to handle requests that do not follow the UNC standard. It is made up of a series of provider .DLLs that provide the ability to communicate with a foreign system, such as NetWare or Banyan Vines.

Resolving Connectivity Problems

Now that the various components that make up the networking environment of the NT operating system have been examined, the objective for this section—how to resolve connectivity problems—can be discussed. Actually, given all of the discussion that led up to this, the resolution process is fairly straightforward.

Most communication problems will revolve around configuration errors rather than problems with specific software modules. The only two software components that might cause problems are the NIC driver and the third-party-provider .DLL files. The solution for either type of problem is simple—install a new copy, preferably the latest available version.

Troubleshooting configuration issues relies upon your knowledge of the various protocols in use on your network. The steps are simple, though:

1. Determine whether the problem is the transport protocol—for instance, if you are using TCP/IP, try using the PING utility to communicate. If this works, you can move up the OSI layers to the next step.

2. Test the NetBIOS connection by using a NET command. At a command line, type **NET VIEW** *Server Name*. This should return a list of all shared resources on that server. If it does, the problem is probably application related.

Exam Essentials

Networking is a complex yet critical piece of most NT environments. It is essential that you know the components involved and how they interact. For the exam, you should concentrate on the following items.

Know the tools used to troubleshoot protocol-related problems. For this examination, a detailed understanding of each protocol is not required. However, it is assumed that you do at least have a firm grasp on the fundamentals. See Table 6.1 for details.

Understand the function of a redirector. A redirector is a software component that provides the ability to access remote resources. Microsoft Windows NT ships with a system redirector that allows communication with each of the Microsoft network–capable operating systems (Windows for Workgroups, Windows 95, and Windows NT), as well as LAN Manager and LAN Server. Other redirectors are used to access foreign systems such as Novell NetWare and Banyan Vines.

Understand the function of the multiple UNC provider (MUP). The MUP accepts requests in which the resource name adheres to the UNC standard. It passes the request to each register's redirector until one of them accepts it.

Understand the function of the multiple provider router (MPR). The MPR handles requests for resources in which the name does not follow the UNC standard. Usually, this will be a request for resources on a server not running Windows NT, such as a Novell NetWare server. The MPR manages a series of DLLs that are designed to talk to foreign servers.

Know the two-step process for troubleshooting connectivity problems. First, determine whether the problem is the transport protocol. Most protocols include a utility to test the ability to communicate, such as the PING utility for TCP/IP. Second, test the NetBIOS connection by using a NET command to access the remote computer.

Key Terms and Concepts

File system driver: Software designed to provide access to a file system. While this definition might seem simplistic and obvious, it is important to understand that this is really all a file system driver is for.

Multiple protocol router (MPR): A user-mode component designed to route requests to resources that do not adhere to the UNC conventions.

Multiple UNC provider (MUP): A user-mode component that interprets UNC names, passing them along to the proper redirector.

Network interface card drivers: Software designed to allow communication between the physical network interface card and the operating system.

Redirector: A file system driver designed to allow access to remote resources.

Transport drive interface (TDI): A component of the Windows NT networking architecture designed to act as an interpreter between the protocols and the redirectors.

Universal naming convention (UNC): An industry standard method of naming resources on the network. All names begin with two backslashes (\\) to indicate a network resource.

Sample Questions

1. Which of the following items accepts and handles network requests that use UNC names?

    A. MUP

    B. MPR

    C. TDI

    Answer: A—MUP stands for multiple UNC provider.

2. Which of the following items accepts and handles requests not formatted using a UNC name?

    A. MUP

    B. MPR

    C. TDI

    Answer: B—MPR stands for multiple provider router.

3. Which of the following utilities is used to test a connection between TCP/IP hosts?

    A. IPXROUTE

    B. IPCONFIG

    C. PING

Answer: C

Choose the appropriate course of action to take to resolve resource access and permission problems.

Permission and resource access problems are usually pretty straightforward. They involve a yes-or-no decision—someone either can or cannot do something to something. If a user is supposed to be able to use a printer and cannot, you have a resource access problem. If a user is supposed to be able to write to a file and cannot, you have a permission problem. The tricky part comes when you try to figure out where the problem lies.

Critical Information

In the case of resource access or permission problems, it is simple to locate the problem. Finding the solution can be more difficult. For example, the problem may be that people cannot access a resource because they cannot log on. Is that a hardware, software, network, or, most likely, an SEU (stupid end user) problem?

Necessary Procedures

Your pager has beeped. You answer the call—it is a frantic end user or help-desk operator. Something isn't working! What do you do now?

Troubleshooting Resource Access and Permission Problems

When a user calls and says that they cannot access the system or a resource:

1. Ask questions. Is it just one person, or is there more than one person involved? What resource is it? Is it a hardware problem; is the printer shut off?

2. If the user cannot log on, make sure that the user is attached to the right domain, is using the right logon name, has the caps-lock key set properly to on or off (*PASSWORD* is not the same as *password*), and is supposed to be on during that time.

3. If the user cannot access a resource, can you access the resource using a different account? If so, you now have a permission problem.

4. When you have determined that the access problem is due to a permission rather than a hardware problem, the next step is to determine how the user was *supposed* to be able to access the account. Were the permissions to be assigned to a group? Can the rest of the group access the resource? If the rest of the group can access the resource, the problem lies with the individual and the group or user memberships they have been given.

TIP Be very suspicious of the no-access permission. If a user belongs to a group that is given no access to a resource, that user will not gain access to the resource, no matter what other group membership they enjoy.

---

5. Make sure that the user is spelling the name of the resource correctly. You would be surprised how fast fingered some users can be, and it is amazing how long you can look at **www.micorsoft.com** before realizing that it is not the same as **www.microsoft.com**.

6. If no one can log on, has the NetLogon service stopped? Check it by going to Start ➣ Settings ➣ Control Panel ➣ Services. While you are there, check the Server and Workstation service.

7. If this is a new server and has never been brought online before, it may not be communicating with the outside world. Check the protocol bindings and make sure you are talking the same languages as everyone else. You can check bindings by choosing Start ➤ Settings ➤ Control Panel ➤ Network.

8. Rights and permissions will take effect the next time the user logs on. If it is a new assignment, have the user log off and then on again.

9. The last place to look is the system policy editor. Is there a new system policy for the user or the user's computer?

10. Is the resource a directory subjected to both NTFS and share permissions?

Exam Essentials

Rights and permissions are favorite topics of the exam writers. Be sure that you understand how the no-access permission can make lives miserable.

Know that the most restrictive rights and permissions are the ones that apply. When you look at the rights and permissions that a user has been granted, take into account all groups the user belongs to, as well as the individual user assignments. The most restrictive rights apply.

Know the impact of the no-access assignment. If a user has been given no-access permissions to a file, folder, or share, that permission will override all others. So, the user TMENDAL may have full control through his membership in the ADMIN group, read access through his membership in the Management group, and no access through his membership in the Accounting group—TMENDAL would be out of luck. No access would override all other permissions.

Know when rights and permissions take effect. A user must log off and then on again to generate a new security identifier (SID). Once the new SID access control list (ACL) has been generated, the new rights or permissions will take effect.

Key Terms and Concepts

SID (security identifier):   Code generated to identify a specific user or group to the NT security subsystem.

Sample Questions

1. The user TMENDAL has full control of a folder through his membership in the ADMIN group, read access through his membership in the Management group, and no access through his membership in the Accounting group. TMENDAL calls and says that he cannot see anything in the folder. How do you solve TMENDAL's problem?

   A. Tell TMENDAL to deal with it.

   B. Grant the group Everyone read access to the folder.

   C. Remove TMENDAL from his membership in the Accounting group.

   D. Copy the information from the folder into a folder TMENDAL can access.

   Answer: C—When you remove TMENDAL from the Accounting group, it will remove the no-access permissions and allow him to see items in the folder.

2. TMENDAL is having a *bad* day. After you removed him from the Accounting group, he still cannot see anything in the folder. Why not?

   A. TMENDAL is a SEU.

   B. You didn't really remove him from the Accounting group.

   C. It isn't midnight, yet. All changes take effect at midnight.

   D. TMENDAL has not logged out and back on to generate a new SID ACL.

   Answer: D—TMENDAL needs to log out and then back on. This will generate a new SID ACL, giving him the rights to access the files.

Choose the appropriate course of action to take to resolve fault-tolerance failures. Fault-tolerance methods include:

- Tape backup
- Mirroring
- Stripe set with parity
- Disk duplexing

Fault tolerance is defined as a system designed so that the failure of one component will not affect functionality. Fault-tolerance failures will not be discussed, because that phrase implies that the fault tolerance itself did not work. The steps involved in reinstating a fault-tolerant state after a component failure has caused the system to switch over to the redundant mechanism will be examined.

Of the three subobjectives, only two really deal with fault tolerance. A tape backup is not fault tolerant in the sense that server functionality is not affected by a failure. When you are forced to use your tape backup to recover from a critical failure, there will be a lapse in network services. Tape backups just allow you to re-create your system from archived data. Those data are only as fresh as the last time you backed them up—any data saved since that time will have to be re-created.

It is fairly easy to calculate the hourly cost of network downtime—count the number of people who rely upon the network to perform their job and multiply that number by an average hourly salary. The resulting figure is the tangible cost per hour of interrupted service. This number does not, however, include the intangibles that are so important in today's competitive market—such as the revenues lost when a client cannot get the service they expect and take their business elsewhere.

Critical Information

As discussed earlier, Microsoft places a lot of emphasis on the various fault-tolerance technologies on NT. Recovery from a failure is part of that emphasis.

Tape Backup

No matter what business you are in, you need a way to archive your data against loss due to hardware failure, user error, and acts of nature. The most cost-effective technology available today is tape backups. While the intent is different, tape backups offer a few advantages over the disk-based fault-tolerance technologies discussed in earlier chapters:

- The hardware and media are fairly inexpensive.

- Tapes can be stored off-site to protect against theft, fire, or flood.

- Tapes can be used for long-term archival of data. Disk-based technology is usually too expensive for long-term storage.

- A backup freezes data at a specific point. If you want an earlier version of a file, retrieve it from one of your older tapes.

- Tapes can be used to protect against mistakes when making changes to your environment. With a disk-based solution, your data are vulnerable when you are working on the server.

Most companies have a tape backup process in place. Many of those companies, however, have no plan of action in the event of a critical failure. The LAN administrators can retrieve files from the tape, but have no idea of the steps involved in recovering a complete server.

This exam objective requires you to understand the basics of server recovery from a tape backup.

1. Fix whatever physical problem is forcing the recovery. This is the step that is ignored most often when administrators put together a disaster recovery plan. If the problem is a hard drive failure, you should know which vendors to call for a replacement part and

what the average turnaround time is on delivery. If your local vendor cannot deliver replacement parts within an acceptable amount of time, consider a contract with a company that guarantees their turnaround time. You should have a plan for the replacement of every critical piece of hardware on your network.

2. The next step will depend upon what piece of hardware has failed. If the disk that died is your boot device, you will have to reinstall the operating system and the partitions that existed before the disaster.

3. After the operating system is up and running, recover the registry from your backup set. Remember that any changes that were made since the backup was created will be lost. Be sure to re-create those changes before continuing with the recovery process.

4. Restore the data from your tape. Remember to check the option that restores file permissions. Once again, the tape will not contain any data created since the backup was done. Have someone from each department verify which data will have to be reentered.

The steps involved in the restoration of your data will depend upon the type of backups that you are doing. There are three main techniques for data backup:

Full backup—Each time a backup is performed, the entire server is backed up. While this method of backing up your server will take the longest amount of time, it is the easiest to use for recovery. To restore you server, just use the latest available backup tape.

Incremental backup—When using the incremental method of backup, first perform a full backup. Each evening after that, you back up only the data that have changed since the day before. This form of backup takes the least time to perform each evening, but can be the most confusing and time-consuming method of backup from which to recover. To recover, you must first restore the full backup, and then each tape, in order, since the full backup was performed.

Differential backup—Once again, start by performing a full backup. Each evening, back up all data that have changed since that full backup. The length of time that it takes to accomplish this will increase each evening until it makes sense to do another full backup and start the process again. Recovery is fairly straight-forward—first, restore the full backup, and then restore the last differential tape.

As you can see, a full recovery from tape backups can be a lengthy process. This is why most consultants suggest using both tape backups and one of the disk-based fault-tolerance technologies. The tape is used to recover from major problems (fire, flood, tornado, etc.), while a fault-tolerant disk system can protect against the more common problem of hard disk failure.

Mirroring

As discussed in Chapter 1, disk mirroring is a software-controlled fault-tolerance system that results in two disks containing the same data. If one disk fails, the other will continue to function and users will not experience any downtime. A subset of mirroring, called duplexing, provides even more redundancy by physically connecting the two disks to two different controller boards. Duplexing not only protects against a disk drive failure, it also provides redundant cabling and controllers.

Since NT's boot and system partitions can be mirrored, this process is used extensively in today's business environments. For this exam objective, you need to know how to reinstate the mirrored state if one of the disks fails.

Correct this problem in the Disk Administration utility found in the Administrative Tools (Common) group. It is a three-step process:

1. Break the mirror set.

2. Install the replacement hard drive.

3. Reboot and re-create the mirrored set.

The operating system will then copy the data from the existing drive to the new one. However, if the primary drive of the mirror set is the one that failed, it requires the extra step of rebooting the computer with a floppy disk containing a modified BOOT.INI file.

Stripe Set with Parity

As discussed in Chapter 1, a stripe set with parity is a software-controlled fault-tolerance disk system in which a series of disks are seen as one logical drive. Each time data are written to this logical drive, the operating system calculates parity information, which is stored on another physical disk in the set. You can use the parity information to re-create the data if one of the disks in the set fails.

When one of the disks in the set dies, the system will automatically begin using the parity information. In this way, the data are still available to users, although there is a performance cost—the data must be rebuilt from the parity information. The process of rebuilding the data can take a large amount of processor time and will usually decrease performance.

The steps to rebuild the stripe set with parity are as follows:

1. Replace the dead drive. On some of the more advanced servers, you can do this while the server is still running; otherwise, you will have to down your server for the installation of the new drive.

2. In the Disk Administrator utility, select the stripe set with parity. Control-click an area of free space (on your new drive), and then choose Fault Tolerance ➤ Regenerate. The regeneration process will not begin until you restart your server.

NOTE   If you have a system with hot-swappable drives (a system that allows the installation of new drives while the server is running), you should be aware of two things. First, your system probably has hardware-controlled RAID technology. Since hardware-controlled RAID is faster than software-controlled RAID, you should implement the manufacturer's version and read the manual for your server to learn about the recovery process. Second, if for some reason you do use NT's stripe set with parity technology, be aware that when you install the new drive and finish the recovery process, the system will not begin rebuilding the data on the new drive until you restart the server. This process will add a tremendous amount of overhead to your server.

Disk Duplexing

Disk duplexing is a subset of mirroring. The only difference is that in a duplexed system, the two drives are attached to different disk controllers. On a mirrored system, if one disk dies, the other takes over with no interruption of service. If the controller fails, however, there is no way to get to the data on either disk.

In a duplexed system, if a controller fails, the other hard drive in the mirrored set is still active. The second controller can still access the redundant disk. Basically, you have extended the fault tolerance to the next piece of hardware—the controller.

Another advantage of duplexing is performance. In a mirrored system, each time data are written to disk, the operating system must first write to one drive and then the other. This is often referred to as a serial procedure. In a duplexed system, the operating system can write to both disks simultaneously, reducing the overall time it takes to write data to disk. This is often referred to as a parallel process.

To create a duplexed system, set up a mirrored set using Disk Administrator. A mirrored set is automatically considered to be duplexed if the two disks are attached to separate controllers. You will not see the term *duplex* in any of the menu choices.

To recover from a disk failure in the duplexed set, follow the same procedure for recovering from a failure in a mirrored set—break the mirror, install the new hardware, and re-create the mirror.

Necessary Procedures

The following procedures are stressed on the MCSE exam. It is critical that you know how to recover from component failures in a fault-tolerant system.

Breaking the Mirrored Set

To break the mirrored set:

1. Highlight the mirrored partitions in the Disk Administrator utility.

2. Choose Fault Tolerance ➤ Break Mirror.

Re-creating the Mirrored Set

To re-create the mirrored set:

1. In Disk Administrator, Ctrl-click the two partitions of equal size.

2. Choose Fault Tolerance ➤ Establish Mirror.

Regenerating a Stripe Set with Parity

To regenerate a stripe set with parity:

1. Install the new hard disk.

2. In Disk Administrator, Ctrl-click the stripe set and an area of free space.

3. Choose Fault Tolerance ➤ Regenerate.

4. Restart the server.

Exam Essentials

The real "exam essentials" for this objective are found above in the "Necessary Procedures" section. Before you continue, be sure that you are comfortable with the following items.

Understand the steps involved to recover a server from a tape backup. Fix the physical problem. Next, reinstall the operating system and restore the registry. Finally, restore the data (remember to choose the option that restores file permissions).

Know the three methods of backup. The methods are full, incremental, and differential.

Know how to use each type of backup in a full recovery. For a full backup, restore the entire tape. For an incremental backup, restore the full backup and then each of the tapes made since that full backup. For a differential backup, restore the full backup and then the last tape made.

Know the process used to reestablish a mirrored set if a disk fails. Break the mirror, install the new disk, and re-create the mirror.

Know the steps involved in recovering from a failed disk in a stripe set with parity. See the "Necessary Procedures" section above for details.

Know the difference between mirroring and duplexing. Mirroring and duplexing are fault-tolerant disk configurations in which two disks contain the same data. The only difference is that in a duplexed system, the two disks are attached to different controllers.

Key Terms and Concepts

Differential backup: A backup system that starts with a full backup and is followed with daily backups of the data that have changed since then.

Full backup: A tape of the entire contents of a server.

Incremental backup: A backup system that starts with a full backup and is followed with tapes of the data that have changed each day.

Regenerate: To rebuild data on a replacement disk in a stripe set with parity.

Sample Questions

1. When restoring from a backup tape, which method requires you to restore the last full backup and each tape since the last full backup?

    A. Full backup method

    B. Incremental

    C. Differential

    Answer: B—In the incremental backup method, you first perform a full backup, and then each day back up only data that have changed. This means that you must first restore the last full backup and then each tape created since then.

2. When using the differential backup method, which of the following statements describes the restoration process?

   A. Restore the full backup.

   B. Restore the full backup and then each tape created since that date.

   C. Restore the full backup and the last tape created.

   Answer: C—The differential method includes a full backup and then daily backups of everything that has changed since that full backup. This results in there being only two tapes necessary for the restoration.

3. Which of the following statements describes the method used to recover from the failure of one disk in a mirrored set?

   A. Install the new disk and the system will automatically remirror.

   B. Break the mirroring using Disk Administrator, install the new disk, and create the mirrored set.

   C. Install the new disk and restore the data from backup tape.

   Answer: B—If a disk in a mirrored set fails, you must break the mirrored set and re-create it.

Index

Note to the Reader: First level entries are in bold. Page numbers in bold indicate the principal discussion of a topic or the definition of a term. Page numbers in *italic* indicate illustration.

A

Access Through Share Permissions dialog box, *205*
account lockout feature, 173
Account Policy dialog box, *172*
accounts. *See also* user and group accounts
administering security policies for, 171–174, 180
Administrator, 166
auditing changes to user account database, 174
deleting user, 178
expiring and reactivating, 180
global user, **165–166,** *167,* 175–177
Guest, 166
local user, 165
password lockout feature, 173
activating disk counters, 270, 276
adapters. *See* network adapters
Add to Chart dialog box, *265*
Administrator account, 166
Alert view (Performance Monitor), 266
Apple Macintosh as client, 155–159
AppleTalk connectivity, 323
applications
implementing permissions and security for, 204
printer problems for non-Windows–based, 311–312
ARC paths
components of, 10, 130
numbering partitions and, 8–10, *9,* 129–130
reading, **17,** 136
Assign Drive Letter dialog box, *15, 129*
ATS permissions, 222
audit policy, 180
Audit Policy dialog box, *174*
auditing
changes to user account database, 174
files
establishing, 211, 220–222, 223
system actions and, 208

B

backup browser, 103, 110
backup domain controllers. *See* BDC
backups
creating or updating an Emergency Repair Disk, 297–298, 300, 305, 307
last known good configuration, **297–298,** 299
methods of, 338
of registry, 303, 307
tape, 333–335
using Registry Editor to back up a key, 305, 307
BDC (backup domain controllers)
difference between PDC and, 55
selecting necessary hardware for, **49–51**
synchronization parameters in registry, **53–54**
synchronizing, **51–53,** *55*
boot failures, 290–301
BOOT.INI file, **294–297,** 299
error messages for, 296–297
example of, 294–295
switches for, 295–296
exam essentials for, 298–300
glossary for, 300
last known good configuration, **297–298,** 299
NT boot phases, **291–294,** 299
overview, 290–291
sample questions for, 300–301
BOOT.INI file, **294–297**
creating FAT partitions for, 11
error messages for, 296–297
exam essentials for, 299
example of, 294–295
switches for, 295–296
bottlenecks. *See* performance bottlenecks
browsers
participating in browser elections, **108–109**
types of, 110
busmaster controllers, 5

C

caching controllers, 6
CAL (client access license), 99
callback modes, 246, 257
carrier lines, 318
CD-ROM
    media failures during installation, 288
    over-the-network installation from,
      61–62
    recreating install diskettes from, 59–61
changing order of protocol bindings, 157
Chart view (Performance Monitor), 265,
    265, 266
client access license (CAL), 99
client computers, **155–159**
    administering remote servers from,
      193–197
    changing binding order of protocols, 157
    exam essentials for, 157
    glossary for, 158–159
    operating system protocols and services,
      155–157
    overview, 155
    sample questions for, 159
Client Service for NetWare (CSNW), 230
command-line switches
    for \i386\WINNT.EXE, 73
    for BOOT.INI file, 295–296
    for COMPACT.EXE, 215
    functions of during installation, 60–61
    for NT Installation Wizard, 40
communication devices, 117–118, *118*
communications. *See* connectivity
COMPACT.EXE command-line switches, 215
Compress Data checkbox (Advanced Con-
    nections Settings dialog box), 118
compressing
    command-line switches for
      COMPACT.EXE, 215
    a file, folder, or drive, 213–215, 222
Computer Browser Services, 102–104
    defined, 96
    types of browsers, 102–103
CONFIG.POL file
    location of, 190
    saving system policy information to, 186
configuration errors, 301–308
    adding or editing key values with Registry
      Editor, 306, 307

backing up and restoring the registry,
    303, 307
creating or updating an Emergency Repair
    Disk, 305, 307
editing the registry, 303–304, 307
overview, 301–303
searching the database with Registry
    Editor, 306, 307
troubleshooting on remote computers
    with Registry Editor, 307
using Registry Editor to back up a key,
    305, 307
Configure Gateway dialog box, *234*
configuring. *See also* configuration errors;
installing and configuring
    client computers, 155–159
    computer for participation in browser
      elections, 108–109
    dial-up networking clients, 248–249,
      256–257
    Directory Replicator service, *105*
    disk drives, **3–19**
    exam objectives for installing and, 36–37
    export server, 105–106, *106*
    hard disks, **127–138**
    import computer, 106–108, *107*
    local printing device, 144–149, *144, 146,*
      147, 148
    modems, 124
    multiple adapters, 89, **90–93,** *92*
    NetBEUI protocol for RAS support, 244
    network adapters, **87–95**
    PPP, 243, 258
    printers, **139–154**
    protocols and protocol bindings, **76–87**
    RAS
      communications, 240–242
      connectivity, 239–260
      protocols, **242–244,** 252–254, *252, 253*
      security, 245–248, *245*
      support for TCP/IP protocol, 243–244
    replication service, **104–105,** *105*
    SCSI devices, 124
    servers, **48–58**
    SLIP, 243, 258
    tape device drivers, 120–121, *121*
    TDI, 242
    UPS, 125
connectivity, 228–260
    configuring RAS, 239–260

communications, 240–242,
250–251, *251*
dial-up networking clients, 248–249,
256–257
overview, 239–240
protocols, 242–244, 252–254, *252, 253*
security, 245–248, *245*, 254–256,
254, 255
exam essentials
for configuring RAS, 257–258
for NetWare networks, 236–237
exam objectives for, 228
glossary
configuring RAS, 258
for NetWare networks, 237–238
for NetWare networks, 229–238
gateway service for NetWare,
230–231, 233–235, *233*
migration tool for NetWare, 231–232,
235–236, *235*
overview, 229
overview, 228–229
sample questions
for configuring RAS, 260
for NetWare networks, 238
troubleshooting, **317–328**
file system drivers, 323
MPR, 324, 326
MUP, 324, 326
NIC drivers, 322
NT server architecture, 321
overview, 320–321
RAS, 317–320
redirectors, 324, 326
resolving, 325
server service, 324
TDI, 323
transport protocols, 322–323
controllers, **4–6**, *4–6*. *See also* BDC; domain
controller; PDC
busmaster, 5
caching, 6
disk technologies and, 4–5
hardware-controlled RAID, 6, 133
optimizing performance with, 271
counters
activating disk, 270, 276
disk-related, 270–271
exam essentials about, 277

memory-related, 269
for NetBEUI and NWLink, 274
network-related, 272–273
processor-related, 267
TCP/IP, 274
Create Volume Set dialog box, *16*
CSNW (Client Service for NetWare), 230

D

data encryption, 246–248, *247*
date and time, 45
default gateway
IP parameters for, 78
knowing about, 85
default groups, **170–171**
deleting user accounts, 178
dependency service, 289
DEVICE.LOG file, 319
Device Settings tab (Properties page), 149
DHCP (Dynamic Host Configuration
Protocol), **25–27**
advantages of, 26–27
configuring servers as DHCP clients, 77
difficulties of IP addressing, 26
overview, 25
reason for using, 32
DHCP service, 101
directories
default directory path, 109
export and import, 97
Directory Replicator
components of, **97–98**
configuring, **104–105**, *105*
defined, 96
directory-level permissions, 209
Disk Administrator
creating
mirror set, 16
stripe sets, **13**, 16, 17, 131, 136
stripe sets with parity, 16
volume sets, **12–13**, 16, 17,
130–131, 136
reassigning drive letters, 15, *15*
disk drive configuration, **3–19**
comparison of disk technologies, 4–5
controllers, 4–6
critical information, 4–15
glossary for, 18

necessary procedures for, 15–16
overview, 4
sample questions about, 19
disk duplexing
defined, 17, 137
failures with, 337
as fault-tolerance method, 14
vs. mirroring, 339
disk space. *See also* hard disks; partitioning
allocating
assigning drive letters, *9*, *15*, **17**, *129*, 134, 136
creating volume sets, **12–13**, 16, 17, 130–131
reassigning drive letters, 15, *15*, 134, 136
summary of, 127–129, *129*
understanding partition numbering and ARC paths, 8–10, *9*, 129–130
installation failure and insufficient, 288
diskettes
creating network client, **70–72**, *70*, *71*
media failures during installation, 288
recreating install diskettes from CD-ROM, 59–61
diskperf command, 270, 276
display drivers
about, 116
changing or updating, 123
menu for setting, 125
DLC (dynamic link control) protocol, 314
DNS (Domain Name System) service
resolving IP addresses, 102
setting IP addresses for, 84, *84*
domain controller. *See also* BDC; PDC
defined, 55
determining hardware needs for, **49–51**, 55
difference between PDC and BDC, 55
understanding the ReplicationGovernor, 56
domain master browser, *102*, 110
domain name assignments, 289
domain server bottlenecks, 281–282
drive letters
assigning, *9*, *15*, **17**, *129*, 134, 136
reassigning, 15, *15*, 134, 136
duplexing. *See* disk duplexing
Dynamic Host Configuration Protocol. *See* DHCP
dynamic link control (DLC) protocol, 314

E

editing the registry, 303–304, 307
end-user printing problems, 311, 314
ERD (emergency repair disk), 297–298, 300, 305, 307
ERROR.LOG file, 236
error messages for BOOT.INI file, 296–297
exam objectives and topics
essential topics
for administering remote servers from client computers, 196–197
for boot failures, 298–300
for choosing a protocol, 31–33
for client computers, 157
for configuration errors, 307–308
for configuring, printers, 151–153
for configuring disk drives, 16–18
for configuring network adapters, 93–94
for configuring protocols and protocol bindings, 85–86
for connectivity problems, 325–326
for fault-tolerance failures, 338–339
for hard drives, 136–137
for identifying performance bottlenecks, 282–283
on installation failures, 289
on installation methods, 73
for Intel-based platforms, 39–47
for managing disk resources, 222–223
for NetWare networks, 236–237
for NT Server core services, 109–110
for Performance Monitor, 276–277
for peripherals and devices, 124–125
for printer problems, 314–315
for RAS installation and configuration, 257–258
for RAS troubleshooting, 319
for resource access and permission problems, 330
for system policies and profiles, 189–190
for user and group accounts, 179–180
for various server roles, 55–56
test objectives for
connectivity, 228
installing and configuring, 36–37
managing shared resources, 162

monitoring and optimization, 262
planning, 2
troubleshooting, 286
export paths, default, 98
export servers
about, 97, 98
configuring, 105–106, *106*
creating subfolders for, 109
exporting log files, 276
Express vs. Custom setups, 63

F

failures. *See* troubleshooting
FAT file system
converting to NTFS, 200, 212–213, 222
creating FAT partitions for NT boot files, 11
extending volume set formatted with,
13, 131
features of NTFS vs., 66
using, 67, 73
fault-tolerance
choosing methods of, **13–15**
disk duplexing, 14, 17, 137, 339
mirror systems, 14
parity sets, 14
troubleshooting failures, **332–340**
breaking a mirrored set, 337–338
disk duplexing, 337
with mirroring, 335
overview, 332–333
re-creating a mirrored set, 338
regenerating a stripe set with parity, 338
for stripe set with parity, 336
for tape backups, 333–335
file auditing, 223
file caching, 268–269
file servers, 279–280
file system drivers
about, 323
server service as, 324
file systems, 10–12
FAT, 11
formatting a partition, 135–136
knowing when to use NTFS or FAT, 73
NTFS, 12
types of, 10
file-level permissions, 210
filenames for FAT file system, 11

files. *See also specific files listed by name*
compressing, 213–215, 222
permissions for, 210
uncompressing, 214
folders
compressing, 213–215, 222
uncompressing, 214
**Forcibly Disconnect Remote Users from
Server When Logon Hours Expire option**
enabling or clearing, 180
function of, 173
frame type, 85

G

Gateway Service for NetWare. *See* GSNW
Gateway Service for NetWare dialog box, *233*
gateways
configuring for NetWare, **230–231,**
233–235, *233*
exam essentials for default, 85
IP parameters for default, 78
General tab (Properties page), 144–145, *144*
global groups. *See also* local groups
about, 170
allocating users to, 171
local groups, users and, 179
global user accounts, **165–166,** *167,* 175–177
glossary
for boot failures, 300
for choosing a protocol, 33
for client computers, 158–159
for configuration errors, 308
for configuring disk drives, 18
for configuring hard disks, 137–138
for configuring network adapters, 94
for configuring printers, 153–154
for configuring protocols and protocol
bindings, 86
for connectivity problems, 326–327
for fault-tolerance failures, 339
for installation failures, 290
for installation methods, 74–75
for Intel-based platforms, 46–47
for managing disk resources, 223–225
for NetWare networks, 237–238
for performance bottlenecks, 283
for peripherals and devices, 125
for printer troubleshooting, 315

for remote server administration, 197
for resource access and permission
  problems, 331
for system policies and profiles, 223–225
for user and group accounts, 180–181,
  190–191
for various server roles, 56
Group Memberships dialog box, *169*
groups, 169–171
default, **170–171**
global, 170, 171, 179
global groups, local groups, and users, 179
local, 170, 171, 179
managing Windows NT groups, **169–171**
system-created accounts, 179
GSNW (Gateway Service for NetWare)
configuring, **233–235**
exam essentials for, 237
overview, **230–231**
Guest account, 166

H

hard disks, 127–138, 198–226. *See also* disk
space; partitioning
assigning drive letters, 9, *15*, 17, *129*,
  134, 136
comparison of disk technologies, 4–5
compressing, 213–215, 222
converting from FAT to NFTS, 200,
  212–213, 222
copying and moving files between file
  systems, 200–202
creating
  mirror sets, 135
  a share, 216–218, 222
  and sharing resources, 202–204
  stripe sets, 13, 16, 17, 131, 136
  stripe sets with parity, 16, 135, 137
  volume sets, **12–13,** 16, 17, 130–131,
    135, 136
establishing file auditing, 211,
  220–222, 223
exam essentials for, 136–137
file caching, 268–269
fixes for bottlenecks, 271, 277
formatting, 134
  a partition, 135–136
glossary for, 137–138

hot swappable drives, 336
implementing
  levels of RAID, **13–15**
  permissions and security, 204–210, 222
improving performance, 133
managing, **12–13**
monitoring performance of, 270–271
overview, 198–200
partitioning, **127–131,** *129*
providing
  redundancy for, 131–133
  security, 134, 137
reassigning drive letters, 15, *15*, 134, 136
sample questions for, 138
setting
  NTFS folder- and file-level permis-
    sions, 219–220, 223
  share permissions, 218–219
sharing a drive using My Computer, *203*
system requirements and recommended
  configurations for, 40, 41
translation methods for, 41
uncompressing, 214
hard page fault, 268
hardware
comparison of disk technologies, 4–5
determining for domain controller,
  49–51, 55
requirements based on SAM size, 50
verifying compatibility of, 58–59
hardware compatibility list (HCL), 40
Hewlett-Packard printers, 314
HKEY_CLASSES_ROOT subtree, 303, 307
HKEY_CURRENT_CONFIG subtree,
303, 307
HKEY_CURRENT_USER subtree, 303, 307
HKEY_LOCAL_MACHINE subtree,
302, 307
HKEY_USERS subtree, 303, 307
Hours button (New Users dialog box), 176
HPMON.DLL file, 141

I

I/O base, 88–89, *88,* 90
I/O port
defined, 94
knowing about address for, 93
IDE (integrated device electronics) drives, 41

implementing permissions and security,
204–210
  for applications, 204
  NFTS file-level permissions, 210
  No Access permissions, 207
  NTFS directory-level permissions, 209
  overview, 204
  share-level permissions, 205–208
  system actions, 207–208
import computer
  about, 97–98
  configuring, 106–108, *107*
import paths, 98
installation failures, 287–290
  error assigning domain name, 289
  failure of dependency service to start, 289
  failure of NT to install or start, 289
  inability to connect to PDC, 289
  insufficient disk space, 288
  media failures, 288
  nonsupported SCSI adapters, 288
  overview, 287–288
installation methods, 58–76
  creating network client diskettes, 70–72,
    70, 71
  exam essentials for, 73
  Express vs. Custom setups, 63
  glossary for, 74–75
  installing NT Server 4, 65–69
  over the network, **61–62**, 70, 73
  recreating install diskettes from
    CD-ROM, 59–61
  sample questions for, 75–76
  upgrading, 64, 73
  using the Network Client Administrator,
    62–63
installing and configuring, 36–159. *See also*
  configuration errors
  client computers, **155–159**
    changing binding order of
      protocols, 157
    operating system protocols and
      services, 155–157
    overview, 155
  dial-up networking clients, 248–249,
    256–257
  exam essentials
    for client computers, 157

  for configuring network adapters,
    93–94
  for configuring printers, 151–153
  for configuring protocols and protocol
    bindings, 85–86
  for hard drives, 136–137
  for installation methods, 73
  for Intel-based platforms, 39–47
  for NT Server core services, 109–110
  for peripherals and devices, 124–125
  for various server roles, 55–56
  exam objectives for, 36–37
  glossary
    for client computers, 158–159
    for configuring hard disks, 137–138
    for configuring network adapters, 94
    for configuring printers, 153–154
    for configuring protocols and protocol
      bindings, 86
    for installation methods, 74–75
    for Intel-based platforms, 46–47
    for peripherals and devices, 125
    for various server roles, 56
hard disks, **127–138**
  allocating disk space capacity,
    127–131, *129*
  creating mirror sets, 135
  creating stripe sets, **13**, 16, 17, 131, 136
  creating stripe sets with parity, 16,
    135, 137
  creating volume sets, 135
  formatting, 134
  formatting a partition, 135–136
  improving performance, 133
  providing redundancy for, 131–133
  providing security, 134, 137
  reassigning drive letters, 15, *15*,
    134, 136
installation methods, 58–76
  creating network client diskettes,
    70–72, *70, 71*
  Express vs. Custom setups, 63
  installing NT Server 4, 65–69
  over the network, **61–62**, 70, 73
  recreating install diskettes from
    CD-ROM, 59–61
  upgrading, 64, 73

using the Network Client Administrator, 62–63
on Intel-based platforms, **39–47**
completing setup, 45
gathering information about system,
43–44
initializing installation, 42–43
installing NT networking, 45
overview, 49–42
network adapters, **87–95**
changing IRQ, I/O base, and memory
address, 88–89, **88**, 90
configuring multiple adapters, 89,
90–93, *92*
NT Server core services, **96–111**
Computer Browser Services, 102–104
configuring computer for participation
in browser elections, **108–109**
configuring the export server, 97,
105–106, *106*
configuring the import computer, 97,
106–108, *107*
DHCP service, 101
Directory Replicator, **96**, **97–98**,
104–105, *105*
DNS service, 102
License Manager, 99–101, *101*, **108**
overview, 96
WINS service, 102
overview, 37–38
peripherals and devices, **112–126**
display drivers, 116, 123
keyboard drivers, 116, 123
modems, 113–114, 117–118, *118*
mouse drivers, 116, 123
overview, 112–113
SCSI devices, 114, 119–120, *119*
tape device drivers, 115, 120–121, *121*
UPS devices and services, 115,
121–123
printers, **139–154**
adding and printers, 140–141
configuring a local printing device,
144–149, *144*, *146*, *147*, *148*
creating a local printer, 143
implementing a printer pool, 142,
150, 152
installing remote printer, 149–150
overview, 139

setting print priorities, 142, **151**,
152, **153**
protocols and protocol bindings, **76–87**
configuring NWLink, 84–85, *85*
installing a network service, 82, *82*
installing a protocol, 81–82, *82*
for NetBEUI, 79
overview of NWLink, **78–79**
protocol bindings, 79–81
setting DNS client information, 84, *84*
setting IP addresses, 82–83, *83*
setting the WINS server address, 83, *83*
for TCP/IP, 77–78
sample questions
for client computers, 159
for configuring hard disks, 138
for configuring network adapters, 96
for configuring printers, 154
for configuring protocols and protocol
bindings, 86–87
for installation methods, 75–76
for Intel-based platforms, 47
for NT Server core services, 111
for peripherals and devices, 126
for various server roles, 57–58
servers, **48–58**
member server, 54
overview, 48
setting up primary and backup domain
controllers, 48–54
Intel-based platforms, 39–47
completing setup, 45
exam essentials for, 39–47
gathering information about system,
43–44
glossary for, 46–47
initializing installation, 42–43
installing NT networking, 45
overview, 49–42
sample questions for, 47
understanding differences in licensing
modes, **46**, 73
interrupt request lines. *See* IRQ
interval, 265
IP addresses
disadvantages of, 26
managing with DHCP, 25–26
parameters for, 78
power outages with DHCP servers and, 77

setting, 82–83, *83*
understanding, 85
IPX network number, 85
IPX/SPX. *See* NWLink IPX/SPX compatible
transport
IRQ (interrupt request lines)
changing, 88–89, *88*, **90**, 93
defined, 94
ISDN service, 241

K

kernel mode for NT architecture, 321
key terms and concepts. *See* glossary
Keyboard control panel, knowing about, 125
keyboard drivers
about, 116
changing or updating, 124

L

LAN adapter settings, 93
LanmanServer, 324
last known good configuration, 297–298, 299
License Manager, 99–101, *101*
choosing right licensing method, 100
client access license, 99
defined, 96
per seat licensing, 99
per server licensing, 99
scope of licenses managed, 109
tracking licenses with, 100, 101, *101*
licensing modes. *See also* License Manager
changing, 67
client access license, 99
differences in, **46**, **73**, 110
with License Manager, 109
per seat, **44**, 47
per server, **43**, 47
Licensing Program, 100
Local Computer Properties dialog box, *185*
local groups. *See also* global groups
about, 170
access permission assigned to, 171
global groups, local groups, and, 179
local user accounts, 165
local user profiles
creating, 187
exam essentials for, 189–190
LOCALMON.DLL file, 141

Log view (Performance Monitor), 266,
275–276
LOGFILE.LOG file, 236
logon times, 180
LPRMON.DLL file, 141

M

Manage Exported Directories window, *106*
managing shared resources, 162–226
administering remote servers from client
computers, 193–197
copying client-based administration
tools, 195–196
overview, 193
from Windows 95, 193–194
from Windows NT Workstation,
194–195
creating and managing policies and profiles, 182–192
creating and implementing system policies, 188–189
creating local user profile and mandatory user profile, 187
creating remote user profiles, 188
creating roaming user profile,
187–188
local user profiles, 183–184
overview, 182–183
roaming user profiles, 184–185
system policies, 185–187
exam essentials
administering remote servers from
client computers, 196–197
for creating and managing policies and
profiles, 189–190
for managing disk resources, 222–223
for user and group accounts, 179–180
exam objectives for, 162
glossary
administering remote servers from
client computers, 197
creating and managing policies and
profiles, 223–225
managing disk resources, 223–225
for user and group accounts, 190–191
managing disk resources, 198–226
compressing a file, folder, or drive,
213–215, 222

converting a drive from FAT to NFTS, 200, 212–213, 222
copying and moving files between file systems, 200–202
creating a share, 216–218, 222
creating and sharing resources, 202–204
establishing file auditing, 211, 220–222, 223
implementing permissions and security, 204–210, 222
overview, 198–200
setting NTFS folder- and file-level permissions, 219–220, 223
setting share permissions, 218–219
overview, 162–164
sample questions
administering remote servers from client computers, 197
for creating and managing policies and profiles, 191
managing disk resources, 225–226
for user and group accounts, 182
user and group accounts, **164–182**
administering account policies, 171–174
auditing changes to user account database, 174
creating global user accounts, 175–177
creating a user template, 177–178
deleting user accounts, 178
managing NT user accounts, 164–166
managing Windows NT groups, 169–171
managing Windows NT user rights, 167–169
renaming users, 178
mandatory user profiles, 187, 189
master browser, 102, 110
measurement databases, 264
media failures, 288
member servers, 55
memory
fixes for bottlenecks, 269, 277
monitoring in Performance Monitor, 268–269

NT's virtual memory model, 268, 276
system requirements for installation, 40–41
memory address
changing, 88–89, *88*, **90**
defined, 94
Microsoft Windows 95
administering remote servers from client computers, 193–194
as client computer, 155–159
Microsoft Windows NT Server
architecture of, *321*
configuring for NetWare networks, 229–238
failure to install or start, 289
installation methods for, **58–76**
installing NT Server 4, 65–69
migrating multiple NetWare servers to, 232
NT boot phases, **291–294**, 299
overview of Performance Monitor, 264–266, *265*, *266*
registry subtrees for, 302–303
software-controlled RAID in, 15, 133
upgrading, 64, 73
virtual memory model, 268, 276
Microsoft Windows NT Workstation, 194–195
Migration Tool for NetWare (MTFN)
about, **231–232**
exam essentials for, 237
using, **235–236**, *235*
mirroring
breaking mirrored sets, 337–338, 339
creating mirrored sets, 16
defined, 17, 136
as fault tolerance method, 14
re-creating mirrored set, 338
troubleshooting, 335
vs. duplexing, 339
modems
compressing data, 118
configuring with Modem control panel, 124
enabling multilink RAS options, 248
installing, 117–118, *118*
overview of, 113–114
troubleshooting dialing problems, 318
using default settings for, 118

monitoring performance, 262–284
    exam essentials
        for identifying performance bottle-
            necks, 282–283
        for Performance Monitor, 276–277
    exam objectives for, 262
    glossary
        identifying performance bottle-
            necks, 283
        for Performance Monitor, 278
    identifying performance bottlenecks,
        279–284
        for applications server, 280–281
        for domain servers, 281–282
        for file and print servers, 279–280
        overview, 279
    improving hard disk performance, 133
    increasing with protocol bindings, **81**, 86
    overview, 262–263
    with Performance Monitor, 263–279
        creating a baseline using Performance
            Monitor, 275
        disk monitoring, 270–271
        exporting information to another
            program, 276
        monitoring memory, 268–269
        monitoring processor, 266–268, 267
        network optimization, 272–275
        overview, 263
        relogging data at longer intervals,
            275–276
        views and features of, 264–266,
            265, 266
    sample questions
        about Performance Monitor, 278–279
        for identifying performance bottle-
            necks, 283–284
mouse drivers
    changing or updating, 123, 125
    overview of, **116**
MPR (multiple provider router), 324, 326
MS-DOS client computers, 155–159
MTFN. *See* Migration Tool for NetWare
    (MTFN)
multilink, 248
multiple provider router (MPR), 324, 326
MUP (multiple UNC provider), 324, 327
My Computer, 216–218

N

NetBEUI protocol
    about, **30–31**, 79
    configuring for RAS support, 244
    limitations of, 33
    NetBEUI counters in Performance
        Monitor, 274
NetBIOS-based networks, 27–29
    name registration, 27–28
    name resolution, 28–29
    tools for troubleshooting, 323
NetWare networks, 229–238
    exam essentials for configuring, 236–237
    gateway service for NetWare, **230–231**,
        233–235
    glossary for, 237–238
    migrating multiple servers to NT Server, 232
    migration tool for NetWare, **231–232**,
        235–236, *235*
    overview, 229
    sample questions for configuring, 238
network adapters, 87–95
    changing IRQ, I/O base, and memory
        address, 88–89, *88*, 90
    configuring multiple adapters, 89,
        90–93, *92*
    exam essentials for, 93–94
    glossary for, 94
    sample questions for, 96
Network Client Administrator dialog box, 70
network client diskettes, **70–72**, *70*, *71*
Network Configuration dialog box, *247*, *255*
Network dialog box, *92*
network interface cards. *See* NICs
networking. *See also* managing shared
    resources
    fixes for bottlenecks, 275, 277
    glossary for configuring NetWare net-
        works, 237–238
    installing NT
        on Intel platforms, 45
        over the network, 61–62, 70, 73
    for NetWare networks, **229–238**
        exam essentials, 236–237
        gateway service for NetWare,
            230–231, 233–235, *233*
        migration tool for NetWare, 231–232,
            235–236, *235*
        overview, 229

optimizing network components, 272–275

sample questions for configuring NetWare networks, 238

troubleshooting on remote computers with Registry Editor, 307

New Share dialog box, *234*

New User dialog box, *167*

NFTS file-level permissions, 210

NICs (network interface cards)

  installing from network client diskettes and unlisted, 72

  questions about, 94

  troubleshooting drivers for, 322

No Access permissions, 207

  effect of, 223

  exam essentials on, 330

  troubleshooting, 329

nonbrowser, 103

nonsupported SCSI adapters, 288

NT Backup Utility

  backing up with, 124

  defined, 125

NT boot phases

  boot loader phase, 292–293

  exam essentials on, 299

  initial phase, 291–292

  kernel phase, 293–294

  logon phase, 294

NT Explorer, 62

NT Server core services, 96–111

  Computer Browser Services, 102–104

  configuring

    computer for browser elections, 108–109

    the export server, 105–106, *106*

    the import computer, 106–108, *107*

    replication service, **104–105**, *105*

  DHCP service, 101

  Directory Replicator, 96, **97–98**, 104–105, *105*

  DNS service, 102

  exam essentials for, 109–110

  License Manager, **99–101**, *101*, 108

  overview, 96

  sample questions for, 111

  WINS service, 102

NT Workstation, 155–159

NTCONFIG.POL file

  location of, 190

  saving system policy information to, 186

NTFS file system

  advantages of, 12

  conversion of FAT file system to, 200

  converting and extending FAT volume sets, 13

  features of FAT 16 vs., 66

  knowing when to use, 73

  setting

    directory-level permissions, 209

    folder- and file-level permissions, 219–220, 223

NTUSER.DAT file, 189

NTUSER.MAN file, 189

NWLink IPX/SPX compatible transport

  advantages and disadvantages of, 32

  choosing, **29–30**

  configuring, 84–85, *85*

  configuring RAS support for, 244

  implementing for Novell NetWare-based file servers, 30

  NWLink counters in Performance Monitor, 274

  overview of, **78–79**

  tools for troubleshooting, 323

  when to install, 32

P

paged and nonpaged memory, 268, 276

PAGEFULE.SYS file, 268, 276

parity sets, 14

partitioning, 6–10

  ARC path components, 10, 130

  formatting a partition, 135–136

  hard disks, **127–131**, *129*

  numbering partitions and ARC paths, 8–10, *9*, 129–130

  placing NT boot files in FAT partitions, 11

  primary and extended partitions, 6–8

  securing files on FAT partition, 134

passwords

  account lockout feature, 173

  Password Uniqueness feature, 173

  RAS authentication protocols, 246–248, *247*

setting length of, 173
setting minimum and maximum ages
for, 172
for special accounts starting service, 176
paths. *See also* ARC paths
default directory, 109
default export and import, 98
to roaming user profile, 185
setting default import and export, 98
PC card setup, *88*
PDC (primary domain controller)
difference between BDC and, **55**
inability to connect to, 289
selecting necessary hardware for, **49–51**
synchronization parameters in registry,
53–54
synchronizing, **51–53**, *55*
per seat licensing. *See also* License Manager;
licensing modes
defined, **44**, 47
with License Manager, 99
unable to change to per server, 67
vs. per server licensing, **46**, **73**, 110
per server licensing. *See also* License
Manager; licensing modes
changing to per seat, 67
defined, **43**, 47
with License Manager, 99
vs. per seat licensing, **46**, **73**, 110
performance. *See* monitoring performance
performance bottlenecks, 279–284. *See also*
Performance Monitor
for applications server, 280–281
for domain servers, 281–282
exam essentials for, 282–283
for file and print servers, 279–280
fixes for hard disks, 271, 277
fixes for memory, 269, 277
fixes for networks, 275, 277
fixes for processors, 267, 277
glossary for, 283
overview, 279
sample questions about, 283–284
Performance Monitor, 263–279
creating a baseline using, 275
disk monitoring, 270–271
exam essentials for, 276–277
exporting information to another
program, 276

glossary for, 278
monitoring
memory, 268–269
processor, 266–268, 267
network optimization, 272–275
real-time chart for, 266
relogging data at longer intervals,
275–276
sample questions about, 278–279
views and features of, 264–266, *265*, *266*
peripherals and devices, 112–126
display drivers, 116, 123
exam essentials for, 124–125
glossary for, 125
keyboard drivers, 116, 124
modems, 113–114, 117–118, *118*
mouse drivers, 116, 123
overview, 112–113
sample questions for, 126
SCSI devices, 114, 119–120, *119*
tape device drivers, 115, 120–121, *121*
UPS devices and services, 115, 121–123
permissions
granting RAS, 245
implementing security and, **204–210**
managing Windows NT user rights,
167–169
for NetWare gateway service, 231
NFTS file-level permissions, 210
No Access, 207, 223, 329, 330
NTFS directory-level, 209
setting
ATS, 222
NTFS folder- and file-level,
219–220, 223
share-level, 205–208
system actions and, 207–208
troubleshooting
exam essentials for, 330
steps for, 329–330
planning, 2–34
disk drive configuration, **3–19**
comparison of disk technologies, 4–5
controllers, 4–6
critical information, 4–15
overview, 4
exam essentials
for choosing a protocol, 31–33
for configuring disk drives, 16–18

fault-tolerance method, **13–15**
a file system, **10–12**, 73
    FAT, 11
    NTFS, 12
    types of file systems, 10
glossary, 18
    for choosing a protocol, 33
    for configuring disk drives, 18
managing hard disks, **12–13**
    stripe sets, **13**, 13, 16, 17, 131, 136
    volume sets, 12–13
objectives for, 2
overview, 2–3
partitioning, **6–10**
    ARC path components, 10, 130
    numbering partitions and ARC paths,
        8–10, 9
    primary and extended partitions, 6–8
protocol, **20–34**
    NetBEUI, **30–31**, 79
    NWLink, 29–30
    overview of, 20–21
    TCP/IP, 21–25
    TCP/IP with DHCP and WINS, 25–29
sample questions
    for choosing a protocol, 34
    for configuring a disk drive, 19
policies. *See* system policies and profiles
Ports tab (Properties page), 146, *146*
power loss, 122
PPP (point-to-point protocol)
    configuring, 243, 258
    exam essentials for, 258
PPTP (point-to-point tunneling protocol)
    configuring, 258
    connecting client to RAS server with, 248
primary domain controller. *See* PDC
print devices. *See also* printers
    categories of, 141
    Hewlett-Packard, 314
    vs. printers, 310
print drivers, 312
    defined, 139
    installing, 151
print servers, 279–280

printer jams, 314, 315
printer pool
    defined, 146
    implementing, 142, 150, 152
    printer jams in, 315
printers, **139–154**. *See also* print devices
    adding and configuring, 140–141
    configuring a local printing device,
        144–149, *144*, *146*, *147*, *148*
    creating
        "hidden" shared, 152
        a local printer, 143
    exam essentials for, 151–153
    glossary for, 153–154
    implementing a printer pool, 142, 150, 152
    installing remote, 149–150
    managing security for, 152
    overview, 139
    printer jams in printer pool, 315
    sample questions for, 154
    scheduling large print jobs, 152
    setting priorities for, 142, **151**, 152, **153**
    sharing, 152
    troubleshooting, **309–317**
        end user problems, 311, 314
        for non-Windows–based applications,
            311–312
        overview, 309–310
        print drivers, 312
        printing speed, 313–314
        spooling, 312–313
        types of problems, 310–311
    using a separator page, 151
printing
    exam objectives for, 38
    printer jams, 314, 315
    speed of, 313–314
privileges, default, 179
processors
    fixes for bottlenecks, 267, 277
    monitoring in Performance Monitor,
        266–268, *267*
    processor-related counters, 267
profiles. *See* system policies and profiles
Properties dialog box, reaching the, 216

protocol bindings, 79–81
  changing order of, 157
  exam essentials for, 85–86
  glossary for, 86
  increasing
    performance with, **81**, 86
    security with, 80, 85
  overview of, 79–80
  sample questions for, 86–87
protocols, 76–87. *See also* protocol bindings;
  and specific protocols listed by name
  available for client computers, 155–157
  choosing, **20–34**
  configuring RAS, **242–244**
  exam essentials for, 85–86
  glossary for, 33, 86
  installing, 81–82, *82*
    network service, 82, *82*
  NetBEUI, 30–31, 79
  NWLink, **29–30**, 78–79, 84–85, *85*
  overview of, **20–21**
  sample questions for, 34, 86–87
  setting
    DNS client information, 84, *84*
    IP addresses, 82–83, *83*
    the WINS server address, 83, *83*
  steps for configuring RAS, 252–254,
    252, 253
  TCP/IP, **21–25**, 77–78
  TCP/IP with DHCP and WINS, **25–29**
  tools for troubleshooting, 322–323

Q

questions. *See* sample questions

R

RAID (redundant array of inexpensive disks)
  about levels, 131–132
  activating disk counters, 270, 276
  hardware controlled, 6, 133
  hot-swappable drives and, 336
  implementing levels of, 13–15
  optimizing disk performance and, 271

RAS (Remote Access Service), 239–260
  configuring communications
    overview, 240–242
    steps for, 250–251, *251*
  configuring dial-up networking clients
    overview, 248–249
    steps for, 256–257
  configuring protocols, 242–244
    NetBEUI, 244
    NWLink, 244
    PPP and SLIP, 243, 258
    steps for, 252–254, *252, 253*
    TCP/IP, 243–244
    TDI, 242
  configuring security, **245–248**, *245*
    callback modes, 246, 257
    multilink, 248
    passwords and data encryption,
      246–248, *247*
    permissions, 245
    steps for, 254–256, *254, 255*
  exam essentials for installing and config-
    uring, 257–258
  glossary for, 258
  overview, 239–240
  sample questions for, 260
  troubleshooting, 317–320
    connection problems, 318–319
    dialing problems, 318
    overview, 317
RAS Server IPX Configuration dialog box, *253*
RAS Server TCP/IP Configuration dialog
  box, *252*
reading ARC paths, 17, 136
reassigning drive letters, 15, *15*, 134, 136
recreating install diskettes from CD-ROM,
  59–61
redirectors, 324, 326
redundancy, for hard disks, 131–133
REGEDIT.EXE file, 306
REGEDT32.EXE file, 306
Registry
  adding or editing key values with Registry
    Editor, 306, 307
  backing up and restoring, 303, 307

editing the, 303–304, 307
searching the database with Registry
   Editor, 306, 307
synchronization parameters for PDC and
   BDC in, 53–54
troubleshooting on remote computers
   with Registry Editor, 307
using Registry Editor to back up a key,
   305, 307
Registry Editor
   adding or editing key values with, 306, 307
   backing up a key with, 305, 307
   searching the database with, 306, 307
   troubleshooting on remote computers
      with, 307
Registry Mode, 186–187, 190
registry subtrees, 302–303
Remote Access Permissions dialog box,
   245, 254
Remote Access Service. *See* RAS
Remote Access Setup screen, 251, *251*
remote server administration from client,
   193–197
   copying client-based administration tools,
      195–196
   overview, 193
   from Windows 95, 193–194
   from Windows NT Workstation,
      194–195
replicating system policy file, 190
replication service
   configuring, 104–105, *105*
   creating subfolders for import and export
      servers, 109
ReplicationGovernor, 56
Report view (Performance Monitor), 266
resource access and permission problems,
   328–331
   overview, 328
   steps for, 329–330
restarting printing, 314
restoring
   from backups, 338
   the registry, 303, 307
roaming user profiles, 184–185

S

SAM (Security Accounts Manager)
   determining load for domain controller,
      49–50
   hardware requirements based on size of, 50
   objects in, 49
sample questions
   about Performance Monitor, 278–279
   on administering remote servers from
      client computers, 197
   for boot failures, 300–301
   for choosing a protocol, 34
   for client computers, 159
   for configuration errors, 308
   for configuring a disk drive, 19
   for configuring hard disks, 138
   for configuring network adapters, 96
   for configuring printers, 154
   for configuring protocols and protocol
      bindings, 86–87
   on connectivity problems, 327–328
   for creating and managing policies and
      profiles, 191
   for fault-tolerance failures, 339–340
   for identifying performance bottlenecks,
      283–284
   on installation failures, 290
   for installation methods, 75–76
   for installing and configuring remote
      access service (RAS), 260
   for Intel-based platforms, 47
   on managing disk resources, 225–226
   for NetWare networks, 238
   for NT Server core services, 111
   for peripherals and devices, 126
   on printer problems, 315–317
   for RAS problems, 319–320
   for resource access and permission
      problems, 331
   for user and group accounts, 182
   for various server roles, 57–58
Scheduling tab (Properties page), 147–148, *147*
scripting, 249
SCSI Adapters dialog box, *119*

SCSI (small computer system interface)
devices
  installation failures and nonsupported, 288
  installing and configuring, **119–120**,
    119, 124
  overview of, **114**
security
  administering account policies,
    171–174, 180
  increasing with protocol bindings, 80, 85
  managing for printers, 152
  providing hard disk, 134, 137
  RAS features, 245–248, *245*
    callback modes, 246, 257
    multilink, 248
    passwords and data encryption,
      246–248, *247*
    permissions, 245
    steps for configuring security,
      254–256, *254*, *255*
  setting minimum and maximum ages for
    ˄asswords, 172
Security Accounts Manager. *See* SAM
security identifier (SID), 331
Security tab (Properties page), 148–149, *148*
**serial cable connections between UPS and
  server,** 125
Server Manager, 98
server service, 324
servers. *See also specific servers listed by name*
  bottlenecks
    for applications server, 280–281
    for domain servers, 281–282
    for file and print servers, 279–280
  cabling between UPS and, 125
  exam essentials for, 55–56
  glossary for, 56
  installing and configuring, **48–58**
    creating network client diskettes,
      70–72, *70*, *71*
    Express vs. Custom setups, 63
    member server, 54
    overview, 48
    primary and backup domain con-
      trollers, 48–54
  on Intel-based platforms
    gathering information for, 43–44

    initializing installation on, 42–43
    setting up, 45
  NT server architecture, 321
  sample questions for, 57–58
Service control panel, *105*
**Share Client-based Administration Tools
  dialog box,** *196*
**Share Network Client Installation Files dialog
  box,** *71*
shared resources. *See* managing shared
  resources
share-level permissions
  about, **205–208**
  creating a share, 216–218, 222
  No Access permissions for user or
    group, 223
  setting, **218–219**
shares, creating, 216
Sharing tab (Properties page), 148
.SHD files, 313
shortcuts on local machine, 189
SID (security identifier), 331
single master model, 51
SLIP (serial line Internet protocol)
  configuring, 243, 258
  exam essentials for, 258
.SPL files, 313
spooling, 312–313
SRV.SYS file, 324
stripe sets
  creating, **13**, 16, 17, 131, 136
  with parity
    creating, 16, 135, 137
    defining a, **18**
    regenerating, 338, 339
    troubleshooting failures for, 336
subnet mask
  IP parameters for, 78
  knowing about, 85
SUMMARY.LOG file, 236
switches. *See* command-line switches
synchronization
  for PDC and BDC, **51–53**, 55
  understanding the ReplicationGovernor, 56
system policies and profiles, 182–192
  creating
    and implementing system policies,
      188–189

local user profile and mandatory user profile, 187
remote user profiles, 188
roaming user profile, 187–188
local user profiles, 183–184
overview, 182–183
roaming user profiles, 184–185
sample questions for, 191
system policies, 185–187
in NTCONFIG.POL file, 190
System Policy mode vs. Registry mode, 186–187
System Policy mode, 190
system requirements
for hard disks, 40, 41
for memory, 40–41
for NT server, 39–40
for Windows 95 client computers, 194

T

tape backups
data backup and recovery with, **333–335**
exam essentials for, 338
tape device drivers
configuring, 120–121, *121*
overview of, 115
TCP/IP protocol, 21–25
common protocols and their functions, 22
configuring RAS support for, 243–244
with DHCP and WINS, **25–29**
exam essentials for, 31–32
functions of utilities, 23
handling IP addresses with DHCP, 25–27
parameters for, **85**
TCP/IP-related counters in Performance Monitor, 274
tools for troubleshooting, 322
WINS with, **27–29**
TDI (transport driver interface)
configuring for RAS, 242
troubleshooting, 323
template
creating user, 177–178
creating user accounts with, 180
terminology. *See* glossary
test questions. *See* sample questions

time and time zone, 45
tools
copying client-based administration, 195–196
for troubleshooting protocols, 322–323, 325
transceivers, 94
translation methods for hard drive, 41
troubleshooting, 286–340
boot failures, **290–301**
BOOT.INI file, 294–297, 299
last known good configuration, 297–298, 299
NT boot phases, 291–294, 299
overview, 290–291
configuration errors, **301–308**
adding or editing key values with Registry Editor, 306, 307
backing up and restoring the registry, 303, 307
creating or updating an Emergency Repair Disk, 297–298, 300, 305, 307
editing the registry, 303–304, 307
overview, 301–303
on remote computers with Registry Editor, 307
searching the database with Registry Editor, 306, 307
using Registry Editor to back up a key, 305, 307
connectivity problems, **320–328**
file system drivers, 323
MPR, 324, 326
MUP, 324, 326
NIC drivers, 322
NT server architecture, 321
overview, 320–321
redirectors, 324, 326
resolving connectivity problems, 325
server service, 324
TDI, 323
transport protocols, 322–323
exam essentials
for boot failures, 298–300
for configuration errors, 307–308
for connectivity problems, 325–326
for fault-tolerance failures, 338–339

on installation failures, 289
for printer problems, 314–315
for RAS problems, 319
for resource access and permission
problems, 330
exam objectives for, 286
fault-tolerance failures, **332–340**
breaking a mirrored set, 337–338
disk duplexing, 337
with mirroring, 335
overview, 332–333
re-creating a mirrored set, 338
regenerating a stripe set with parity, 338
for stripe set with parity, 336
for tape backups, 333–335
glossary
for boot failures, 300
for configuration errors, 308
for connectivity problems, 326–327
for fault-tolerance failures, 339
installation failures, 290
printer problems, 315
for resource access and permission
problems, 331
installation failures, **287–290**
error assigning domain name, 289
failure of dependency service to
start, 289
failure of NT to install or start, 289
inability to connect to PDC, 289
insufficient disk space, 288
media failures, 288
nonsupported SCSI adapters, 288
overview, 287–288
overview of, 286–287
printer problems, **309–317**
end user problems, 311, 314
for non-Windows-based applications,
311–312
overview, 309–310
print drivers, 312
printing speed, 313–314
spooling, 312–313
types of problems, 310–311
RAS problems, **317–320**
connection problems, 318–319
dialing problems, 318
overview, 317

resource access and permission problems,
328–331
overview, 328
steps for, 329–330
sample questions
for boot failures, 300–301
for configuration errors, 308
connectivity problems, 327–328
for fault-tolerance failures, 339–340
on installation failures, 290
printer problems, 315–317
for RAS problems, 319–320
for resource access and permission
problems, 331
turning disk counters on and off, 270, 276

U

UDF (uniqueness database file), 63
uncompressing files, folders, and drives, 214
uniqueness database file (UDF), 63
updating Emergency Repair Disk, 297–298,
300, 305, 307
upgrading NT server, 64, 73
UPS (uninterruptable power supply)
configuring with UPS control panel, 125
defined, 125
installing, **121–123**
insuring data with, 6
overview of, **115**
User Environment Profile dialog box, *168*
user and group accounts, 164–182
about global user accounts, **165–166**, *167*
administering account policies, 171–174
allocating users to global groups, 171
auditing changes to user account
database, 174
creating
global user accounts, 175–177
user accounts with template, 180
a user template, 177–178
deleting user accounts, **178**, 178, 179
expiring and reactivating accounts, 180
local user accounts, 165
managing
NT user accounts, **164–166**
Windows NT groups, **169–171**
Windows NT user rights, 167–169

renaming
    user accounts, 179
    users, 178
user mode, 321
user profiles
    defined, 167–168
    exam essentials for, 189
    paths to roaming, 185
    user policies and, 169
user template
    creating, 177–178
    creating user accounts with, 180
users
    global groups, local groups, and, 179
    logon hour restrictions and, 180
    renaming, 178
Users Must Log On in Order to Change
    Password option, 173

V

volume sets
    creating, **12–13**, 16, 17, 130–131, 136
    extending, 13, 131

W

WINNT default root folder
    defined, 46
    disk space requirements for, 40
WINNT.EXE
    disk space requirements with /b
        parameter, 40
    knowing command-line switches for, 73
    using /u parameter with, 73
**WINS (Windows Internet Name Service),
27–29**
    advantages of, 29
    installing, 102
    name registration, 27–28
    name resolution, 28–29
    reasons for using, 32
    setting address for WINS server, 83, *83*

MCSE EXAM NOTES®

MCSE CORE REQUIREMENT STUDY GUIDES FROM NETWORK PRESS®

Sybex's Network Press presents updated and expanded second editions of the definitive study guides for MCSE candidates.

ISBN: 0-7821-2220-5
704pp; 7½" x 9"; Hardcover
$49.99

ISBN: 0-7821-2223-X
784pp; 7½" x 9"; Hardcover
$49.99

ISBN: 0-7821-2222-1
832pp; 7½" x 9"; Hardcover
$49.99

A $50.00 SAVINGS!

ISBN: 0-7821-2221-3
704pp; 7½" x 9"; Hardcover
$49.99

ISBN: 0-7821-2256-6
800pp; 7½" x 9"; Hardcover
$49.99

MCSE Core Requirements
Box Set
ISBN: 0-7821-2245-0
4 hardcover books;
3,024pp total; $149.96

Microsoft® Certified
Professional
Approved Study Guide

NETWORK PRESS®
SYBEX

STUDY GUIDES FOR THE MICROSOFT CERTIFIED SYSTEMS ENGINEER EXAMS

MCSE ELECTIVE STUDY GUIDES FROM NETWORK PRESS®

Sybex's Network Press expands the definitive study guide series
for MCSE candidates.

ISBN: 0-7821-2224-8
688pp; 7¹/₂" x 9"; Hardcover
$49.99

ISBN: 0-7821-2261-2
848pp; 7¹/₂" x 9"; Hardcover
$49.99

ISBN: 0-7821-2248-5
704pp; 7¹/₂" x 9"; Hardcover
$49.99

ISBN: 0-7821-2172-1
672pp; 7¹/₂" x 9"; Hardcover
$49.99

ISBN: 0-7821-2194-2
576pp; 7¹/₂" x 9"; Hardcover
$49.99

ISBN: 0-7821-1967-0
656pp; 7¹/₂" x 9"; Hardcover
$49.99

Microsoft® Certified
Professional
Approved Study Guide

NETWORK PRESS®
SYBEX

STUDY GUIDES FOR THE MICROSOFT CERTIFIED SYSTEMS ENGINEER EXAMS

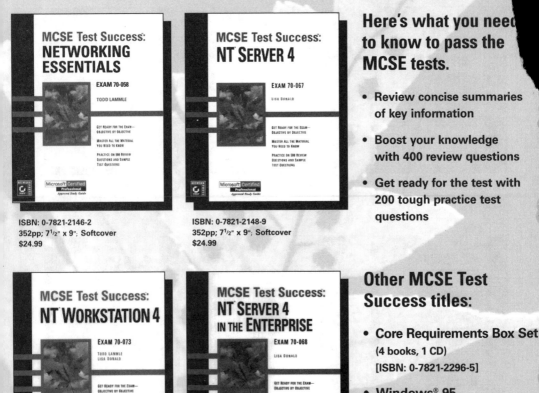